SILVER STATE
DREADNOUGHT

★

Also by Stephen M. Younger

Endangered Species: How We Can Avoid Mass Destruction and Build a Lasting Peace

The Bomb: A New History

Calculating Chiefs: Simulating Leadership, Violence, and Warfare in Oceania

SILVER STATE DREADNOUGHT

★

THE REMARKABLE STORY OF BATTLESHIP *NEVADA*

★

STEPHEN M. YOUNGER

Naval Institute Press
Annapolis, Maryland

This book has been brought to publication with the generous assistance of Edward S. and Joyce I. Miller.

Naval Institute Press
291 Wood Road
Annapolis, MD 21402

Library of Congress Cataloging-in-Publication Data
Names: Younger, Stephen Michael, date, author.
Title: Silver State dreadnought : the remarkable story of Battleship Nevada / Stephen M. Younger.
Other titles: Remarkable story of Battleship Nevada
Description: Annapolis, MD : Naval Institute Press, [2018] | Includes bibliographical references and index.
Identifiers: LCCN 2018026934 (print) | LCCN 2018028511 (ebook) | ISBN 9781682472903 (epub) | ISBN 9781682472903 (ePDF) | ISBN 9781682472897 (alk. paper)
Subjects: LCSH: Nevada (Battleship) | United States—History, Naval— 20th century. | World War, 1914-1918—Naval operations, American. | World War, 1939-1945—Naval operations, American. | Battleships—United States—Design and construction.
Classification: LCC VA65.N4 (ebook) | LCC VA65.N4 Y68 2018 (print) | DDC 359.3/252—dc23
LC record available at https://lccn.loc.gov/2018026934

♾ Print editions meet the requirements of ANSI/NISO z39.48-1992 (Permanence of Paper).
Printed in the United States of America.

26 25 24 23 22 21 20 19 18 9 8 7 6 5 4 3 2 1
First printing

To
Chief Petty Officer James Younger, USN (Ret.)
and
Petty Officer Second Class Joel Younger, USN

Contents

Preface

The Marines were having a tough time. Getting to the beach on Iwo Jima had been hard enough, but once ashore they came under withering fire from carefully concealed Japanese guns. Bunkers and artillery emplacements seemed to appear out of nowhere, and the Marines' light weapons were incapable of knocking them out.

"Pop" Grosskopf, captain of the battleship *Nevada*, was watching the action through binoculars. Something needed to be done—and fast. When the ship's 5-inch guns failed to take out a particularly troublesome Japanese bunker, he turned the job over to the massive 14-inch barrels of *Nevada*'s main turrets. An initial salvo swept away the sand covering the bunker but failed to penetrate the reinforced concrete. Grosskopf ordered armor-piercing rounds into the big guns and blew the bunker to pieces. That afternoon a cannon hidden in a cave again pinned down the Marines. *Nevada* turned her main guns to the challenge and scored a direct hit on the first shot. After that they called her the "Sweetheart of the Marine Corps."

Nevada witnessed the making of the American century. Her keel was laid in 1912, an exciting time for the U.S. Navy as America assumed the role of a major power that could project power across the globe. During World War I she fired only a few shots in anger, but she protected American doughboys on their way to France, ready to sink any German ship that tried to harm them.

Nevada benefited from the arms control treaties of the 1920s, which prohibited navies from building new battleships. Existing ones were refurbished instead, and *Nevada*'s rebuild during 1928–30 gave her a new lease on life.

On December 7, 1941, she was the only battleship to get under way at Pearl Harbor, although damage from bombs and a torpedo caused her to sink later in the day. Within a year she was raised and rebuilt, and in May 1943 she took part in the recovery of the Aleutian Islands. A year after that she was providing fire support for the Normandy invasion, seemingly oblivious to shells from German shore batteries landing all around her. *Nevada* was gaining a reputation as a sharpshooter, a welcome sight to men on landing craft who knew that the ship's big guns were there to pave their way ashore.

After steaming south to take out German gun emplacements during the invasion of southern France, *Nevada* moved to the Pacific. She was with the Marines at Iwo Jima and Okinawa and then patrolled the waters around Japan in preparation for the invasion of the home islands. At the end of the war she was old and tired, her guns and speed outclassed by newer battleships. But there was to be no scrapyard for *Nevada*. The Navy wanted to assess the effect of the new atomic bomb on warships, and *Nevada* was chosen as ground zero. The bomber missed its target, and she survived. The second atomic blast, underwater this time, was expected to break her into pieces, but again the old lady stood her ground. Because she was too radioactive to be of any value even as scrap, the Navy towed her to Hawaii for use as a target in gunnery practice. All calibers of shells, bombs, and rockets pounded her hull, but *Nevada* did not budge. Somewhat in exasperation, the Navy called in an airstrike, and for the second time in her life a torpedo sank her.

This is the story of a remarkable vessel, the first warship built by the United States that was the equal of any ship afloat. It is the story of a nation coming of age, reluctantly putting aside small-town life to accept the mantle of a global superpower. Most of all, it is the story of the men and women who built her and the men who served on her, all of whom were fiercely determined to create the best ship, the most accurate guns, and the finest crew in the Navy.

This is also a love story, of men for their ship and, I think, of a ship for her men. *Nevada* represents the best of American ingenuity, American dedication to a righteous cause, and American heroism. She rests in the deep now, but her spirit lives on as an inspiration to all who know that it is by strength of arms and dedication to duty that peace is maintained.

Whenever possible I used primary sources in documenting *Nevada*'s history. Especially useful were the ship's logbooks and war diaries. On a number of occasions during my research I noted discrepancies between the log—the legal record of the ship—and published histories. For the most part I have relied on the logbooks, with the notable exception of the record for December 7, 1941, which the logbook jumbled a bit—a forgivable error given the awful events of that day. For details of construction and refurbishment I used the correspondence files of the Bureau of Construction and Repair, and for target practice and other exercises I sorted through the voluminous files of Commander Battleships. I also consulted records from the Bureau of Ordnance, the Office of the Secretary of the Navy, the General Board, and other sources.

Even for a single ship, it is virtually impossible to evaluate *all* of the available documentation, and I make no claim of completeness. However, I have tried to access what I thought were the most important records—those that most clearly and accurately tell *Nevada*'s history. Omissions are my responsibility. I intentionally left out details in some cases, such as in describing repetitive training missions and changes in command involving *Nevada*'s twenty-six commanding officers.

Acknowledgments

It is a pleasure to thank the many people who helped make this book possible. At the top of the list are many whose names I shall never know: the people who typed and filed the records that enabled me to better understand *Nevada*'s story. As I sorted through thousands of letters and documents and tens of thousands of pages of logbooks, I silently thanked those unknown men and women who so carefully recorded the details of an amazing ship. I would like them to know that many decades after they left their desks, someone really appreciated their work.

There are others whose names I do know and whose help I gratefully acknowledge. Susan Abbott, Chris Killillay, and Mark Mollan of the National Archives were especially helpful in finding material on *Nevada*'s early history. Paul Stillwell guided me to additional sources. Janis Jorgensen and Anne Rehill of the U.S. Naval Institute assisted in finding oral histories and photos. Robert Nylen provided access to a number of scrapbooks and other memorabilia at the Nevada State Museum in Carson City. My agent, Don Lamm, read early versions of the manuscript and offered his usual sage advice on making it more readable. Adm. Richard Mies, USN (Ret.), put me in contact with the Naval Institute Press, for which I am most grateful. Glenn Griffith, acquisitions editor at the Naval Institute Press, was both encouraging and patient in my first foray into naval history. I would like to thank an anonymous reader at the Naval Institute Press who offered exceptionally helpful advice that greatly improved this book. Thomas Hone, another reader at the press, corrected a number of errors and suggested several important improvements. Mindy Conner was invaluable in editing the manuscript for publication. Finally, I would like to thank my wife, Mari, for her patience and encouragement throughout this project, and for accepting *Nevada* into our home.

To the Old Maru (an affectionate nickname for *Nevada*): I never sailed with you, but I feel that I have come to know you as I researched your story. Thank you for the privilege.

1

Building a Better Battleship

On January 23, 1911, Phillip Andrews sent a handwritten note to Rear Adm. Spenser Wood of the U.S. Navy's General Board:

Wood,

The Secretary would like today an informal memorandum showing how the all-big-gun battleship was proposed by the G.B. [General Board]—recommended to the Dept. How the Bu. of C&R [Bureau of Construction and Repair] delayed a year or more in preparing sketch designs. Whether it went to the Board of Construction or not & what their action was. In other words how we lost first blood on the Dreadnoughts.[1]

ANDREWS

Andrews was the aide to Secretary of the Navy George von Lengerke Meyer, and his note has all the hallmarks of a senior official's panic about being asked embarrassing questions. The navies of the world had been surprised in 1906 when Britain introduced the first all-big-gun battleship, HMS *Dreadnought*, which vastly outgunned anything afloat. The ever-parsimonious U.S. Congress fretted that another technological leap forward might again render millions of dollars' worth of U.S. Navy ships obsolete.

Wood replied the same day with a tersely written summary of U.S. dreadnought history.[2] The Navy was thinking about an all-big-gun ship as early as 1903 but lacked the technical capability to deliver a workable design. Struggling just to catch up on such basic issues as guns, armor, and engines, the Navy did indeed fail to appreciate the significance of losing "first blood" to Britain on the all-big-gun ship. The clear implication in the exchange of notes was that such a slip-up should not happen again; if there were to be another leap forward on battleship design, that leap would be made by the United States.

As Rear Admiral Wood penned his response to the secretary, the U.S. Navy had thirty-three battleships in the water or being built, an astonishing feat given that the first of these, *Indiana*, had entered service only in 1895. America's first all-big-gun battleship, USS *South Carolina*, was approved on March 4, 1905, seven months before *Dreadnought* was laid down. But the final designs were not complete until November 1905, and construction did no start until a year after that, well after the British ship was in the water. Chronic delays pushed completion of *South Carolina* to early 1910.

South Carolina and her sister ship, USS *Michigan*, were a thousand tons lighter than *Dreadnought*, but they were of a more advanced design. To maximize flexibility, the Navy's Bureau of Construction and Repair focused on providing the greatest weight of broadside fire possible. *South Carolina*'s eight 12-inch guns were placed along her axis so that all could fire to either side. *Dreadnought*, in contrast, had three turrets on the centerline and two "wing" turrets, one on each side of the superstructure, so she could fire only eight of her ten guns in a broadside. To avoid having a long hull on *South Carolina*, with associated costs for engines and armor, designers elevated the second and third turrets so that they would fire over their (fore and aft) neighbors. Even so, there was still a problem with speed. *South Carolina* could make only eighteen and a half knots, significantly slower than the twenty-one-knot *Dreadnought*.

USS *Delaware* and USS *North Dakota* followed *South Carolina* and *Michigan*, each mounting two more 12-inch guns and power plants that could drive them at a respectable twenty-one knots. *North Dakota* was given turbine engines, simple in concept and very compact compared with the reciprocating machinery standard at the time, but a challenging technology for American shipyards.

Four ships were authorized in 1908 and 1909—USS *Florida*, USS *Utah*, USS *Wyoming*, and USS *Arkansas*—all of them stretched-out versions of *Delaware* that mounted even more 12-inch guns along the centerline. USS *New York* and USS *Texas* were given ten of the Navy's new 14-inch guns, arming them comparably with the most modern British ships.

The Navy was on a solid path of battleship construction, but stretching and modifying the *Delaware* design could be carried only so far. On May 24, 1910, Secretary Meyer asked the General Board to recommend what ships should be built the following year. Was there a smarter approach to battleship design? Britain had stunned the world with *Dreadnought*—what was the next step, and how could the United States take the lead in a new class of *super*-dreadnoughts?

The General Board shared the secretary's frustration that the United States had given up first blood in dreadnought design to the British and gave the Navy's Bureau of Construction and Repair a demanding set of requirements. The ships needed to carry as many of the biggest guns as possible and have armor sufficient to protect them from long-range gunfire. Ten 14-inch guns were considered the minimum. Speed was important to enable a commander to choose the time and place for battle. Finally, because the fleet might have to operate at great distances from a friendly port, the steaming radius had to be maximized and the logistical problems associated with refueling minimized.

Mounting ten 14-inch guns on a hull costing no more than the $6 million Congress authorized meant that one of the other two criteria—speed or armor—had to suffer. The General Board's specification of twenty and a half knots was already a compromise; just as the United States was starting on the new design, the Japanese began laying down two ships (*Fuso* and *Yamashiro*) that could make twenty-three knots. The Germans had already laid down four ships (the *König* class) designed to make twenty-one knots.

With guns and power plant fixed, the only place left to look for savings was in armor protection. Here the bureau proposed a brilliant solution that came to be known as the "all-or-nothing" concept. Rather than trying to protect *everything* on the ship, designers focused on protecting only the *most important* elements—guns, ammunition, engines, and conning tower. Around these critical elements they placed enough armor to stop anything the enemy was likely to throw at them. Other areas deemed not vital to the survival and performance of the ship were left relatively unprotected. Shells might even pass through them without exploding, because fuses were often set to detonate only after the shell had passed through heavy armor plate. With the same weight and cost, a ship would be better protected with the all-or-nothing concept than with the traditional approach of distributing the available armor weight over the entire ship. The idea quickly became standard practice among the major navies of the world.

Another innovation for the new design was the choice of oil rather than coal as fuel. Since oil has a higher energy density than coal, it would enable a ship to steam farther per ton carried in the bunkers. Oil also made the ship easier to refuel because it could be transferred quickly by hoses rather than by the backbreaking human labor required for coal. Boiler room crews could be reduced by more than 80 percent, and ships would not have to slow down every few hours to remove coal ash from fire grates, a potential problem in battle. Only one smokestack would be required for an oil-fueled set of boilers, simplifying the interior design of the ship. Finally, oil was plentiful—by the early twentieth century the United States had become one the world's leading producers of petroleum products. (Britain also understood the advantages of oil but lacked a reliable source and was forced to rely on domestic coal.)

The arrangement of the big guns posed another challenge to the super-dreadnought designers. Naval tacticians wanted at least ten 14-inch guns, but they were not happy with the cumbersome five- and six-turret arrangements of *Florida* and *Wyoming*. Supplying shells to so many turrets was a logistical nightmare, and closely spaced guns interfered with one another during battle. The Bureau of Ordnance solved this problem by means of a triple-gun main turret.

On March 4, 1911, Congress authorized Battleship No. 36 and Battleship No. 37, later to be named USS *Nevada* and USS *Oklahoma*. A week afterward, the Bureau of Construction and Repair proposed a design concept that met all of the General Board's requirements. The new ships would indeed be revolutionary—the first in the world to adopt the all-or-nothing concept of armor, the first to be oil fired, and the first (American) dreadnoughts with triple-gun turrets. Weighing 27,000 tons, they would be 565 feet long at the waterline and, with a beam of 95 feet, able to pass comfortably through the Panama Canal.

The main armament of 14-inch guns was distributed in two triple-gun turrets and two twin-gun turrets, which were numbered 1 through 4, starting at the bow. The heavier triple-gun turrets—turrets 1 and 4—were mounted at deck level, and the lighter twin-gunned turrets 2 and 3 were elevated to fire over the top of them.

Secondary armament consisted of twenty-one 5-inch guns and a variety of smaller arms for saluting, mounting on small boats, and other purposes. Significantly, the design included four air defense guns, a harbinger of the future

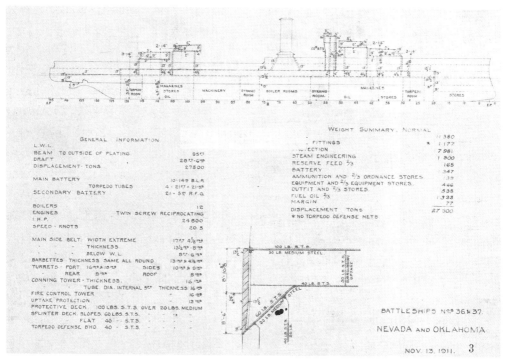

Rough plan for Battleships Nos. 36 and 37 prior to their authorization by Congress and naming as *Nevada* and *Oklahoma*. *National Archives Photo Collection, RG 19*

of naval combat. Two 21-inch torpedo tubes were located below the waterline, although the possibility that a capital ship might come within torpedo range of the enemy was increasingly remote as effective gunnery ranges increased.

Nevada and *Oklahoma* differed in meeting the last element of the guns-armor-speed trio of requirements. Turbine engines had been tried on *North Dakota* with dismal results, but the promise of easier maintenance and compact designs was highly attractive. The Navy decided to hedge its bets by putting turbines on *Nevada* and reciprocating engines on *Oklahoma*.

Curtis turbine engines with a combined 24,800 horsepower would drive *Nevada* at 20.5 knots by means of 2 propellers. With a full load of 2,000 tons of oil, the ship would have a steaming radius of 8,000 miles—more than enough to reach America's most distant possessions in the Pacific. To fuel the other component of the ship—the crew of more than 1,000 men—there were storerooms capable of supporting a cruise of up to 90 days.[3]

Nevada was a technological leap forward, an ambitious and risky design that would be either a brilliant success or a failed experiment.[4] History would vote for success, since *Nevada* became the first of a "standard design" battleship that navies around the world would copy. While bigger guns, more powerful engines, and other technologies such as radar would follow in time, the general scheme implemented on Battleship No. 36 would persist until battleship construction ended in the 1940s. *Nevada* took the design of *Dreadnought* to its logical conclusion—she was the first super-dreadnought.

In addition to being a technological marvel and a potent weapons system, *Nevada* was a political symbol of an ascendant America. Other countries watched closely what America did in naval construction, as did the U.S. Congress. Would *Nevada* and *Oklahoma* set off an arms race that could cost tens of millions of dollars? Would the two ships exacerbate the already expensive arms race between Britain and Germany? Many members of Congress saw battleships as offensive weapons that had only one use: the pursuit of territorial ambitions that could embroil the United States in costly foreign wars. The Navy walked a fine line between giving America the ships it needed to ensure its defense and alarming other countries and Congress.

The naval architects at the Bureau of Construction and Repair had more immediate concerns. While they had a workable sketch, it was far from something that could be turned over to a shipyard for construction. The triple-gun turret planned for *Nevada* was an untried concept for the U.S. Navy. Ordnance experts fretted that the blast from one gun would throw off the aim of the other two. Also, three openings for gun barrels in a single turret increased the probability that a lucky enemy shot might enter the turret, destroying three rather than two guns and possibly setting off an explosion in the magazine below. Still, there were compelling advantages to the three-gun arrangement: it allowed more guns to be put into fewer turrets, which in turn meant more guns for a given length (and cost) of ship. Ammunition supply was simplified, and armor that would have been used on an additional turret could be used elsewhere in the all-or-nothing concept.

Squeezing three guns into a turret posed challenges. In two-gun turrets, each barrel operated independently, enabling one to be loaded while the other was elevated to fire. But there was not enough space in the triple-gun turrets to accommodate three sets of elevation gear. Ordnance designers had to mount all three guns on a common horizontal mounting post (a trunnion), which meant that they were raised and lowered together. It was a necessary solution, but designers still worried that the enormous shock produced by firing would throw off the alignment of the guns, something that might be difficult or impossible to fix at sea.

To better assess these risks the Navy ordered the construction of an experimental triple-gun turret that could test performance under realistic operating conditions. Unfortunately, the results of the experiments would not be available until *after* the contract for *Nevada*'s construction was fixed. If it didn't work, costly design changes would be necessary.

The Bureau of Construction and Repair had overall responsibility for implementing the General Board's recommendations, but the Navy was keenly interested in getting the thoughts of line officers before finalizing the ships' plans. Sketches of *Nevada* were sent to the Atlantic Fleet for review, and many officers submitted their opinions. On May 24, 1911, Adm. George Dewey advised the Navy Department that "such of the comments and criticisms of these officers which the General Board regarded as being practicable and useful in connection with these designs have been submitted to the technical bureaus through the Aid for Material."[5] The bureau's March 11 design survived these comments largely intact—the designers added 10 feet to the length of the hull and 500 tons to the displacement to accommodate the fleet officers' recommendations, making her final length 575 feet at the waterline (583 feet overall) and her displacement 27,500 tons.[6] Some of the added weight went to heavier deck armor, a change that would prove especially beneficial decades later at Pearl Harbor.

Once *Nevada*'s general characteristics were confirmed, her designers focused on the details. Experts asked the most basic questions, starting with: Will she be stable in heavy seas, including after sustaining various forms of battle damage? Will she fit in available dry docks? What new equipment will be required, and where, to service her?

To minimize the probability of sinking if she took one or more hits below the waterline, the ship was divided into watertight compartments, one or more of which could flood while allowing the ship to continue to float and fight. Ensuring that the compartments would *remain* watertight was complicated because nearly every bulkhead had to be pierced in one way or another by hatches, ventilator shafts, electrical conduits, steam pipes, or voice tubes. Major pieces of equipment such as oil tanks, boilers, guns, and armor had to be distributed so that the ship floated properly, a nontrivial task given that the hull was narrow at the front and wide at the rear and thus varied in buoyancy along its length.

It was one thing to figure this out for a stationary ship in calm water, quite another to ensure that balance was maintained when the ship was under way, fuel was burned, ammunition was expended, and battle damage sustained. What would happen to the stability of the ship if shellfire or torpedoes ripped open the hull, allowing seawater to flood compartments on one side? At what point would the resulting list become so great that the ship capsized? If the captain decided to flood a compartment on the other side of the ship to bring her to an even keel, how much lower in the water would she ride? How would doing that affect speed and armor protection?

Many parameters were impossible to estimate by paper-and-pencil calculations, so accurate scale models of the hull were constructed and tested in the Navy's model basin in Washington, D.C. These experiments yielded empirical data on water resistance for a particular hull shape, data that would help designers estimate probable speeds for a given set of engines. Stability against rolling could be studied, as well as the maximum list the ship could sustain before she "turned turtle" and capsized. Rules of thumb linked the models—which could be as much as twenty feet long—to full-size ships.

Nevada was more than just a fighting machine—she was a floating city with machine shops, a hospital, galleys, crew quarters, and everything else needed to meet the needs of a thousand men at sea. Designers paid close attention to requirements for food storage, berthing, ventilation, recreational facilities, and a host of other human issues.

By the fall of 1911 the Navy was confident enough in its design to open the contract for bid. On October 18 Secretary of the Navy Meyer approved the *Circular of Requirements for Bidders, Battleships Nos. 36 and 37, Authorized by Act of Congress Approved March 4, 1911*. Potential builders could propose to build the ship just as specified in Navy plans or suggest a design "in general accordance" with the Navy's specifications. The unique characteristics of warships meant that commercial builders could seldom produce a superior design, but the Navy wanted to leave

Drafting room at the Fore River Shipyard, circa 1917. An army of draftsmen drew plans for every part of *Nevada* by hand. *With permission from Massachusetts Institute of Technology Museum, BSVP632*

the door open for new ideas. The successful company would have three years to complete the ship, and there would be a stiff fine for each day of delay.

Bidders had only sixty days to respond—a remarkably short time by twenty-first-century standards. In addition to cost, the Navy assessed the bidder's ability to complete the contract and the probable quality of the finished product. Bids were opened at noon on January 4, 1912, and on January 22 the Fore River Shipbuilding Company in Quincy, Massachusetts, was awarded a fixed-price contract to build *Nevada*. The $5,895,000 cost did not include armor, guns, and other government-supplied equipment.[7] By the time she was completed, *Nevada* would cost American taxpayers $11,518,763.13.[8]

The Fore River Shipbuilding Company had a long and distinguished history. Founded in 1883 by Thomas Watson, Alexander Graham Bell's former assistant ("Watson, come here, I need you"), its initial focus was on building engines for small ships. Soon boat building was added, and by the end of the century Fore River was competing for significant Navy contracts. When his business outgrew the original site, Watson built a new shipyard at Quincy in 1901 that included machine shops, foundries, carpentry shops, and vast storehouses, making it one of the largest shipyards in the United States.

Battleships became a specialty of Fore River. The new shipyard had barely opened when the Navy awarded it a contract to build the battleships *Rhode Island*

and *New Jersey*. Watson's insistence on quality was a significant factor in winning the competition, as was his ability to deliver a product at the lowest possible cost.

Fore River was an innovative operation for its time. The same act of Congress that authorized *Nevada* mandated an eight-hour day for battleship construction, increasing the cost from $177.25 to $215.26 per ton but greatly easing the lives of shipyard workers.[9] But Fore River went beyond the letter of the law by creating an extensive environment of social activities for its employees that included glee clubs, sports teams, and a newsletter highlighting family events. Management's philosophy was that well-cared-for workers were productive workers who would put personal pride into their products. There were occasional labor problems—twelve strikes occurred during construction of *Nevada*—but in general Fore River was a well-run establishment.[10]

Even with a contract in hand, Fore River's naval architects still had hundreds of questions to answer. While engineers ordered materials, construction foremen assembled teams of skilled laborers and worked out the inevitable scheduling conflicts between *Nevada* and other projects at the yard. A scale model of the ship was constructed to help in the estimating process and to plan the sequence of assembly. It would be embarrassing and costly if, during construction, builders realized that they could not fit a big piece of equipment through a previously installed narrow hatch.

Following the maxim "measure thrice and cut once," shipwrights made a full-sized paper or wooden template for each component of the ship. These templates would later be laid over steel plates to show where they should be cut and where openings for hatches, pipes, and wiring needed to be made. Given *Nevada*'s size, the creation of a full set of templates required a small army of draftsmen and carpenters. Further complicating the process was the fact that some of the metal plates on the ship had to be bent in two dimensions, such as the bow plates, which curved outward along the length of the ship and inward toward the keel. By using a combination of scale models and full-size templates, the fabricators learned how to cut and bend a plate to fit.[11]

Most of the steel involved in the construction of a battleship consisted of rolled or hammered sheets. Major components such as the stem at the forward end of the ship and the struts that held the propeller shafts were cast to shape. While the armor was to be as tough as possible, softer steel was used in hull plating because its ductility allowed the ship to flex rather than crack as she rode the seas.[12]

To satisfy the Navy that the ship was being built according to rigid specifications, the builders tested every batch of metal before cutting it to shape. By the time a part was accepted it might have four separate quality control stamps. Every

View of the keel and the inner and outer hulls, January 1, 1913. *National Archives Photo Collection, RG 19*

item was inspected, including tens of thousands of nuts, bolts, and rivets. The failure of one of these fasteners could be as serious as the failure of a hull plate.

To oversee *Nevada*'s construction the government assigned Naval Constructor Thomas G. Roberts of the Bureau of Construction and Repair. Roberts was a dedicated Navy man who in 1910 had written a prize-winning essay on the merchant marine for the Naval Institute *Proceedings*, the premier journal of naval affairs. Just prior to joining the *Nevada* project he wrote a highly mathematical description of how to estimate the displacement, center of gravity, and other properties of ships. His new assignment was distinctly more practical. Roberts was in the unenviable position of having responsibility for the completion of the biggest ship the Navy had ever constructed, but he had no authority to direct specific work at the shipyard.

In a large, open space that sloped gently toward the river, workmen carefully positioned a line of large wooden keel blocks. Once the blocks were in their proper places, the men constructed a wooden cradle matching the shape of the ship's bottom around the blocks. On November 4, 1912, nearly ten months after the award of the contract to Fore River, skilled ironworkers laid two flat steel plates, each approximately twenty feet long and four feet wide, on the forward-most keel blocks. These plates were the beginning of the "outer bottom" of the ship. A vertical plate parallel to the length of the ship was positioned on the seam between the bottom plates to make an inverted T, and two more horizontal plates were put on top to create an I-beam. The upper horizontal plates were the start of the "inner bottom" of the ship. This pattern was continued along the length of the ship to complete her keel. The plates varied in thickness from five-eighths of an inch to one inch, so, with some effort, they could be moved into position by hand; an experienced crew could install upward of one hundred plates in a single day.[13] There was no ceremony, nor were any important witnesses present to commemorate the start of construction.[14]

From the central keel, the shipwrights worked outward to create the rest of the ship. Plates forming the outer hull were laid flat on the wooden cradle, starting from the keel and extending outward. Vertical plates, this time running perpendicular to the ship's length, were affixed following the curve of the hull. If the keel was the ship's spine, these vertical plates constituted the beginning of her ribs. Details were important. The joints between the hull plates were staggered to increase strength,

The sides of the hull are rising, and transverse bulkheads are being installed, April 1, 1913.
National Archives Photo Collection, RG 19

much as the planks in a hardwood floor are staggered. Rivet and bolt patterns were designed to transmit stress as evenly as possible. Everything, it seemed, had been thought through, and rules of thumb incorporated lessons learned through painful prior experience.[15]

Having built the foundation, the workers proceeded to assemble the sides of the hull and the transverse bulkheads (the internal walls running from side to side). Decks and compartments were built inside the hull, and the stem—the heavy steel casting that formed the bow of the ship—was connected. The first compartment was tested for watertight integrity on September 10, and the first armor plate was installed on October 27.

Accurate scheduling was critical to construction. There was not enough room at the construction site to store all the components of the ship, and ensuring that each part arrived at the right place at the right time was a mammoth logistical task. Such planning was all the more impressive because no computers or sophisticated project planning tools were available at the time—carbon paper copies and handwritten notebooks were the order of the day. One might say that *Nevada* first floated upon a sea of paper. Through it all, she was constructed by an experienced team of professionals under the watchful gaze of a demanding Navy customer.

Which is not to say that there were no problems. John C. Niedemair, who worked at Fore River during summer vacations while studying at the Webb Institute, learned one of *Nevada*'s big secrets from friendly yard workers.

> One of the frames had missed the shell by several inches, so we crawled in through the inner bottom to show me this. They were really interested in showing me what goes on and, sure enough, there was the frame two inches away from the shell, filled in with wood, and they had put in a fake that looked like a rivet on the outside, but it was really a bolt on the inside, because they couldn't put a hot rivet through the wood.[16]

The fix never caused a problem for the ship.

As the hull rose from its wooden cradle, workers installed the boilers and engines. Twelve Yarrow Express water-tube boilers, four each in three watertight compartments, drove the engines and a pair of 300-kilowatt dynamos that supplied electricity to the ship. The boilers produced steam at 295 pounds per square inch by sending water through an array of 1,092 1.75-inch-diameter tubes. Seven oil burners heated each boiler, spraying a fine mist of preheated heavy oil to extract the maximum energy from the fuel. Assembling such a complex array of piping and making sure there were no leaks or weak points that could fail when the ship was at sea required skill and dedication to detail.

Construction workers take a break while completing the bow. *National Archives Photo Collection, RG 19*

Steam from the boilers went via 9-inch-diameter pipes to four engine rooms, two on each side of the ship. High-pressure Curtis turbines in the forward engine rooms, designed to spin at a maximum of 222 rpm, had blades measuring 11 feet in diameter. At full power, each could generate 6,625 horsepower. To squeeze the maximum amount of power from each ton of oil, steam exiting the main engines was sent to lower-pressure turbines in the aft engine rooms, generating still more power.[17] Reversing turbines were mounted in the same casing as the low-pressure turbines in the aft engine rooms.

Even though oil contains more energy per ton than coal, the Navy's insatiable desire for cruising range meant that fuel efficiency was critical. A contract change in July 1914 provided for two geared turbines to be installed in the forward engine rooms, increasing efficiency at nominal cruising speeds. Manufactured by the General Electric Company, the cruising turbines spun at 3,200 rpm to generate 1,750 horsepower each. A specially designed gearbox reduced the rpm by a factor of 23.85 to connect to the propellers. The cruising turbines, as their name implies, were intended for use at lower speeds, below 15.5 knots, and were disconnected at higher speeds. A type of clutch shifted the 14.5-inch-diameter propeller shafts from cruising to main engines.

Two fourteen-foot-diameter three-bladed propellers, each cast in one piece of manganese bronze, drove the ship through the water. At the ship's normal load the top of each propeller was nearly fourteen feet below the surface of the water. Propeller design was an art in itself, since the goal was to *push* water and not just stir it up. An efficient propeller was essential to both speed and steaming radius, and naval architects conducted numerous theoretical and experimental studies to optimize its design.

Tests of a full-scale mockup of the triple-gun turret performed at the Naval Proving Ground during 1912 proved "satisfactory," "subject to minor modifications."[18] This was a relief to the Bureau of Ordnance and an even greater relief to the Bureau of Construction and Repair because manufacture of the triple-gun turret was well under way by the end of the year. Any changes in turret design might have delayed the delivery of the ship.

USS *Nevada* was launched on July 11, 1914, twenty months after the first keel plates were laid. Distinguished guests at the launch included Secretary of the Navy Josephus Daniels, Assistant Secretary (and later president) Franklin D. Roosevelt, Nevada governor Tasker Oddie, Massachusetts governor David Walsh, and several members of Congress. VIPs crowded shoulder to shoulder on a reviewing platform facing the massive bow of the ship, and hundreds of spectators lined the ways. Admission to the yard was by ticket only, so many spectators took to the river in small boats or stood on the shore opposite the shipyard. Red, white, and blue bunting created a patriotic and festive atmosphere.

The honor to christen *Nevada* went to ten-year-old Eleanor Anne Siebert, niece of Governor Oddie. As she swung the bottle of champagne against the bow, saying, "I christen thee *Nevada*," workmen cut away the last restraints holding the hull in position and the cradle carrying *Nevada* slowly slid backward into the river. Although eight tons of grease had been applied to the ways to ease her progress, the friction caused smoke to flare from the skids.

Once *Nevada* was moving, the challenge was to keep her from picking up so much speed that she would cross the Fore River and run aground on the other

Secretary of the Navy Josephus Daniels, Eleanor Anne Siebert, and Nevada governor Tasker Oddie just prior to launch. *Library of Congress LC-B2- 3148-11*

USS *Nevada* enters the water for the first time. *Nevada State Museum*

side. To retard her motion, heavy ropes and chains connected the cradle carrying the ship to stakes sunk into the ground. Each of these "stops" snapped in turn, momentarily slowing the ship's progress.

The launch went off without a hitch, and following the formal ceremony Fore River president J. W. Powell hosted a luncheon for 130 dignitaries at the Copley Plaza Hotel in Boston. Among other gifts, Miss Siebert was presented with a diamond-studded gold locket to commemorate the occasion.[19]

T. G. Roberts, who had been in the reviewing stand with his wife, described the event in a July 23 letter to Washington:

1. The NEVADA was launched at the works of the Fore River Shipbuilding Co., Quincy, Mass., on July 11, 1914, at 1:53 P.M.

2. The NEVADA was christened by Miss Eleanor Anne Siebert of Carson City, Nevada, niece of the Governor of Nevada. One quart bottle of Mumm's Extra Dry Champagne was used, manufactured by G. H. Mumm and Co., of Reims, France. The bottle was enclosed in a network of red, white and blue ribbon, but was not suspended from the vessel. The bottle was broken by Miss Siebert, by swinging it in a horizontal plane against the stem casting.[20]

Nevada in the Fore River immediately after launch. The tugs will push her to a nearby dock for completion. *National Archives Photo Collection, RG 19*

Roberts' report on Eleanor Anne Siebert's swing was important information for Navy personnel. Old sea lore suggested that failure to break a christening bottle on the first attempt would result in bad luck for the ship. In launching HMS *Dreadnought*, for example, King Edward VII failed to break a bottle of Australian wine on his first attempt. Misfortune followed months later when the completed *Dreadnought* ran aground on her way out of the shipyard.

Launching was a milestone, but much work remained before *Nevada* was a functioning warship. Before the VIPs had even left the shipyard, six tugs maneuvered the hull to a nearby dock where construction continued.[21] By August 12, 1914, a month after launch, the ship was 72 percent complete. Still to come were the side armor, turrets, guns, and hundreds of other pieces of equipment. Two masts extending 114 feet from the waterline were installed, atop which were placed spotter platforms, searchlights, and radio antennae. The masts were of a "cage" design constructed of steel pipes woven in a spiral pattern that provided strength while minimizing the probability that a single enemy hit would collapse the mast.

The Navy's interest in completing *Nevada* increased as international tensions rose during the summer of 1914. On July 28, following continuing unrest in the Balkans and the assassination of Austrian Archduke Franz Ferdinand, Austria-Hungary declared war on Serbia. Russia mobilized its enormous army the next day. Germany followed suit on July 30. The Germans invaded France, violating Belgian neutrality in the process. Interlocking alliances quickly brought Great Britain into the war.

Most Americans were more than happy to keep out of what they expected to be a short-lived European dispute. Even the combatants thought that the war would be over "before the leaves fall" or at worst by Christmas. But modern weapons such as machine guns caused shocking carnage on the battlefield, and, unable to advance, each side dug in for what would become four years of trench warfare.

The all-or-nothing concept employed first on *Nevada* included an armor belt extending along the side of the ship, 13.5 inches thick above the waterline tapering to 8 inches below. By the end of 1912 the Bureau of Construction and Repair had let contracts for 15,300 tons of Krupp-type armor for *Nevada* and *Oklahoma*, dividing the large order between the Bethlehem Steel, Carnegie Steel, and Midvale Steel companies.[22]

To deal with the growing problem of plunging fire—shells arriving at a steep angle at the end of long-range flight—five inches of deck armor were provided in two parts, each composed of several layers of armor plate. The thicker top part would not stop an armor-piercing shell, but it would cause it to detonate before it

Portside view, October 1, 1914, nearly two years after the keel was laid. Note the swinging bridge in the background. *Nevada* would have to squeeze between the bridge and the roadway when leaving the shipyard. *National Archives Photo Collection, RG 19*

reached critical systems below. To absorb the blast of the shell and stop shrapnel, a second "splinter deck" was installed. Such an arrangement was common on battleships of the time, but *Nevada* excelled in the thickness of her horizontal armor. Combined with the thick side armor and armored bulkheads at the forward and aft ends of the ship, the deck armor enclosed nearly all of the ship's critical systems within a well-protected box.

The front faces of the main turrets were protected with an incredible eighteen inches of armor, and the cylindrical barbettes on which they rested and through which ammunition was passed had thirteen inches of armor around them. *Nevada* was one of the best-protected battleships in the world.

Four manufacturers operating under the direction of the Washington Navy Yard fabricated *Nevada*'s massive main armament.[23] Each 14-inch gun had a barrel 52.5 feet long—45 times its diameter—and weighed more than 140,000 pounds. Constructed of a set of concentric steel tubes reinforced by steel hoops, the innermost tube had spiral grooves (rifling) cut into its interior face. These grooves spun the shell as it was accelerated down the barrel, greatly improving its stability during flight. Constructing guns out of several tubes rather than one piece of steel had an important economic consideration: only the innermost one—the rifled liner—had to be replaced after the wear and tear of repeated firings.

Curiously, the 1,400-pound armor-piercing shells the main guns fired contained only 31.5 pounds of high explosive. It was the momentum of the heavy steel shell that enabled it to penetrate enemy armor. The relatively small amount of explosive was intended to cause damage once the shell was *inside* the enemy ship. Four silk bags containing a total of 365 pounds of smokeless powder provided the motive force of the guns. At the maximum gun elevation of 15 degrees, *Nevada* could lob shells in an accurate salvo pattern out to 23,000 yards. The guns' maximum range was 36,000 yards, but the designers' desire to keep the openings in the turret faceplate as small as possible limited their maximum elevation to 15 degrees. In any event, 23,000 yards was close to the maximum distance at which shipborne observers could spot the fall of shells.

An unexpected problem arose in mid-1915: the war in Europe was consuming everything the world's munitions plants could produce, and the Navy was having trouble buying shells to put into the guns. The cost of a 14-inch armor-piercing shell jumped from $320 in January 1914 to $415 in March 1915.[24]

The original contract for building *Nevada* demanded completion in thirty-six months, by January 22, 1915. But as early as November 1913 it was clear that construction was falling behind schedule; only 49.2 percent of the work was done

New Year's Day 1915. Guns are being installed in the forward turrets. *National Archives Photo Collection, RG 19*

by November 1, 1913, and the best estimates placed completion at April 22, 1915, three months late.[25] A year later the completion date had slipped to August 13, 1915, nearly eight months late.

The delay did not escape the attention of Congress. On January 4, 1915, Representative A. P. Gardiner of Massachusetts wrote to Secretary of the Navy Daniels inquiring about the cause of the schedule slips. Daniels replied that strikes caused fifty-three days of delay, rejection of material seventy-five days, and late delivery of material an additional seventy-five days. Other delays beyond the responsibility of the shipyard brought the total to ten months.[26] (Ultimately, the Navy would call it even and declare the commissioning date to be the new contractual delivery date, canceling all penalties for late completion.)[27]

A contract modification in July 1914 granted an additional five months to install cruising turbines, and workers used this respite to make up most of the lost time. On May 29, 1915, the president of Fore River Shipbuilding Company wrote to the Navy saying that he hoped to have the ship ready to leave the yard by August 29, only slightly more than a two-month delay from the contract requirement.[28] Last-minute problems proved this an optimistic guess. It was not just a matter of assembling parts. As major systems were completed they went through a rigorous set of tests. Sometimes modifications were required to solve unanticipated problems—modifications that took time to design, fabricate, install, and validate. While Secretary Daniels tried to put the best face on the delays, tempers began to flare at what the Navy saw as foot dragging by the contractor. On September 22, 1915, less than a month after the company president's optimistic estimate of completion, T. G. Roberts wrote his boss at the Bureau of Construction and Repair that "up to the present date it has appeared to me that the Contractors were aiming at a date of docking and trials immediately thereafter wholly incompatible with the state of the work on this vessel." Furthermore, "the Contractors have not applied themselves to the rectification of known difficulties in such a way as to warrant a belief that they expect the testing program completed." Roberts warned the Navy to expect Fore River to defer "a whole lot of testing until after the trials," which he viewed as wrong.[29] The purpose of trials was to prove that the ship met specifications, and he did not see how that could be confirmed with so many things left to do. The date for *Nevada*'s departure from the shipyard was pushed back until early October.

A strike of Fore River's coppersmiths further complicated matters. At the request of the shipyard, Acting Secretary of the Navy Franklin D. Roosevelt authorized a slip in the departure date to October 23 or 25. Familiar with Roberts' complaints, he added, "These dates are set with the understanding that the testing of systems and auxiliaries shall be completed and errors rectified and the remainder of the work completed."[30]

Ready for engine trials dockside, October 1, 1915. *National Archives Photo Collection, RG 19*

One of the most important of these tests occurred on Sunday, October 3, 1915, when steam was admitted to the portside main and cruising turbines for the first time. It was a tense few moments. Turbines were still relatively new technology, and to achieve high efficiency they had to be built to demanding specifications. The eleven-foot-diameter rolled-brass blades in the main turbines had to be installed precisely to within thousandths of an inch; if a blade rubbed against the housing or was even slightly off-balance it could shatter and destroy the entire engine. The engine room crew was relieved to hear the turbines hum into operation as the steam valves were opened. Six days later, tests began on the starboard engines with similar positive results. The run-ups used only low-pressure steam because full power would have damaged the dock to which *Nevada* was moored.

Powering up the turbines was one of the final tests *Nevada* had to pass at the shipyard. On October 4, 1915, H. G. Smith, manager of Fore River, wrote to the Navy's superintending constructor that the ship would be ready to leave the works on Friday, October 22, at about 0900.[31] The first trip would be to Dry Dock 4 at the New York Navy Yard, where *Nevada*'s bottom would be cleaned and painted, the propellers polished, and other minor work performed. Marine growth that had accumulated since launch would cause drag on the hull and propellers, and both Fore River and the Navy wanted *Nevada* at her best during speed trials. Smith expected the ship to be in dry dock about three or four days and requested approval to work overtime to complete all tasks on time.

Arranging dry dock time was a special problem for *Nevada*, because only the New York yard had a berth big enough to hold her. Scheduling was further complicated by the need to depart Fore River on a daylight high tide. A ship of *Nevada*'s size required deep water; no one wanted a repeat of *Dreadnought*'s grounding on her first day out. Just to make sure, the Navy contracted with the Bay State Dredging and Contracting Company to dredge the shoals of the Weymouth Fore River, which linked the Fore River works to the sea.

As the date of departure approached, provisions were loaded, the ship took on oil, and men reported for duty. The massive boilers were lit to make steam. *Nevada* was ready to go.

2

Trials at Sea

"The USS *Nevada* left the works of the Fore River Shipbuilding Company at 9:17 a.m. 22 October, 1915, and proceeded to sea passing Boston Light abeam at 11:10 a.m."[1] Lt. R. W. Mathewson's matter-of-fact description of *Nevada*'s departure from Fore River belied the complexity of moving a 27,500-ton battleship from the narrow confines of her birthplace to the open sea.

The Fore River was barely 1,000 feet wide at the shipyard—less than twice the length of *Nevada*. Just north of the yard was a bridge that rotated at its center to let ships and boats pass. The gap between bridge and shore was challenging enough to navigate, and a wooden causeway—the extension of Washington Street in Quincy—further constrained the channel to less than 110 feet, barely 15 feet wider than *Nevada*. Several sharp turns had to be negotiated after the bridge to get to deep water. It was a difficult passage.

Since *Nevada* was not yet commissioned as a Navy ship, she flew the big blue flag of the Fore River Shipbuilding Company. Command during trials was the responsibility of thirty-two-year-old Capt. Joseph Kemp, marine superintendent at Fore River, who had five years' experience taking new ships out of the yard.[2] Some of the workers thought he had seawater in his veins; Kemp's father and five of his six brothers were ship captains as well. He knew *Nevada*, he knew the river, and perhaps most important, he had nerves of steel.

After the last lines connecting Battleship No. 36 to the pier were cast off, tugs pulled her back and turned her clockwise to point down the channel. The river was much too shallow and narrow for *Nevada* to move on her own—her massive propellers would only stir up the mud, creating unpredictable eddies that might pull the stern in unwanted directions.

A temporary catwalk spanning the width of the ship had been erected atop the conning tower to give the pilot a good view of the squeeze past the bridge. *Nevada* would be the first battleship to negotiate the newly dredged east side of the channel, and Kemp had handpicked a group of assistants to man the sides of the ship and be ready to call out corrections to the shepherding tugs. Cables pulled on her bow, and tugs pushed on her stern, but *Nevada* had to go through the gap alone.

There was no hurry—it took twenty minutes to ease the 575-foot-long ship past the bridge.

Once she was through the gap, the tugs helped *Nevada* negotiate a sharp turn to the right and another to the left. The channels here were scarcely wider than the Fore River, and "turning" really meant rotating the ship about her center point. Finally, after the second turn, the open water of Quincy Bay beckoned and Captain Kemp could relax. *Nevada*'s giant turbines spun into action, and she quickly left the tugs behind, making her own way into the Atlantic. Kemp knew to take care on that first trip out of the yard. *Nevada*'s engines had been tested dockside, but never with high-pressure steam and never to actually propel the ship. Equally significant, for all of her life *Nevada* had rested in calm water. As she passed Boston Light she encountered the rolling waves of the open ocean for the first time, and a thousand new stresses pushed and pulled on her hull, challenging every rivet, weld, and joint.

The Navy had insisted on strict quality control during construction, and numerous tests had been conducted before *Nevada* left the yard, but most of these tests involved individual components of the ship. Now it was time to see whether all of them worked in harmony on a fully operational vessel. Kemp expected a few problems, and he was not disappointed. A pump in the steering compartment short-circuited on the first night out, and at 0815 the following day rudder control had to be shifted from the steam-driven steering unit to the electrical unit. A test of the cruising engine had to be abandoned when a thrust bearing on the starboard turbine overheated. Minor things: nothing that couldn't be fixed when they reached New York.

The ship was not due in dry dock until October 25, and Kemp used the three days allotted to the journey to put *Nevada* through her paces. As he began to get a feel for how she performed at sea, he spun the main turbines up to 215 rpm, close to the design maximum of 222 rpm. The ship surged to nineteen knots, and Kemp had little doubt that when she came out of dry dock clean and smooth she would reach twenty-one knots, just over the design specification of twenty and a half knots. Pushing hard, she might even make twenty-two knots.

Kemp was relieved to know that *Nevada*'s engines could reach near full power without incident. Memories of turbine problems in *North Dakota*, an earlier product of Fore River, were fresh in his mind, and there was still debate in naval circles about the suitability of the new type of engines to drive a big ship. Two problem children within a few years would be bad for business.

Kemp dropped anchor off Tompkinsville, Staten Island, at 2234 on October 24. There was no need to chance a nighttime passage into dry dock, and both the Navy and Fore River wanted to maximize the publicity value of *Nevada*'s arrival. For the last few months the *New York Times* had made the ship's debut an event to

Nevada at trials, November 3, 1915. Note the very clean lines topside. The ship consisted of a hull with four turrets, a conning tower, a smoke pipe, and two cage-style masts. *National Archives Photo Collection, RG 19*

be anticipated: "In appearance, in arrangement of her batteries, and in many other important ways the *Nevada* is a ship the like of which was never before seen in New York."[3] *Nevada* was something to be proud of, a national achievement, and she was coming to New York first. Kemp raised anchor at 0918, and the vessel began her stately progress up New York Harbor escorted by tugs and pleasure craft packed with people who wanted to get a good view of the ship.

By 1104 she was safely tucked up in Dry Dock 4 at the New York Navy Yard. There was not a moment to waste. The day after *Nevada* left Fore River, T. G. Roberts wrote a blistering thirty-page letter to the Secretary of the Navy: "As before stated, the Contractors have adopted a somewhat irrational program of work by deferring the great volume of work to the very last." He attached a list of 597 items that needed to be done before he considered the ship complete, including repairing a gasket, stopping a minor leak, fitting locking devices on a watertight hatch, clearing a louver jammed between pipes, and patching a seam in a duct.[4] It was rather like the punch list that a homebuyer provides a builder. Roberts was determined that Fore River would *finish* the ship before she underwent formal trials.

Washington had already gotten the message. Crossing Roberts' letter in the mail was a short directive from David W. Taylor, chief of the Bureau of Construction and Repair, ordering Roberts to telegraph Washington "if items do not progress to your satisfaction or should the items not be completed to your satisfaction at the time NEVADA leaves New York."[5]

Nevada left Dry Dock 4 at 1330 on October 28 and made her way to Tompkinsville and then Rockland, Maine, the site of the formal trials. It was a leisurely trip at low speed, and the ship did not arrive at Rockland Breakwater until 0705 on October 30.[6]

Since the formal inspection was not due to start until November 3, Captain Kemp had an opportunity to perform his own tests on the now-pristine *Nevada*. Lieutenant Mathewson reported: "At 6:45 a.m. 31 October, 1915, the ship got underway and made runs at various speeds over measured mile for Contractors' benefit at speed varying from 10 knots to full power. The average of the three longest full power runs was 20.707 knots per hour."[7] *Nevada* had beaten the specification for maximum speed by just over 0.2 knot.

Nevada at trials, November 3, 1915. Moving at a stately 10.51 knots, she hardly raises a bow wave. *National Archives Photo Collection, RG 19*

Nevada making 16.13 knots at trials, November 3, 1915. *National Archives Photo Collection, RG 19*

Next came a test of the cruising turbines. Kemp had cause to be anxious because one of the main bearings had overheated on the trip down to New York. This time all went well, and the crew was able to get useful data on oil and water consumption using the ship's more efficient cruising engines.

One of the key remaining requirements for the ship was her commanding officer. Joseph Kemp was a civilian employee of the Fore River Shipyard; after *Nevada* was commissioned, a U.S. Navy officer would take command. Being assigned command of the most powerful battleship in the world was a plum assignment, and there were more than a few contenders. Capt. William Sowden Sims got the job.

Sims was an ideal choice for *Nevada*. After graduating from the Naval Academy he had proven himself a rebel and, more important, a reformer. Beginning with his first cruise as a midshipman on board *Tennessee* he had sent a fusillade of letters to high officials about deficiencies in ships and operational practices. Sims was a dedicated officer who constantly sought ways to improve the efficiency of the service, especially in the area of gunnery. After observing superior gunnery practices on British ships he wrote a monograph suggesting improvements to U.S. aiming and firing procedures. The Navy responded to the troublemaker by making him inspector of target practice, where he could propagate his ideas throughout the fleet. William Sims was the man who taught the Navy to shoot straight.

Cdr. William Sowden Sims, *Nevada*'s first captain, shortly before he was promoted and given command of *Nevada*. *Library of Congress, Lot 12362*

Sims' detailed reports gained the notice of President Theodore Roosevelt, who appointed him his naval aide. Sims so impressed the president that Roosevelt proposed promoting him to rear admiral, over the heads of more senior Navy captains. The Navy bureaucracy proved too strong for even the president, and as a consolation prize Sims was given command of the pre-dreadnought battleship USS *Minnesota*. Once on board, he promptly implemented "Sims' Way" of command and control, which emphasized teamwork, respect for skills in the enlisted ranks, and an unswerving focus on excellence.

Blasting along at 20.81 knots, above the designed top speed of 20.5 knots. The heavy smoke is the result of a poor air-to-fuel ratio. *National Archives Photo Collection, RG 19*

Stern view of *Nevada* at trials, running at 19.5 knots. The small craft near the bow is due for a rough ride as the bow wave passes. A Sailor is poised on the bridge extension watching the close call. *National Archives Photo Collection, RG 19*

"To command a successful battleship is the best job in the world," Sims wrote to a friend.[8] Being the first captain of *Nevada* was a dream come true, a chance to shape a brand-new ship and crew into the finest vessel in the fleet. Sims arrived at Fore River in October 1915, in time to get familiar with his new charge before she left the yard for her acceptance trials.

The inspectors from the Board of Inspection reported to Rockland at 1700 on November 1 and spent the next day reviewing data on the ship and plans for the trials. They were well armed for their work with copies of the Navy's contract with Fore River, a full set of specifications, and a formal charge from Assistant Secretary of the Navy Franklin Roosevelt. In addition to the board members, VIPs on board included David W. Taylor, chief of the Bureau of Construction and Repair, and Rear Adm. Victor Blue, chief of the Bureau of Navigation. Taylor and Blue were ostensibly there to verify that the trials were fair and complete, but there was an element of fun as well. *Nevada* was a brand-new battleship, the best in the world, and they relished the chance to be out of Washington and part of the action.

Formal trials started before dawn on Wednesday, November 3, and continued through November 10. Kemp took the ship through full-speed endurance runs, efficiency runs using the cruising turbines, and various tests of her steering. *Nevada* passed every test with flying colors, but she was by no means ready to join the fleet. Numerous items still had to be addressed before the ship was ready for commissioning. Kemp reversed *Nevada's* tortuous path back to Fore River, and yard workers got busy readying the ship for her official handover to the Navy.

With each passing week, Washington pressed more emphatically for *Nevada* to be delivered as quickly as possible. The war in Europe seemed deadlocked, and the Navy worried about the consequences of a British defeat. If England lost the war, would part of the Royal Navy pass into the hands of the Germans? And if so, would Berlin make a play for colonial territories in the Western Hemisphere, perhaps taking on the United States in the process? In late February the Navy Department informed Fore River that it wanted the ship in Boston on March 1. H. G. Smith, vice president and general manager of the company, wrote back that March 2 was preferable to take advantage of high tides. He added that "there will probably be a few minor items of uncompleted work at the time of delivery," and that yard workers would complete those items at Boston immediately after the delivery of the ship.[9]

T. G. Roberts reported from Boston on March 10 that Fore River had gotten nearly everything done and that the acting commanding officer, Cdr. J. T. Tompkins, was pressing for commissioning the very next day, Saturday, March 11.[10] There were two reasons for the rush. First, the Navy was paying a substantial sum to keep supplies sitting in railcars on the dock. The faster the ship was

Commissioning of USS *Nevada*, March 11, 1916. *Naval History and Heritage Command, NH 45458*

commissioned, the faster those supplies could be unloaded. Second, should commissioning not take place on the eleventh, the next available date was the inauspicious thirteenth. (According to tradition, commissioning could not take place on the twelfth because it was a Sunday.) The Navy Department agreed and telegraphed the commandant of the Navy Yard on Saturday morning: "Immediate delivery 'Nevada' authorized. Preliminary acceptance effective on delivery. Contractors' liability period beginning today there being only five items of work unfinished." The government would do the remaining work after the ship was delivered and charge the costs to Fore River.[11]

All of this was happening without the presence of Captain Sims. In what must have been a supreme frustration, the CO of America's newest battleship had been called to Washington to testify before the House of Representatives Committee on Naval Affairs. The ostensible reason for the hearings was to discuss the Navy appropriations bill, but Sims spent all day March 10 responding to a wide range of questions on Navy Department organization, the value of the Naval War College, results of target practice, and the role of submarines in warfare. It was a friendly hearing, and Sims even managed some humor. In response to Representative Calloway's comment "We have been told that naval officers never have any faults," Sims replied, "That is all right, but they are made out of the same kind of stuff that Congressmen are."[12] The committee adjourned on Friday afternoon, but the chairman told Sims to return on the following Tuesday. Sims was stuck in Washington.

Nevada's logbook started at the moment of her commissioning.

FROM 1:42 to 2:00 PM

At 1:42 with the USS NEVADA moored to the south west side of pier #9, Navy Yard, Boston, Mass., with the officers and crew in mass formation on the after end of the main deck, and after Commander R. D. Hasbrouck, U.S. Navy, Captain of the yard, read telegraphic orders from the Navy Department authorizing the acceptance of the ship from the Fore River Ship Building Corporation, in accordance with contract agreement and directing that ship be placed in commission, the national colors and commission pennant were hoisted in accordance with the ceremonies prescribed by the Navy Regulations. In the absence of Captain, W. S. Sims, U.S. Navy, ordered to command, Commander, J. T. Tompkins, U.S. Navy, read his orders from the Navy Department as Executive Officer and assumed command.[13]

"Tommy" Tompkins, the ship's executive officer and later a close friend of Sims, thus brought *Nevada* into the fleet. "This is a great day for the Navy," he said in his address to the crew. "The *Nevada* is without doubt the finest ship in this part of the world and one of the most powerful of any Navy in the world." But he knew that a battleship is more than steel. "This ship will be run by good men and I assume all here are good men . . . I trust every man on this splendid battleship will do his full duty." Chief Boatswain C. W. Antonson called for three cheers for the ship, and then the assembly dispersed.[14]

The remainder of *Nevada*'s first day as a U.S. Navy warship was uneventful. Sailors loaded 1,400 pounds of bread and other commissary stores from Henry's Bakery in Chelsea, Massachusetts. The evening brought 808 pounds of ham, 178 pounds of sausage, 201 pounds of luncheon meat, 1,469 pounds of beef, 7,200 pounds of potatoes, and an additional 1,129 pounds of bread. With a complement of 1,134 to feed, even this massive amount of food would last only a short time.

Not everyone was happy to be on the ship. Three days after she was commissioned, W. Leddy, a construction apprentice, was reported absent during ship's muster. He wandered back on March 19 and was discharged the following day "from this vessel and the naval service with a Bad Conduct Discharge." It would not be the last instance of bad behavior on *Nevada*. A substantial part of the log for the early months consists of disciplinary actions taken against crewmembers for offenses such as smoking belowdecks, reporting late for work, failing to carry out orders promptly, and, as in Leddy's case, absence from the ship without leave.

One man *was* exceptionally happy to come on board: Captain Sims reported on March 16, fresh from his ordeal with the House Committee on Naval Affairs. It

Nevada leaves Boston Navy Yard on March 23, 1916, shortly after her commissioning. *National Archives Photo Collection, RG 19*

was a proud day for Sims. His pennant flew over the newest battleship in the world, and the captains of other vessels came to pay their respects. For a Navy man, life did not get much better.

Sims was soon to have more visitors. On March 19 the ship was opened to the public, and more than two thousand people came to see America's first super-dreadnought. The guests were awed by this technological marvel of the age. Here floated a self-contained community with its own telephone network, water supply, sanitation system, and laundry. Cooking, baking, and most heating units were powered by electricity, a relative novelty for the day. Every surface gleamed, and the Sailors showed manifest pride in their ship. The open house was a chance to show citizens what their money had bought; few came away unimpressed.

Nevada left Boston on March 23 and arrived two days later at Berth 11 at the New York Navy Yard. Though now a commissioned warship, she was not yet fully operational: ammunition hoists had to be installed as well as torpedo tubes and other ordnance-related equipment. She remained in New York for more than two months, ending her stay with a stint in dry dock to clean her hull. On May 25 Sims ordered her anchor raised and headed to Newport, Rhode Island, for almost a month of mini–shakedown cruises.

Next up was a trip to Hampton Roads, Virginia, where *Nevada* would try out her guns. As she lay at anchor on the Navy's shooting range on May 22, gun crews started systematic target practice using the 5-inch secondary armament. The next day *Nevada* opened up with her 14-inch main battery, firing at targets 18,000 yards away. Sims, the former director of target practice, was in his element. But his pride was bruised when an accident occurred on the very first shot of the 14-inch guns. Chief Turret Officer C. N. Curtis suffered lacerations and shock when a recoiling gun struck him in the head. He was lucky not to have been killed, and Sims could not have been happy that a turret captain had been injured by one of the guns in his charge.

The next morning turret 2 fired three single shots and a two-gun salvo. And then *Nevada* showed what a super-dreadnought could do: "Fired 2 gun salvo from No. 3 turret; 3 gun salvo from No. 4 turret; 3 gun salvo from No. 1 turret and ten gun salvo from all turrets." It was a grand display of firepower. With each of the ten guns loaded with a full charge of four bags of smokeless powder, nearly two tons of explosive were propelling the shells. The noise was deafening, and fore and aft the side of the ship appeared to erupt in flame. The recoil force ejected dust from every nook and cranny, creating a gray haze belowdecks. For several minutes after the ten-gun salvo, *Nevada* rocked gently side to side.

Captain Sims was quick to institute his unique brand of leadership in the wardroom and throughout the ship. No dictator, he believed in developing initiative by delegating work to capable people. If someone could not handle the responsibility, better to find out now than when the ship was in a fight for her life. Sims was a superb communicator, and he spent hours talking with people individually and in groups, winning them over by persistence as well as by logic. Always ramrod straight in an immaculate uniform, he set an example that he expected others to emulate. Enlisted men got used to the captain showing up at unexpected times in unexpected places, always with the admonition, "Cheer up!" The phrase was the title of Sims' favorite poem, an uplifting verse by James R. Gooding that began:

> We cannot, of course, all be handsome,
> And it's hard for us all to be good;
> We are sure now and then to be lonely,
> And we don't always do as we should.

The poem encapsulated Sims' brand of management: people are imperfect, but they can be pleasant to one another and at least try to do the right thing. He had the poem printed on small cards and posted throughout the ship.

"The Cheer Up Ship" soon became the first of several nicknames for *Nevada*. Crewmembers made a mat for the captain's stateroom inscribed with the motto and even fitted an electric "Cheer Up!" sign behind Sims' desk. Electricians arranged a hidden switch so that he could flash the sign at anyone who came to his cabin to complain. Sims' spirit was infectious, and word that *Nevada* was a good ship quickly made its way around the fleet.

Sims was careful about his use of pronouns. "She is our ship, say 'we' and 'our,' for she belongs to us. When you go ashore on liberty remember that we are all in this together." He knew that many in his crew were young and away from home for the first time and more than ready to sample what the world had to offer. He preferred the men to stay away from bars, but if they did imbibe they should remember, "We are your friends—we will take care of you." "I would rather you came back with too much than stayed ashore and took more. If you come back, turn in and do your work next day, I promise you no trouble."[15] During one particularly long stay at Boston there were no reports of drunkenness or desertions in *Nevada's* crew,[16] remarkable for a time when drunken brawls and desertions often marked port calls. *Nevada's* Sailors took pride in their ship and didn't want to let down their commander or their shipmates. Such dedication paid off in performance—*Nevada* had excellent ratings for efficiency and, comforting to Sims, gunnery.

William Sims did not see command of a battleship as any reason to interrupt his tradition of afternoon tea, and he insisted that high standards be maintained. Coming into the wardroom one day he was shocked to see the makeshift manner in which his officers were brewing his favorite beverage. Without delay he fired off a letter to the paymaster general of the Navy: "Our Junior Officers are serving tea in a pitcher or a three-inch cartridge case, cream in a toothbrush mug. This is not proper for a first-class battleship. Assuming, therefore, that you are an advocate of adequate preparedness, can you allow us enough for tea tools? Peary drank tea at every meal on the dash for the Pole and I take it every afternoon. It is the Warrior's beverage."[17] Sims got his "tea tools" later that year when the state of Nevada presented its namesake with a magnificent sixty-eight-piece silver service made from three hundred pounds of silver and gold mined in the state—tea tools befitting a first-class battleship indeed!

After a quick protocol stop at Philadelphia, *Nevada* steamed south to join the Atlantic Fleet. On July 10 she took position astern of *Arkansas* for tactical and battle maneuvers that were to include a realistic war game. *Nevada* was finally doing what she was designed to do, steaming with the Atlantic Fleet to ensure that no enemy could approach American shores uncontested.

August 7 saw *Nevada* again steaming with the fleet. On the eighth she had to sheer out of line to avoid running down *Arkansas* when the latter made an unanticipated turn. On the eleventh, lookouts "sighted *North Carolina* and destroyers on port bow. Went to General Quarters and formed for attack." The ships took turns playing the role of enemy, with both sides learning important lessons. The attackers practiced how they would engage the enemy line of battle, and the defenders learned how to respond to surprises. This was before radar or aerial reconnaissance might reveal distant fleets, and, especially in bad weather, surprise was a real possibility.

Surprises occurred even in port. While *Nevada* was anchored at New York on September 27, the crew realized that something was amiss. "At 12:00 the ship began to list to starboard and listed about 3 degrees." Surely the ship was not sinking at anchor in calm water! Detailed depth soundings made along the length of the hull revealed that "the ship was aground on the port side." No damage was done, and the Cheer Up Ship refloated when the tide came in.

———

William Sims was promoted to rear admiral in August 1916, an overdue recognition of his many contributions to the Navy. He had mixed emotions about the promotion: he got his pick of future assignments (he chose president of the Naval War College), but never again would he walk the bridge of a ship as its commanding officer. With the normal delay attending a change in rank, he did not leave *Nevada* until December 30, 1916. As he went over the side for the last time the crew broke into a thunderous three cheers, a heartfelt tribute to a respected commander. "It was a sad business," he wrote to his wife.[18]

Sims' replacement was Capt. Joseph Strauss, former head of the Bureau of Ordnance. Strauss had spent much of his career creating the weapons that Sims had so ably perfected in practice, including the 12-inch gun that formed the main armament of the early U.S. dreadnoughts. It was Strauss who worked out the concept of the super-firing turret, in which one turret was raised so as to shoot over the top of another. Like Sims, Strauss had a strong practical bent. He established the Naval Proving Ground at Indian Head, Maryland, to verify that the big guns the Bureau of Ordnance developed did the job they were intended to do. Also like Sims, Strauss had previously commanded a pre-dreadnought battleship, *Ohio*.

After a pleasant New Year's in Norfolk, Strauss took *Nevada* to sea on January 9, 1917. A week's battle practice with the fleet at the Southern Drill Grounds was followed by what a rather romantically inclined lieutenant (jg) described in the logbook as "cruising in the Caribbean Sea," with stops at Puerto Rico, Haiti, and Cuba. On January 24 there was a challenging set of torpedo defense exercises in which ships from the destroyer flotilla "attacked" the line of battleships from behind. They reached *Utah*, immediately astern of *Nevada*, but never achieved a firing position for the Cheer Up Ship.

Euphemisms aside, life on a warship in the tropics was anything but a pleasure cruise. Men sweated and food spoiled. A ton and a half of potatoes had to be thrown overboard when they rotted in the hot, humid air. Boiler room crews were thankful that *Nevada* was oil fired and they were spared the agony of shoveling coal in roasting boiler room temperatures. Everyone—officers and enlisted men alike—suffered in the heat.

Nevada spent the remainder of February at Guantanamo Bay, the fleet's winter headquarters. The bay was large enough to hold the entire Atlantic Fleet at anchor while still leaving room for seaplane operations. Recreational facilities ashore included swimming pools, tennis courts, baseball diamonds, and even a golf course.[19] Less wholesome amusements were available in the nearby towns of Caimanera and Bucorón, where "rum, roulette, and ruin might be had at a price."[20]

During the time at Guantanamo the fleet practiced torpedo defense, gunnery, and fleet maneuvers of various kinds. On February 28 Vice Adm. DeWitt C. Coffman, commander of the Battleship Force, transferred his flag from *Wyoming* to *Nevada* to observe one of the target practices. *Nevada* fired ten rounds from her main guns at targets 20,000 yards off her starboard beam. Firing continued after lunch with single-gun shots and two-gun salvos. Strauss was beaming; he knew every aspect of the big guns and knew that Sims had brought the gun crews to the peak of perfection. It was a proud day for *Nevada*, even overriding the stress of having an admiral on board.

March 6 was another matter. The electric steering gear broke down an hour out of port, and Strauss had to raise the breakdown flag and steer the ship by engines alone. Five minutes later the crew had it fixed, only to have it fail an hour later. The breakdown flag was again raised and again the crew fixed the problem, this time in less than ten minutes. When the electric steering gear failed a third time after lunch, Strauss had had enough. He shifted to the steam-driven steering system for the balance of the day. Despite the problems, *Nevada* managed to complete her assigned gunnery drills.

Torpedo practice on March 8 turned into an exercise in trust. *Nevada* left Guantanamo Bay early in the morning, steaming in company with *Wyoming*. First up to shoot, *Nevada* fired two torpedoes at a target towed by *Wyoming*, in both cases achieving "partial hits." Then it was *Wyoming*'s turn to fire at a target towed by *Nevada*. *Wyoming* scored a hit—on *Nevada* herself. The wide-eyed crew watched the wake of the torpedo converge on the starboard side of the ship, knowing that it *must* be a practice round but with that faint fear that a mistake had been made. The torpedo bounced off the hull. An inspection revealed no damage, save perhaps to the uniform of the lieutenant who had to enter the space between the inner and outer hulls.

The fleet returned to Norfolk and remained there until the end of March. Sports competitions occupied the ships' crews, and *Nevada* won first place in the punt and dinghy boat races. The Navy was its own little world. But that world was about to change.

3

The Great War

In a rousing speech on February 3, 1916, President Woodrow Wilson called for construction of "incomparably the greatest navy in the world."[1] It was a turnabout for the president who just months before had based his election campaign on keeping America *out* of the war. But if Germany should win in Europe and come across the Atlantic in search of colonies and markets, the United States had to be prepared. Congress endorsed the need for naval preparedness by authorizing the construction of dozens of warships, including ten battleships and six battle cruisers. The number of uniformed officers and Sailors in the service would expand accordingly. All of these additions were to be funded over a three-year period, starting with a doubling of the Navy's budget in the first year.[2]

The money came just in time. On February 3, 1917—one year to the day after Wilson's speech—Washington broke off diplomatic relations with Berlin. The proximate causes were Germany's resumption of unrestricted submarine warfare, including the sinking of the passenger liner *Lusitania* with American citizens on board, and the leak of the Zimmerman telegram. The latter, an attempt by the German Foreign Ministry to bring Mexico into the war in exchange for promises of future territorial concessions, was the final straw for Wilson. On April 2 he asked Congress for a declaration of war. Four days later Congress passed a joint resolution endorsing the president's request, and Wilson signed it the same day.

At 1350 on April 6, 1917, Vice Adm. DeWitt Coffmann signaled all ships under his command that war with Germany had commenced. Two minutes later he sent a message indicating that the president had signed a declaration of war. The timing was interesting. The fleet was informed that it was at war before it was told that Congress and the president had legally authorized that war.

In fact, the U.S. Navy had been on a war footing since early February.[3] On February 4 the General Board sent the Secretary of the Navy a list of twenty-two steps that should be taken "to meet a possible condition of war with the Central European Powers."[4] A detailed mobilization plan followed on March 23 specifying where ships should rendezvous upon a declaration of war, what should be done to prepare them for battle (such as storage of nonessential equipment), and the priority that shipyards should give to completing work on various types of vessels.[5]

———

Nevada, assigned to Division Eight, Squadron Four of the Battleship Force of the Atlantic Fleet, was undergoing a minor overhaul at the Norfolk Navy Yard when the war began. Captain Strauss informed the crew of America's entry into the war and "gave . . . a serious talk on our war duties."[6] Within weeks the ship's complement grew by 301 to a total of 51 officers and 1,263 Sailors, ensuring sufficient manpower to run the ship, fire the guns, and repair damage even after taking casualties in battle.

Sailing orders arrived at 2300 on April 21, and arrangements were made to get under way at 0700 the following morning. Problems with the steering gear continued to plague the ship, however, and when the mechanism failed a test at 0100 on the day of departure, parts had to be sent to the yard's machine shop for modification. *Nevada* did not get under way as a battleship at war until April 24.

She spent the following weeks at anchor in the York River conducting intensive training for the new men, focusing on gunnery and defense against submarines. The latter mission was made more realistic by having U.S. submarines move through the fleet, challenging those on watch to spot the telltale periscope wake or other disturbances created by submerged craft. The loss of several British warships to submarine-launched torpedoes gave added emphasis to torpedo defense, as did regular sightings of German U-boats off the east coast of the United States. Fire drills became a routine practice, crucial on a vessel containing huge quantities of explosive and flammable materials.

Nevada remained in the York River until May 15, when she stood up Chesapeake Bay to conduct short-range battle practice for 5-inch gun crews. Judging from the initial results (two hits for twelve shots, both hits made by the same gun), practice was definitely needed. Within a few days the score improved to twenty-two hits out of thirty-six shots.

Some of the new men assigned to *Nevada* were learning how to operate 5-inch guns before being shipped off to armed merchant ships or newly commissioned destroyers. Gunnery practice was held nearly every day. *Nevada* would leave her moorings at around 0600, steam up Chesapeake Bay to a predetermined anchorage, and conduct "sub-caliber" firing practice with her main and secondary batteries. To save wear and tear on the big guns, a small gun firing a miniature projectile was strapped to the gun barrel—not quite the same as shooting a three-quarter-ton armor-piercing shell driven by hundreds of pounds of smokeless powder, but more realistic than simply going through the motions without shooting at all. The

14-inch guns used 1-pounder rounds in their sub-caliber attachments, and the 5-inch guns used .30-caliber ammunition. Sub-caliber guns were fired electrically, just like the actual guns, so the fire control system got a full workout.[7] "Sky gun" (antiaircraft gun) crews practiced by shooting at balloons released by other ships.

On May 30 *Nevada* welcomed thirty-nine midshipmen from the Naval Academy for the annual summer cruise. The cruise gave the students an opportunity to leave their books and experience life on a commissioned warship, the beginning of a practical naval education that would continue throughout their careers. This group of future officers arrived on a good day because the ship was in dry dock having her bottom cleaned and painted. The midshipmen got the full tour of the ship, inside and out, including seldom-seen views of the massive propellers, the rudder, and the bulbous bow that was designed to enhance the ship's speed and fuel efficiency.

During their weeks on board *Nevada* the midshipmen participated in routine drills and observed gunnery exercises with both sub-caliber and full-scale guns. Part of their wish to see a battleship in action was granted when the 14-inch main armament was fired during target practice near San Marcos Island. *Nevada* traded target practice observers with her sister ship *Oklahoma* to keep scoring honest and stimulate a healthy sense of competition between the two battleships.

Tragedy struck on July 2 as *Nevada* was heading out the York River when Seaman 2nd Class Henry Middleton jumped overboard through the port of a 5-inch gun compartment. The logbook reported that "the ship was at the time

The galley circa World War I. Food was collected in the galley and taken to berthing spaces to be eaten. *Naval History and Heritage Command, NH 104610*

passing through the 35 foot dredged channel and could not turn around. A life buoy was dropped close to the man but he made no effort to swim for it." *Wyoming*, following astern, lowered a boat, and *Nevada* turned around as soon as she could, but despite a thorough search Middleton was never found. Interviews with crewmembers suggested that he suffered from mental problems. Training resumed within hours of the accident.

During short-range battle practice on July 5 the 5-inch gun crews scored fifty-five hits out of ninety shots. But "numerous shell[s] were seen to break up on leaving muzzle,"[8] a phenomenon Captain Strauss found particularly frustrating. As the former head of the Bureau of Ordnance, which oversaw the Navy's ammunition supply, he knew that faulty ammunition could have disastrous consequences if the target was a German submarine or a destroyer launching a torpedo attack. Exacerbating his worry, the radio room copied a signal that a submarine had been sighted in Chesapeake Bay. *Nevada* immediately returned to her protected anchorage. There was no question of bravery in such a situation—a battleship was too valuable an asset to risk when there was nothing to be gained.

On August 13 the Battleship Force proceeded to sea for a week's maneuvers. Torpedo defense watches were set, and gun crews continuously manned their weapons, even sleeping next to them at night. Five days later the Battleship Force split into two parts: Battleship Force One posed as the enemy and "attacked" Battleship Force Two, which included *Nevada*. This type of exercise added an element of real-time initiative to maneuvers, something that could be lacking in tightly scripted practices in which ship movements were known in advance. Signalmen needed to be on the alert for commands from the flagship and send their own reports of enemy sightings. Bridge crews and gun directors had to be ready to repel attacks and launch salvos of their own. When a ship was sighted emerging from the mist, there were precious few seconds to determine if it was a friend joining the formation or an enemy about to open fire.[9] Two American ships had already been fired upon for not returning the correct signals when challenged.

After these initial wartime training exercises, *Nevada* spent the next five months undergoing an extensive overhaul at the Norfolk Navy Yard. A great deal of work had been authorized during a readiness-for-war assessment the previous July, but there had been no time to do it. The pneumatically driven ammunition hoists had to be modified to reduce the probability that battle damage would put them out of action, and special expansion chambers had to be installed on the 14-inch guns so that the recoil dampeners would return the guns to their original position after firing. Nine of the twenty-one 5-inch guns—those at the bow and stern—were removed during the overhaul and their gun ports plated over. Experience had demonstrated that sea spray rendered these guns useless except in the calmest weather.

Nevada needed to be in the best possible condition to operate on a prolonged assignment in distant waters.

———

As early as July 1917 British admiral John Jellicoe had lobbied his American counterparts to send battleships to serve with the Grand Fleet, thinking such a move would serve two major goals. First, the presence of American capital ships in European waters would be a potent political symbol of America's commitment to the war effort, vital to the morale of the Allies. Second, the presence of modern battleships would enable the British to decommission some of their old pre-dreadnoughts, releasing crews to serve on new ships. One dreadnought was the fighting equivalent of two or three pre-dreadnoughts, so there was great leverage in the exchange.[10]

On November 24, 1917, five coal-burning battleships (*Delaware*, *Florida*, *Wyoming*, *New York*, and *Texas*) under the command of Rear Adm. Hugh Rodman sailed for Scapa Flow to form Battle Squadron Six of the Grand Fleet.[11] *Nevada* and *Oklahoma*, two of the most modern dreadnoughts in the U.S. fleet, would have been welcome additions, but the British were critically short of oil and could not guarantee that fuel would be available for them. The sisters would remain on the East Coast as protection against a breakout of the German fleet.

———

After five months in the yard and with many new men on board—including recently assigned Capt. Andrew T. Long—the first order of business for *Nevada* was a return to proficiency in basic routines. The crew repeated fire quarters, collision quarters, man overboard drill, and all of the other standard procedures until they knew them by heart. In April 1918 Long took his new command out for maneuvers with the fleet, an opportunity to test both ship and crew against other members of the battle line.

The cruise did not start out well. Despite all her time in the Norfolk Navy Yard, *Nevada*'s perennial steering problems reasserted themselves. On May 2 *both* the electric and steam systems failed, causing her to fall out of formation. Repairs were quickly made, but Captain Long knew that such a failure in battle, or even while steaming in submarine-infested waters, would draw the enemy to his ship like vultures to carrion.

Intensive gunnery exercises continued on a near-daily basis. On May 10 *Nevada* fired 67 rounds of 14-inch ammunition and 149 rounds of 5-inch shells, all with full powder charges. This was comparable to what might be expended in a running battle and was a rigorous test of the crew's ability to rapidly transfer ammunition from the magazines, load it into the guns, aim, and fire on a sustained basis. Further practice in shooting service rounds—the same type that would be used in battle—was held on June 6 when two 10-gun salvos were fired, an enormous stress on the ship but a spectacular show for surrounding vessels. On July 12 the secondary gun crews got their turn, firing 127 5-inch shells and an additional 20 rounds of 3-inch (antiaircraft) shells. Four days later *Nevada* fired five practice torpedoes. Both ship and crew were getting a thorough workout in their prime mission— delivering ordnance on target. Admiral Jellicoe had been disappointed with the shooting of the five American battleships assigned to the Grand Fleet because the scatter in their shooting was greater than that on British ships of similar type. The U.S. Navy was determined to fix the problem.

Indeed, the importance of accurate gunnery, especially against submarines, was brought home nearly every week. An American destroyer had recently depth-charged a U-boat off the coast of North Carolina not very far from the fleet's anchorage near Norfolk. On July 19, 1918, the cruiser USS *San Diego* hit a mine and sank off the coast of New York. William Sims' old command, the pre-dreadnought *Minnesota*, sustained serious damage when she hit a submarine-emplaced mine while steaming off Delaware. Secondary gunnery practice was survival practice.

Amid the hectic schedule of exercises and drills, time was set aside for recreation. The log entry for May 14 records that the crew was "marched aft for singing instructions" (no indication is given as to what songs they sang). The Fourth of July celebration included a twenty-one-gun national salute and a minstrel show in the evening. Athletics—from boxing to rowing to baseball—were encouraged as a means to build morale.

Captain Sims' enlightened treatment of officers and crew continued to pay off long after he left *Nevada*. During the period from July 1, 1917, to June 30, 1918, the Cheer Up Ship had the lowest rates of all forms of courts-martial of the four battleships in her group. Desertions were about average, as were certain classes of petty offenses (disobeying orders, drinking, etc.), but discipline on board the ship was generally good,[12] a considerable accomplishment given the constant stream of new men coming on board. The good discipline may have been partly attributable to the continuity of the ship's petty officers—the backbone of the Navy. It was not unusual for petty officers to remain on board the same ship for a decade or more, rising in seniority and authority. These senior enlisted men, who often counseled junior officers on the best way to get things done, refreshed the brushstrokes that Captain Sims had made on the blank canvas of *Nevada*.

In Europe, Germany's position was becoming increasingly desperate, and Allied planners worried that the High Seas Fleet might try to break out into the Atlantic to attack American troop convoys. As a counter, the Navy decided to send Battleship Division Six—*Utah*, *Nevada*, and *Oklahoma*—to Queenstown, Ireland, where they could sail on short notice to escort convoys on the last, most dangerous, leg of their journey. Rear Adm. Thomas Rodgers, in command of the division, chose *Utah* as his flagship. While the fuel oil situation had eased a bit in Britain as a result of the successful convoy system, the Navy decided to send a dedicated oiler with the battleships just in case, along with a tug.

Command of the new Battleship Force would remain in American hands, in contrast to the situation at Scapa Flow where Rear Admiral Rodman's ships served under Admiral Jellicoe. Rodgers would work closely with British admiral Lewis Bayly in Ireland, but Battleship Division Six's mission was to protect American convoys, and it would remain under the command of an American.

Although the ship's new assignment had not yet been announced, *Nevada*'s crew suspected that something was up when the ship was recalled from gunnery practice on July 29 and ordered to proceed immediately to the Norfolk Navy Yard. This was surely preliminary to a long overseas deployment. The frantic pace of activity at the yard only confirmed the men's suspicions; work that would have taken two months in normal times was completed in ten days.

Since *Utah* was not ready to sail, Rear Admiral Rodgers raised his flag on *Nevada*, and at 1315 on August 12, Captain Long cast off all lines and moved the short distance from the Norfolk Navy Yard to Hampton Roads. After taking on fuel, *Nevada* and *Oklahoma* weighed anchor at 1545 on August 13. The ships zig-zagged according to plan, making a standard speed of fourteen and a half knots and darkening ship at sunset to avoid presenting a target to submarines. The 5-inch antisubmarine guns and 3-inch antiaircraft guns were continuously manned. Two days out from port the ships steamed through a large field of floating wreckage, a sobering reminder of the potential for submarine attack.

On August 19 lookouts reported a submarine periscope on the port bow. "Speed was immediately increased to eighteen knots . . . and the port torpedo defense battery opened fire. Only four shots were fired." The "periscope" was later thought to have been a floating spar; "however, no chances were taken . . . the NEVADA had fired her first shots of the war."[13] Aside from this scare the trip was uneventful, and experienced Sailors said that they had never made a crossing with such fine weather and smooth seas.

An escort of six U.S. destroyers came out to meet *Nevada* and *Oklahoma* on their arrival at Bantry Bay on August 23. All ships increased speed to twenty and a half knots; the faster they were through the submarine danger zone the better. Captains and crews breathed easier when the ships were through the harbor's anti-submarine net and anchored in friendly waters.

Thirsty from her transatlantic crossing, *Nevada* took on 467,879 gallons of fuel oil the next day. Official visits were exchanged between the ships' captains and

Nevada in Queenstown, Ireland, awaiting the call to protect American convoys en route to France. *Naval History and Heritage Command, NH 013684*

the local British commodore, and the Navy paymaster brought on board 1,500 pounds in English currency. Despite being in a harbor protected by an antisubmarine net, Captain Long kept torpedo defense guns manned as a precaution against German intruders.

Utah joined Battleship Division Six on September 10 flying the flag of Atlantic Fleet Commander in Chief Adm. Henry Mayo, who had hitched a ride on *Utah* to inspect American naval forces in European waters. Rear Admiral Rodgers transferred his flag from *Nevada* to *Utah* on the fifteenth.

Nevada, *Oklahoma*, and *Utah* were kept on four hours' notice to sail, but they spent most of their time in Ireland at anchor—battleships were not to be risked at sea without a strong destroyer escort, and destroyers were in short supply owing to the need for convoy escorts. When screening destroyers were available, the American ships maximized their opportunity by conducting a full range of training exercises, including target practice with the main batteries, torpedo defense, and mine clearing.[14]

Despite being confined to port most of the time, Battleship Division Six may have had more opportunity to conduct realistic training in Ireland than would have been the case back home. Nearly all of the U.S. Navy's destroyers had been sent to Europe for convoy duty, and there were not enough left to provide essential screening duties for American battleships on the East Coast.[15]

Nevada's crewmembers enjoyed their new surroundings, and small liberty parties were allowed to go as far afield as London. Nearby Bere Island contained both a British Army camp and football fields, and "friendly relations soon developed between ship and shore."[16] It was the first time that many of the crew had been out of the United States, and they reveled in the quaint Old World customs.

In what was becoming a tradition for *Nevada* commanders, Captain Long was promoted to rear admiral and given a new assignment: Navy liaison to the Allied Supreme War Council. Capt. William C. Cole, who had served in the Spanish-American War, took command on October 14. Most of Cole's sea experience was as an engineering officer, not a bad thing for a ship that suffered occasional mechanical malfunctions.

Cole knew that he had inherited a good ship, and the crew liked him. Behind his back the enlisted men referred to him as a "gob," Sailor slang for a regular guy. He liked to hear the crew sing and attended many of their athletic events. Cole was a disciplinarian, but like Sims, he saw punishment as a transition to a new start. "No matter what you are punished for today—tomorrow you start a clean slate." He wanted *Nevada* to be the "cheeriest 'Cheer Up' ship in the Navy."[17]

The new skipper had little time to adjust to his ship. On the very day he took command, the Navy received a warning that German cruisers had escaped into the

Atlantic. Since there were two American troop convoys approaching Europe, the battleships were ordered to prepare for immediate departure. Battleship Division Six got under way at 1755, steaming west at fifteen knots with an escort of eight destroyers. Since the ship was sailing through an area known to contain enemy submarines, Cole ordered torpedo defense and antiaircraft guns continuously manned. All twelve boilers were producing steam in case the formation needed to go to high speed on short notice.

At 2257 the next day, lookouts sighted a convoy of eleven troop ships en route from America, and the three battleships slipped into formation astern. After escorting their charges through the most dangerous part of their journey, the battleships and destroyers turned westward again and, the following morning, picked up the second convoy, also consisting of eleven ships. After safely escorting the second convoy to port, *Nevada*, *Oklahoma*, and *Utah* set course for Bantry Bay. As it turned out, there were no German cruisers in the area, but it was better to be safe than sorry when thousands of soldiers' lives were at stake. It was to be *Nevada*'s only combat mission of the war.

Another deadly enemy began to attack *Nevada* in October: influenza (referred to in the log as "pneumonia"). Seaman 3rd Class Stephen Murray and Seaman

Deck view taken in Queenstown, Ireland. *Naval History and Heritage Command, NH 092621*

H. G. Hyre died on October 21, and Seaman 2nd Class Bernard Nicklas died the following day. Six more crewmembers succumbed by the end of the month, and the ship lost a total of eleven during her wartime deployment.[18] With more than a thousand men crammed belowdecks, the probability of contagion was high; the only surprise was that there were so few cases.

———

By early fall 1918 the armies of the Central Powers were exhausted. With American forces in Europe approaching 2 million men, all but the most ardent militarists in Berlin recognized the situation as hopeless. On November 11, 1918, in a quiet ceremony in a railway car near Compiègne, France, the opposing commanders signed an armistice to take effect on the eleventh hour of the eleventh day of the eleventh month.

At 0645 on Armistice Day, Allied commander Marshal Ferdinand Foch signaled "All Ships and Stations": "From Marshal Foch, Commander-in-Chief quote hostilities will cease upon the whole front from the eleventh of November, eleven o'clock French time period the Allied troops will not cross until a further order the line reached on that date and hour."

Two hours later a message went out to naval forces: "The armistice is signed. Hostilities are to be ceased forthwith unless their hostile intent is obvious. Submarines on the surface will not be attacked."

Celebrations erupted around the world. On *Nevada* the officers and crew commemorated the occasion in their own special way.

> Then came our little celebration on shipboard. [Marine] Major Brumbaugh donned a bathrobe and, with a Turkish towel entwined about his head in true turban style, acted as the drum major, leading the band in our parade about the ship. Following the band came the crew, headed by the majority of the officers, dressed in any costume that was available on short order, all marching in the prison lock step and forming a seemingly endless line wriggling about the upper decks. Others grouped on the tops of the turrets and in the masts or any other point of vantage. When the quarterdeck was reached speeches were the order of the day and all the spokesmen were enthusiastically cheered. It was a glorious day as, according to our President, we had accomplished everything for which we had fought.[19]

Lt. (jg) J. M. Williams recorded the event with one sentence in the logbook: "Received information from the force Commander to the effect that an armistice has been signed with Germany." An unknown hand later added an arrow in blue pencil to call attention to the entry. It was, after all, "the greatest day in history," and it deserved a bit more emphasis in the ship's official record.[20]

Florida, serving with Rear Admiral Rodman in the Grand Fleet, was going home for a much-needed overhaul, and on November 18 *Nevada* was ordered to sail to Rosyth Harbor on the east coast of Scotland to replace her. For a few days, at least, *Nevada* would be a part of the Grand Fleet.[21] The ship's Marine band played "Auld Lang Syne" as she steamed slowly past *Oklahoma*, which would remain at Bantry Bay. The two crews had become close, and despite the spirit of competition between them, many men regretted parting from comrades.

Although hostilities had formally ceased, no one could be sure that all elements of the Central Powers had gotten the word or would abide by it. Screened by a destroyer escort, *Nevada* zigzagged north. Captain Cole ordered torpedo defense guns and antiaircraft guns manned throughout the journey, which was a rough one. At one point on the nineteenth, *Nevada* had to stop zigzagging and slow to one-third speed to allow the number 2 magazine crew to secure a 14-inch shell that had come loose from its storage mount. Heavy seas carried away a whaleboat, the forward life buoys, two booms, and forty-seven drums of gasoline.

Passing through the outer boom at Rosyth Harbor at 0810 on November 23, *Nevada* joined Rear Admiral Rodman's Battle Squadron Six and was formally attached to the British Grand Fleet. She was two days too late to witness the greatest naval parade in history.

Per the terms of the armistice, major elements of the German High Seas Fleet left their bases on November 21, 1918, for internment by the British. Admiral David Beatty (who had replaced Jellicoe as commander of the Grand Fleet) met them partway on their journey and gave them a fitting reception. Standing on the bridge of his flagship, *Queen Elizabeth*, Beatty surveyed two columns of Allied ships that stretched nearly to the horizon. Three hundred and seventy warships, including the American battleship division with Admiral Sims on *New York*, were on hand to witness what was, in all but name, the surrender of the High Seas Fleet. German dreadnoughts, battle cruisers, cruisers, destroyers, and other craft steamed between the two columns with Allied gun sights firmly locked upon them. While the guns were not loaded, ammunition was at the ready, and any wrong move would have brought an instant and fatal response.

When the armada reached Rosyth Harbor Beatty signaled all assembled ships: "The German flag is to be hauled down at three thirty-seven P.M. (sundown) and is not to be hoisted again without permission." "It was a pitiful day," he later told men on board *New York*, "to see those great ships coming in like sheep, being herded by dogs to their fold, without an effort on anybody's part, but it was a day that everybody could be proud of." Regarding the disappointment of not engaging

Nevada escorting *George Washington* (background) carrying President Woodrow Wilson to peace talks in France. *National Archives Photo Collection, RG 19*

the High Seas Fleet in a decisive battle, Beatty said, "The prestige of the Grand Fleet stood so high that it was sufficient to cause the enemy to surrender without striking a blow."[22] Good words, but many officers—on both sides—secretly regretted missing the opportunity to do what they had been trained to do—fight a great battle at sea.

There was no fraternization when British and American officers and men boarded the German vessels to ensure that the terms of the internment were being honored. *Nevada's* Yeoman S. E. Wilkinson later wrote, "Although orders forbidding it had been issued, they were unnecessary as our men certainly would not seek to communicate with or respond to overtures from sailors who had previously manned the murder-stained boats. No unnecessary sentences were spoken." He went on to remark that the German crews had "very little respect for their officers."[23] A few days later *Nevada's* officers and crew watched the German ships start on their final voyage to Scapa Flow.

Nevada left Rosyth soon afterward, on December 1, bound for Portland on the south coast of England. The crew was delighted to see the "homeward bound" pennant raised, a poignant symbol of the end of the war. Admiral Sims paid a short visit to the ship on the twelfth to address her officers and crew. As he climbed up on one of the ventilators on the quarterdeck, long-serving members of the crew thought it was just like old times. Battleship Division Six got under way that afternoon to perform one final escort duty: it accompanied SS *George Washington*, carrying President Wilson to the peace talks, into Brest Harbor.

Nevada topped off her fuel tanks from a French oiler on December 14 and joined Battleship Divisions Six and Nine for the long-awaited journey home. The trip was smooth, the only lament being that the ships did not arrive off New York until December 25, scotching crewmembers' hope to spend Christmas with their families.

On the day after Christmas, America threw a grand homecoming for its fleet. An ecstatic *New York Times* reported that "every craft in the harbor which had a whistle joined in a noisy welcome which was reinforced by the cheers of the tens of thousands who witnessed the spectacle from Battery Park, from the windows of tall buildings, and from pierheads."[24] Secretary of the Navy Josephus Daniels stood on the naval yacht *Mayflower* and reviewed the battle force as it steamed past the Statue of Liberty. USS *Arizona* led the column of battleships. On passing Daniels' yacht she fired a nineteen-gun salute while her Marine band played "The Star-Spangled Banner." *Nevada* was third in the line of the ten battleships and flew a homeward-bound pennant more than one hundred feet long—one foot for each day she was overseas.

After the battleships were securely anchored, *Mayflower* circumnavigated the fleet. Each ship's crew manned the rail in salute, and each ship's band played the national anthem. It was a bitterly cold day with heavy snow and mist, but Secretary Daniels stood hatless for more than an hour in honor of the men he passed.

That afternoon six thousand Sailors and Marines marched through the city, cheered by one of the largest crowds ever assembled on Fifth Avenue. In interviews later that day, Rear Admiral Rodman struck a diplomatic note, saying, "The Allies won because of that Grand Fleet in the North Sea. But for the Grand Fleet

Nevada with the fleet returning from Europe at the end of the war. *National Archives Photo Collection, RG 19*

. . . the war would have been lost."[25] After the formal events, five thousand men were granted liberty. Dances and parties were held around the city, with various venues vying to outdo one another in offering the warmest hospitality. Given the occasion, the men were models of good behavior, with few incidents of fighting or drunkenness.

———

The Great War was the worst cataclysm the world had ever seen. When the guns fell silent on November 11, 1918, the toll came to 16 million dead and 20 million wounded. The German, Austro-Hungarian, Russian, and Ottoman empires had ceased to exist. Britain and France were physically and financially exhausted. The battles to win the war were over, but the battles to win the peace were only just beginning.

4

Battleship Diplomacy

After a pleasant January spent enjoying the delights of New York, Captain Cole ordered anchors aweigh for battle practice at Guantanamo Bay. The U.S. Navy had learned much in the Great War and was eager to apply those lessons to fleet operations. The maneuvers of early 1919 focused on integrating surface ships, aircraft, and submarines into a combined fighting force, recognizing that new technologies were transforming naval combat from a two-dimensional to a three-dimensional affair.

Above the surface, aircraft had the range and endurance to serve as spotters for battleships, enabling the big guns to engage at longer range and with greater accuracy. Special "flying-off platforms" were constructed on the upper turrets of battleships. No catapults were needed because the speed of the ship was sufficient to give planes enough lift to take off even on such short "runways." Unfortunately, the flight was one way because the fifty-foot-long platforms were too short to permit landings. A plane either flew to shore or ditched in the sea at the end of a flight. It was a good bargain, however, because aircraft could spot targets beyond the range of mast-top observers and could assist in placing "indirect fire" when smoke or mist obscured the target.

Below the surface, advances in the range and speed of submarines enabled them to sail with the fleet. Subs could be used as pickets to warn of an approaching enemy or as attackers to whittle down an opposing battle line before a major surface engagement.

New radios were installed on major ships, and dedicated communications officers were brought on board. One of the key lessons of the May 1916 Battle of Jutland—the greatest naval engagement of the Great War—was that maneuvering a complex fleet in bad weather against a clever enemy required constant contact between a fleet commander and his ships. Lack of tactical awareness had cost Admiral Jellicoe a resounding victory, and the U.S. Navy was determined not to make that mistake in a battle involving American ships.

Nevada's crew got a break from the routine of drills and exercises when the fleet made a three-day call at Bridgetown, Barbados, in March 1919. Officers of

After the war, *Nevada* was fitted with a flying-off platform on the forward raised turret. The plane could take off from the ship but had to ditch at sea or return to land. *Naval History and Heritage Command, NH 013631*

Crew relaxing by the aft turrets, 1919. *Naval History and Heritage Command, NH 013688*

Squadron Three (*Wyoming*, *Nevada*, *Texas*, and *Oklahoma*) were treated to a dance hosted by the U.S. consul, and leading citizens of the island took them on drives and picnics. Enlisted men were granted liberty, one-third at a time, but were sternly warned "as to the evil effects of the native rum and the prevalence of venereal diseases on shore." To help ensure good behavior, each battleship sent ashore two patrols to assist the Bridgetown police. The warnings and shore patrols seemed to work, because "there was comparatively little drunkenness and but few instances of disorder."[1]

By June 1919 *Nevada* had been running hard for more than a year, including seven months in Europe. Numerous systems needed attention, and on June 15 the ship's newly assigned commander, Capt. T. P. Magruder, took her into the Philadelphia Navy Yard, where she would remain until December 15. Then it was back to Norfolk, where the crew had the pleasure of painting the ship's bottom while she rested in Dry Dock 3. Only the prospect of celebrating New Year's in New York consoled the men as they spread paint over more than an acre of steel plating.

The new year began with a heavy schedule of exercises including full-power trials, gunnery practice, and antiaircraft drills. During February the crew enjoyed

Fire at Guantanamo Bay, January 14, 1920. *National Archives Photo Collection, RG 19*

a return to Barbados but was disappointed that a subsequent visit to Trinidad was canceled due to "local conditions."[2] Instead, *Nevada* and the other ships of Squadron Three, Division Seven, steamed to Colón in the Canal Zone—hardly a consolation prize.

The fleet's movements remained unsettled in 1920. On February 2 Adm. Henry B. Wilson, commander in chief of the Atlantic Fleet, wrote to the Chief of Naval Operations (CNO) asking about plans for the balance of the year. The longer the Navy delayed in identifying fleet movements, the harder it was for

Nevada in dry dock, 1921. The torpedo tube opening is clearly visible beneath the waterline. Crewmembers spread paint over an acre of hull. *National Archives Photo Collection, 461423*

men to find housing for their families, and that in turn had an impact on morale and efficiency. The CNO responded with a rambling letter outlining the complications of fleet operations, including the need to schedule ships in Navy yards. The Navy Department had not yet pinned down when it would conduct joint exercises between the Atlantic Fleet and Pacific Fleet, and its best advice to Admiral Wilson was to assume that "the Fleet be based in a general way on New York City, using adjacent waters for drill grounds." One can only imagine ship commanders' frustration in trying to interpret what "in a general way" meant with regard to maneuvering tens of thousands of tons of battleships manned by thousands of frustrated men.

The Atlantic Fleet ended up splitting the summer between Hampton Roads and Guantanamo, where the battleships conducted torpedo defense practice, fired slugs (shells without explosives) from the main guns, and exercised at antiaircraft tactics. Gunnery practice paid off in improved performance: the four ships of Division Seven (including *Nevada*) fired thirty-two 14-inch salvos, thirty-one of which straddled the target.[3]

Ens. Dan Gallery related events inside turret 1 during one such gunnery exercise:

> From the time of commence firing till "cease" that turret and every man in it worked like a machine. At "stations" the gun captains, plugmen, powdermen, etc. seemed to fill up all the available space as they stood by their guns ready to snap to it at "load." When "load" was given everyone jumped to his job at once. The three huge plugs dropped down together and with the same movement that dropped the plug the gun captain reached down for a powder bag as the shell was slammed into the hissing jaws of the guns by the rammer. Then as the long fisted arm of the rammer shot back out, the powder bags were lifted into the tray and shoved home, and then as the tray was thrown back and the plugs snapped shut, the gun's crews disappeared into little nooks and corners that you would hardly think could hold a man. Then an angry grinding of gears as the guns crouched down to let drive, the powdermen flattening out as the guns came down till they could not roll over without touching them. A few seconds in this position, then the stand by bell, a few more tense seconds with no signs of life at all in the turret, then a heavy jar as the guns recoiled, and the turret's crew sprang into life again jumping to their stations as the guns came up for another load.[4]

Three days later Gallery observed operations in a 5-inch gun emplacement:

> Said gun is on the topside just aft of turret 2 so in action it is just under the muzzles of turret 2 and above those of turret 1. I knew I was in for a stormy session so I went up there in dungarees, left my cap below, and stuck a bale of

Secondary gun, circa 1921. It was hot inside the hull when the ship was in the tropics. The bare-foot Sailor was probably taking things a bit too far. *Naval History and Heritage Command, NH 013625*

cotton in my ears. I thought old Gabriel had blown his horn when the first salvo went off. All five of those babys [*sic*] let go at once, everything turned lurid red, and I got a jar like I had let out a tremendous sneeze and saw all my papers go flying into scraps. Our little pop gun then fired its ten shots and we rushed over to the lee side but we had to take three more big salvos first. All I got from my observers was one tattered and forlorn looking remnant.[5]

Even routine maneuvers had moments of excitement. The officers and men on *Nevada*'s quarterdeck held their breath on June 10 as *Oklahoma* ran up to within fifty yards of the stern. *Nevada* sounded her collision alarm, and one can easily imagine the dressing down that occurred on the bridge of *Oklahoma*.

The largest fleet maneuvers since the end of the war were conducted off the west coast of South America in early 1921. In this massive exercise involving both the Atlantic and Pacific Fleets, the column of warships stretched nearly four miles. Aside from a diplomatic motive of showing the flag in the domain of the Monroe Doctrine, the Navy wanted to practice integrated operations between what had become two distinct fleets. Each had evolved its own command structure and procedures, and getting them to function as a single fighting force would require practice.

To spice things up, there was a competition: the two fleets were to engage in simulated combat against one another. They were evenly matched—each had seven battleships and eighteen destroyers—so tactical skill factored highly in the outcome. In a letter to the CNO, Admiral Wilson said that he might personally command the Battleship Force, a perk that he would very much enjoy.[6]

The instant the crews got wind that they were to cross the equator, preparations began for a hallowed tradition on warships of all nations: the arrival of King Neptune and his court. The purpose of the royal visit was to oversee the induction of landlubbers—those who had never "crossed the line"—into the fraternal order of shellbacks, subjects of the king of the deep. No opportunity was lost to frighten initiates regarding the severity of the ceremony they were to undergo, and no expense was spared on costumes and stage sets. The battle fleet of 1921 may have represented the greatest single induction into Neptune's society up to that time—fully 25,000 men spread over 60 ships—so the effort seemed worth it if only for the stories that would be told, embellished, and retold for years to come.

Although the fleet actually crossed the equator at 0400 on January 24, the official ceremony was delayed to a more civilized 0800. The first order of business was to ensure that the "line" did not foul the ships' propellers, so a cadre of men was assigned to "lift it over the masts." This feat accomplished, the entire fleet stopped all engines for ten minutes to enable King Neptune, attended by his retinue of counselors, prosecutors, family members, clergymen, and other retainers, to climb onto the forecastle.[7] (Through some undisclosed magic the king appeared on all the ships simultaneously.) Capt. Luke McNamee relinquished command of the ship to the king's navigator, and every member of the crew not performing essential duties moved to the bow.

The dual meaning of Neptune's "court" soon became clear to the inductees. In a brief appearance before the king, every landlubber was found guilty of some infraction of royal law, from singing out of tune to having had a silly nickname at school. The miscreant was called forward, put in a barber's chair, and asked to verify his name. When he opened his mouth to speak, a foul-tasting gob of grease was thrust inside and a "barber" slathered him with a concoction of flour paste. After the man was "shaved" with a wooden razor, the barber's chair was tilted backward, spilling the unfortunate into a tank of water. Waiting hands dunked him until the flour paste was washed away, at which point it was time for the next victim. With hundreds of men to process, it was a prolonged affair, and there were few of the speeches that would accompany the ceremony on a smaller vessel.[8] Officers were not exempt from Neptune's justice, although they were treated somewhat more respectfully.

With sister ship *Oklahoma* (*left*) in the early 1920s. The two sisters led very different lives. *Naval History and Heritage Command, NH 50109*

The more serious work of the cruise began a few days later. At 2045 on January 27, screening vessels of the Atlantic Fleet sighted "enemy" destroyers. Searchlights were trained on the attackers, and guns were loaded and trained. A real enemy would have been able to conduct a devastating torpedo attack from a range of two thousand to five thousand yards of the battle line, a sobering reminder of the need for constant vigilance.

The Navy took its recruiting slogan, "Join the Navy and see the world," seriously, and part of the winter maneuvers of 1921 included visits to South American ports. The Atlantic Fleet stopped in Peru while the Pacific Fleet steamed on to Chile. The 13,000 officers and men of the Atlantic Fleet received a warm welcome on their arrival at Callao, Peru, on January 31, including an effusive speech from Peruvian president Augusto B. Leguia.

The National Geographic Society had worked with the Navy to provide Sailors with an information booklet about Peru, "in which the things worth seeing had been set forth, a plan of the city given, and the monetary system explained."[9] Lima, located eight miles inland of Callao, was the principal destination of liberty parties, and Sailors swarmed over the city. With the men having received stern warnings of the power of pisco, the indigenous liquor, there were few incidents.

As a special treat, the Peruvians scheduled a demonstration bullfight for the Sailors that included some of the city's most famous bulls and bullfighters. Many Sailors found the spectacle appalling and shocked their hosts by rooting for the bull, shouting, "Go get him, bull!"[10] All ended well, but it was a culture clash neither side anticipated.

The Americans thanked their hosts by giving a farewell ball on *Nevada* on February 4. It was a clear night, and the electric lights on the ships crowding the harbor created a gala atmosphere. The ship's kitchens provided food in abundance, and two bands accompanied dancing until 0100, when officers and men reluctantly escorted their guests ashore.

The Atlantic Fleet left Callao the following day to rejoin its Pacific counterpart for joint maneuvers, including another simulated battle that almost ended before it began. Steaming in heavy fog on the evening of February 6, *Nevada*'s bridge crew was horrified to see the stern of *Oklahoma* appear immediately ahead. Collision Quarters was sounded, both engines were thrown into full reverse, and the port anchor was let go to help prevent a crash. The emergency measures were successful, but the sister ships were now one-to-one for near collisions at sea.

There were no real winners in the simulated battles between the two fleets—their main purpose was to develop tactics benefiting both. Back in Panama, however, *Nevada* emerged the clear victor in another type of battle: the Battenberg Cup boat races. Started in 1905 by Prince Louis of Battenberg and Rear Adm. Robley Evans of the U.S. Navy, the hotly contested race between cutters of British and American ships had been won two years in a row by *Arizona*. This year *Nevada*'s crew brought home the ornate trophy, a happy day for the Cheer Up Ship.

Success followed success. On April 21 the fleet athletic completion was held at Guantanamo Bay. Six thousand Sailors jammed the stands around a ring built for wrestling and boxing, and chairs twenty rows deep were set up for officers. When *Nevada* won the trophy for general excellence the crew went wild. Dan Gallery reported: "After the bouts, in which she carried off the big honors, they had a triumphant torch light parade around the field. It was led by the officers who marched about 20 abreast arm in arm with the skipper in the center . . . then the ship's company carrying lurid torches and large banners, and in the center of it were the ships fighters and wrestlers each borne on the shoulders of four or five hilarious sailors."[11]

Nevada's crewmembers had to adjust their attitude toward the Pacific Fleet when, in July 1921, the CNO transferred *Nevada, Oklahoma, Arizona,* and *Maryland* from the Atlantic to the Pacific and sent four older battleships in the reverse direction. The nine battleships in the Pacific Fleet now included many of America's newest and most powerful, while the seven in the Atlantic Fleet were the Navy's older coal-burning battleships. In 1922 the Atlantic-based ships would be organized into the Scouting Fleet, and the newer units in the Pacific would be designated the

Nevada at San Pedro, California, 1920s. It was good to be in home port. *Naval History and Heritage Command, NH 013697*

Battle Fleet. En route to the transfer, *Nevada* returned to Peru to commemorate the Peruvian Centennial Exhibition, a happy event for many in the crew.

Prior to the transfer, a drama of considerable importance to *Nevada's* crew played out between Captain McNamee, the Navy Department, and the Robbins & Myers Manufacturing Company. On January 19, 1921, McNamee wrote to the Bureau of Construction and Repair that the motor of the ship's potato peeler, built by Robbins & Myers, had burned out. Construction and Repair promptly wrote to the Motor Sales Department of Robbins & Myers, which replied with a copy of the test data for the motor in question. The company assured the Navy that the motor met all of the original contract requirements, and Construction and Repair dutifully sent this information, along with its own suggestions for repairing the motor, to *Nevada*. While additional exchanges were taking place between the Navy Department and Robbins & Myers (which suggested returning the defunct motor to the factory for further examination), the ship's crew fixed the problem. There was no way that the galley crew was going to peel potatoes for more than a thousand hungry men while bureaucrats sorted out contract liabilities.

While the Navy's performance during fleet maneuvers and gunnery exercises was improving, a new threat was emerging in the air. In April 1919 Gen. William "Billy" Mitchell of the Army Air Service arrogantly asserted that his bombers could sink any ship afloat, including battleships. A panel of admirals assembled by Assistant Secretary of the Navy Franklin D. Roosevelt scoffed at the idea that flimsy airplanes could sink a heavily armored capital ship. Roosevelt himself called the claim "pernicious."[12]

Mitchell refused to back down, and finally the Navy agreed to a series of landmark tests that were performed during the spring and summer of 1921. An assortment of target vessels, including the ex-German battleship *Ostfriesland*, was assembled fifty miles outside the Chesapeake Bay, and Army bombers set out to sink them.

To no one's surprise, Mitchell's bombers made short work of two destroyers and a light cruiser. Then they turned their attention to the ten-year-old *Ostfriesland*, a fine ship with tough armor and excellent watertight integrity. The German battleship endured a number of direct hits that did little damage, but when two 1-ton bombs hit the water close to the hull, the resulting explosions pushed in the armor plates and started serious leaks. *Ostfriesland* sank twenty-two minutes later.

The tests were supposed to be done under "wartime" conditions, but that was hardly the case. The ships were not under way, there was no antiaircraft fire, and no attempt was made to repair damage between bomb hits. Nevertheless, the sight of canvas-covered biplanes sinking a first-class battleship made a strong impression on the observers—and eventually on Congress.

The Navy had, in fact, already embraced aviation and was investing in its future. Immediately after the Great War, the General Board recommended that an aircraft carrier be assigned to each division of battleships.[13] A separate administrative

Scrubbing the deck, spring 1921. Maintenance of wood and steel in a saltwater environment was a constant chore. *National Archives Photo Collection, RG 80, no. 460938*

structure, the Bureau of Aeronautics, under the command of Rear Adm. William Moffett, was created within the Navy Department in 1921, and the Navy's first aircraft carrier, the converted collier *Langley*, gave the fleet a chance to experiment with integrated air-sea operations. On battleships, catapults replaced the crude "flying-off platforms" so that seaplanes could be launched and then hoisted back on board for their next flight. Aviation was becoming a true and valued part of the fleet.

The Navy could deal with threats from new technologies, but political threats proved much more challenging. President Warren G. Harding entered office on March 4, 1921, with a profound belief in small government and a return to "normalcy," a term that many saw as the equivalent of isolationism. He was not alone in this belief. Naval historians Harold Sprout and Margaret Sprout explain: "The United States Navy held indisputable sway over the Eastern Pacific and over that part of the Western Atlantic which lay north of the Equator. The continental United States, therefore, enjoyed a measure of security unapproached by any other great nation in modern times."[14] If there was no real threat to the continental United States, why go to the expense of a huge navy? With a keen sense of public

The Washington Naval Conference of 1921 helped *Nevada* escape the scrapyard. *Library of Congress, LC-H27- A-4041*

Transiting the Panama Canal, February 15, 1921. *Nevada* has evidently paused in her progress. *Naval History and Heritage Command, NH 73829*

opinion, the former newspaperman Harding proposed a major international conference to discuss ways to limit armaments, particularly expensive capital ships.

The Washington Naval Conference opened with great fanfare on Saturday, November 12, 1921, one day after the third anniversary of the Armistice. Secretary of State Charles Evans Hughes opened the proceedings with an electrifying speech outlining the failure of previous arms control efforts and the disastrous consequences of the Great War. "If we are to be spared the uprisings of peoples made desperate in the desire to shake off burdens no longer endurable, competition in armament must stop."[15]

Hughes proposed a ten-year "holiday" in capital ship construction for the United States, Great Britain, and Japan. America would halt construction on nine battleships and six battle cruisers, even though some were nearly complete. All pre-dreadnoughts would be scrapped. Thirty American battleships would be sent to the breakers. Similar measures were suggested for Great Britain and Japan. To address the *causes* of international tensions Hughes negotiated a parallel agreement that froze the fortification of Pacific bases, making it virtually impossible for the United States or Japan to attack one another in home waters.

The Washington Naval Treaty limited battleships and battle cruisers to a maximum of 35,000 tons with no bigger armament than 16-inch guns. Aircraft carriers were limited to 27,000 tons and could carry no more than 10 guns of 8 inches or less. Cruisers were limited to 10,000 tons and 8-inch guns. There were total tonnage limits for capital ships (500,000 tons for the United States and Britain, 300,000 tons for Japan, and 175,000 tons for France and Italy) and aircraft carriers (135,000 tons for the United States and Britain, 81,000 tons for Japan, and 60,000 each for France and Italy), but none for cruisers, a situation that led to a huge increase in the construction of these fast warships in the next decade.

More troubling than the lack of limits on cruisers was the complete absence of constraints on submarines and aircraft. Both had proven their utility in combat—submarines in the Great War and aircraft in Billy Mitchell's bombing demonstrations—but the conferees could not agree on how to limit them. The best they could do was to outlaw the type of unrestricted submarine warfare the Germans practiced during the Great War.

In hindsight, it might seem that the Washington Naval Conference attendees went to great trouble to limit ships that were already becoming obsolete. However, all of the major navies recognized that while the submarine and airplane had the *potential* to change the strategic equation, it was still only a *potential*. Not a single modern battleship was sunk by a submarine during the Great War. Billy Mitchell had demonstrated that aircraft could sink a well-armored battleship, but admirals reckoned that the solution to that threat was better antiaircraft defenses and armor protection against bombs. For now, the battleship still reigned as the supreme instrument of national power projection.

5

The Great Cruise

Battleship diplomacy continued to be important in the wake of the Washington Naval Treaty. In August 1922 *Nevada* and *Maryland* were ordered to Rio de Janeiro to pay America's respects to the newly elected president of Brazil and to attend the Independence Centenary International Exposition celebrating the one-hundredth anniversary of Brazil's independence.

The visit was fraught with political sensitivities. The United States and Brazil were on friendly terms, but Great Britain was keen to develop stronger economic ties in South America, and Washington worried that enhanced trade between the two nations might be the start of political or even military cooperation. The dispatch of two of the U.S. Navy's most powerful battleships to Rio was a clear demonstration of America's dominance in the western Atlantic.

The visit went well, and *Nevada* and *Maryland* were scheduled to leave for home on November 5. However, the late arrival of the new president extended their stay in Rio by an extra week. The delay was to have significant benefits on the diplomatic front. An "American Day" celebration, long planned for November 8, was in danger of cancellation because the buildings at the Exposition grounds were not finished; such a gaffe would be embarrassing to the United States. Capt. Douglas E. Dismukes and the American ambassador put their heads together and came up with a remarkably simple solution: rename November 8 "*Nevada* Day" with parades and a concert by the ship's band. A check for $1,041 raised from *Nevada*'s officers and crew was presented to the American grade school in Rio de Janeiro, complementing a previous contribution of $500 raised by a benefit performance of *Nevada*'s theatrical troupe.[1] *Nevada* saved the day.

The crew was not always as sensitive to the niceties of international relations, and the log records a number of instances of Sailors being arrested for drunkenness, overstaying their liberty, and theft. A record-breaking 291 cases of venereal disease were diagnosed following the visit. The Navy noted in its annual report that "moral and medical advice does not seem to suffice when opportunity is present."[2] Overall the men's behavior was good, but the attractions of Rio de Janeiro were simply too tempting to maintain *Nevada*'s sterling reputation.

Even departing Rio proved a challenge. When Captain Dismukes attempted to raise the anchor at 1601 on November 16, it snagged on undersea cables. The crew struggled for more than six hours to free it, at last succeeding at 2225. Thirty-five minutes later *Nevada* was under way on six boilers, headed for Hampton Roads.

———

The challenge of defending American interests in two oceans increased markedly with the restrictions imposed by the Washington Naval Treaty. Strict limits on the number of battleships and aircraft carriers meant that no country could rely on overwhelming superiority in a fleet engagement—victory would go to the fleet that was best able to create and exploit a tactical advantage, often on the spot.

The U.S. Navy broke that problem into three parts. First, the Naval War College conducted a wide-ranging series of board games pitting the fleet against different adversaries under various conditions. What was the best distribution of ships in the Atlantic and Pacific if threats arose in both oceans? If the United States had to carry a naval war into the western Pacific, how would ships perform far from bases or friendly ports? On the tactical level, how should the U.S. fleet, which lacked fast battle cruisers, deal with an enemy battle line that was faster but had thinner armor than American ships carried? Board games provided a systematic way to address these and many other questions.

The second component of the Navy's solution was a series of annual fleet problems—massive exercises that involved nearly every vessel in the U.S. Navy. Board games were helpful in thinking through new strategy and tactics, but real ships had to deal with variable weather conditions, mechanical breakdowns, communication failures, and the numerous other unknowns affecting war at sea. The purpose of the fleet problems was to "train the fleet for war" by having it engage in realistic simulations of what it would face in actual battle.[3]

The third component of the solution involved the human element: mold a group of ship commanders into a coherent team that would respond to unknown situations in a known manner. Modern naval battles—which might include ships, submarines, and aircraft—were simply too complex to rely on a fixed playbook. Nor could a battle be trusted to chance, hoping that captains would respond correctly to a situation as it unfolded. The fleet problems sought that happy medium wherein officers had the flexibility to take advantage of opportunities but the discipline to do so within carefully thought-out guidelines. Ship commanders would be able to anticipate what actions their peers would take in any given situation, a tremendous advantage in the chaos of battle: "I know what he will do because I would do the same thing myself."

With the fleet in heavier seas, 1920s. Even 27,000 tons of steel was affected by the waves. *Naval History and Heritage Command, NH 013600g*

The decades between the world wars were a time of intense experimentation and change in nearly every aspect of naval doctrine. Early fleet problems focused on tactics, assuming that fleets had already come into contact, but they quickly evolved into major strategic exercises in which ships steamed thousands of miles in a realistic rehearsal of naval war from start to finish.

The Navy put considerable effort into understanding optimal formations for the fleet during the critical phases of cruising (prior to sighting the enemy), approach (configuring for battle), and engagement (the battle itself). In the cruising phase, battleships steamed in three parallel columns centered within an inner screen of cruisers and an outer ring of destroyers, both intended to protect the capital ships from submarine and air attack. Aircraft carriers followed the battleships in the inner core of the formation. At first sight of the enemy, either from mast top or scouting aircraft, the fleet would close ranks, with a heavy concentration of cruisers and destroyers in front and a smaller group in the rear.

When the enemy was nearly in range, the three parallel columns of battleships would turn to port or starboard to create the battle line, a single column that could direct its full broadside on the enemy. They would not wait until they were in the optimum position to open fire. According to the War Instructions of 1923, "The fundamental tactical principle is that of superiority of force at the decisive point of contact."[4] Battleships were to start firing as soon as the enemy came into the maximum effective range of their guns. The probability of hitting a target at ranges in excess of 30,000 yards (the maximum range of the newest U.S. battleships) was low, but the chance of disabling an enemy combatant early in the fight was too attractive to miss. At the very least, coming under fire might disrupt the enemy's intentions, forcing him to react rather than implement a more carefully considered plan of his own.

Engaging the enemy at maximum range exploited a strength of American ships and a weakness of foreign ones. To reach extreme range, guns had to fire at a high angle. Shells would strike the target at roughly that same angle, landing on the relatively thin deck armor of the target rather than its much thicker side armor. American ships were fortunate to have much thicker deck armor than their counterparts, an advantage that could be exploited in battle, where the key was to inflict maximum damage while being able to absorb hits without sinking.

The opposite problem occurred at short range. Side armor could be penetrated at about 6,000–20,000 yards depending on the caliber of shell and the angle of impact. (The angle at which a shell struck the armor of a ship would influence whether it penetrated to a vital area or merely glanced off.) Clearly one wanted to avoid a slugging match at point-blank range, where both sides were evenly matched and the rate of fire alone determined the outcome.

The optimum fleet engagement scenario was to occupy the "immune zone" between 20,000 and 30,000 yards, where enemy fire was unlikely to penetrate either side armor or deck armor and where maximum damage could be inflicted on a less-armored enemy.[5] Having thus identified where the U.S. battle line *should* be, the next challenge was achieving and maintaining that position against an enemy that might be faster and more maneuverable.

Decisions codified in the Washington Naval Treaty put American battleships at a decided disadvantage with regard to speed. Great Britain and Japan had fast battle cruisers that could steam at thirty knots or more, but the United States had converted its *Lexington*-class battle cruisers to the aircraft carriers USS *Lexington* and USS *Saratoga*. This implied that in any major fleet engagement the enemy might have big-gun ships with an eight-to-ten-knot speed advantage that could easily "cross the T" of the American battle line. ("Crossing the T occurred when the enemy passed in front of the American battle line, enabling it to fire its full broadside at the lead U.S. ships while the American ships could only shoot back with their forward turrets.) The fleet problems worked out a solution to this dilemma: deploy on a parallel course and then reverse direction to put the enemy's fastest ships in the rear, nullifying any advantage in speed.

Maneuvering by itself did not sink ships, however; winning a battle required directing the maximum firepower on the target at the earliest opportunity. There were two challenges to long-range fire—one related to the character of the guns and one related to targeting. Minor variations within bags of smokeless powder and the movement of shells down rifled barrels created dispersion in the pattern of shells landing near the target. Side to side the pattern could be quite compact, but along the line of flight there was greater variation. Even if the center of a salvo pattern was right on top of an enemy ship, high dispersion reduced the probability that an individual shell would strike the target. Every effort was made to compensate for dispersion—such as maximizing rate of fire to increase the probability of a hit—but nothing could be done to eliminate it entirely.

The second problem affecting long-range fire was aiming the guns. The maximum range at which shell splashes could be spotted from a mast top was about 24,000 yards; beyond this the curvature of the earth prevented seeing impact on the surface. If aimers could not see where shells were landing, they could not adjust the range and angle of the next salvo. The solution to this problem was to put spotters in aircraft where they would be higher in altitude and closer to the enemy and could direct the fire of the big guns via radio.

Much-debated rules regulated the fleet problems, the most hotly contested being the number of hits achieved by different types of guns and by aircraft dropping bombs. For example, umpires ruled that a 14-inch gun had a 26 percent probability of hitting when fired from 14,000 yards, and that a modern American battleship could absorb 18.6 such hits before sinking. (In World War II the hit rates were much lower, but the number of impacts a ship could survive was greater.) Aircraft bombing was an even less exact science, since naval aviators had little experience with bombing ships under way. Moreover, aviation technology was changing so rapidly that it was difficult to keep track of what had actually been demonstrated versus what was likely to occur in a future battle.

The fleet problems became more realistic when some ships assumed the specific characteristics of enemy vessels; a fast cruiser, for example, might represent a more heavily armed battle cruiser. Phantom ships were created to expand the fleets—a single ship might represent a division, a single aircraft a squadron. To make matters more interesting still, umpires could introduce surprises by deeming a fleet commander killed, by declaring communications cut off, or by granting special intelligence on enemy intentions. Thus the element of surprise—so important in actual battles—was explicitly included.

A ruthless critique followed each fleet problem, often in front of hundreds or even thousands of officers. Professional courtesy was left at the door of these reviews, and even senior officers came in for withering criticism. "You should have known from prior intelligence that the enemy was going to appear at that time," or "Why didn't you deploy your fast cruisers to cut off the destroyer attack?" There was nothing personal in the criticism—the intent was to improve the Navy's chances of winning a war, not prove which fleet commanders were smarter or luckier.

By the time the U.S. Navy entered World War II, nearly all of the challenges that it would face at sea had already been simulated in one or more fleet problems. Moreover, many unsuccessful strategies that could have led to disaster were eliminated from consideration. The Navy trained the way it would fight.

The first fleet problem was held February 18–22, 1923, off the west coast of Panama. This massive tactical exercise involved 165 ships—including 14 battleships —and nearly 40,000 personnel. The premise was that "Black" forces (Japan) were attempting to destroy the Panama Canal, the vital link between the Scouting Fleet in the Atlantic and the Battle Fleet in the Pacific. If successful, they would prevent the two American fleets from joining up and create a situation in which the Black forces might prevail in the "decisive battle" naval strategists predicted— a battle that would settle a naval war in a single engagement.[6]

A follow-on exercise conducted in March simulated a full battle in which the radio-controlled target ship *Iowa* (built in 1896 and woefully obsolete) was sunk by gunfire from USS *Mississippi* using aircraft spotting to control long-range fire. This was a different type of target practice for most of the men involved because their guns were directed not against target panels mounted on rafts but against an actual ship that eventually capsized and sank. The fact that she was an American vessel familiar to some of the men added a particular poignancy to the exercise.

Nevada arrived at Guantanamo Bay on January 17, 1923, fresh out of her overhaul at Norfolk Navy Yard. She sortied nearly every day for short-range battle practice, alternating between shooting her own weapons at towed targets and towing targets for other ships. On February 5 this led to tense moments when a torpedo fired from *North Dakota* went astray (or was misaimed) and hit *Nevada* on the starboard quarter.

With gunnery exercises complete, *Nevada* left Guantanamo Bay, passed through the Panama Canal a few days later, and steamed forth with the Scouting Fleet to engage the Battle Fleet in Fleet Problem I. Once begun, the action was nonstop. During a massive torpedo attack on March 19, *Nevada* had to maneuver sharply to avoid being hit. One torpedo passed within twenty yards of the ship; others passed several hundred yards ahead, and more were spotted on the starboard beam.

The lessons learned from Fleet Problem I confirmed many of the conclusions naval strategists had reached in Naval War College board games. On the surface, the fleet was critically short of screening units—cruisers and destroyers—that were essential to protect battleships from torpedo attacks by destroyers. In the air, planes were useful in scouting missions and spotting the fall of shot, but they could not yet carry enough bombs to represent a serious threat to a battle line. Below the surface, the maximum speed of submarines was too slow to permit them to accompany the fleet in long-range deployments. The same was true of the fleet train (tankers, supply and repair ships). Neither submarines nor supply ships would be of much use if they were hundreds of miles behind the main body and were themselves vulnerable to enemy attack.

Following Fleet Problem I and its follow-on exercises, *Nevada* steamed with the Battle Fleet to San Pedro, California, and spent the next several months engaged in long-range battle practice. The remainder of 1923 saw her ranging up and down the West Coast, paying port calls at San Francisco and Port Angeles and participating in Battle Fleet maneuvers off the coast of Washington. The routine of practice and training was pleasantly interrupted on September 1 when the ship was awarded the Secretary of the Navy's Prize for Engineering Excellence for 1922–23. The recognition was nice, and the money that accompanied the award was even nicer.

Nevada spent a few weeks in dry dock at the Puget Sound Navy Yard in November for replacement of worn-out gun barrels, and then it was back to sea, where the long December nights were optimal for night battle practice. She arrived back at San Pedro a few days before Christmas 1923.

The holidays were cut short when *Nevada* left San Pedro on January 1, 1924, to accompany the Battle Fleet to Panama. Old problems with the steering gear recurred on the way down when both steam and electrical steering systems failed with the rudder jammed at 5 degrees. Capt. J. M. Luby managed to keep her in formation by adjusting the rpm of the two engines to compensate for the jammed rudder.

The Battle Fleet passed through the Canal and arrived in the U.S. Virgin Islands in late January 1924 to conduct exercises with USS *Langley*, the first aircraft carrier in the U.S. Fleet. Navy aircraft practiced dropping simulated bombs on ships, and ships practiced antiaircraft fire against the planes.

Fleet Problems II, III, and IV were conducted during January and February 1924. Each was part of an overarching scenario that postulated war between the United States and Japan. As an added complication, the fleet problems assumed that the British, who had a close relationship with Japan, were undecided on their intentions. With threats in both the Atlantic and Pacific, U.S. commanders had to balance their forces in order to defend the East Coast while launching a transpacific attack on the Japanese.

Included in the mix was a "Grand Joint Army-Navy Exercise" in which the Army conducted an amphibious assault on Panama. A prelude to the massive amphibious operations of World War II, the exercise stressed the ability to land troops and equipment under fire and practiced coordinating bombardment from

Navy ships with the Army's ground assault. While Panama was the exercise location, the real target was assumed to be an island in the western Pacific where a base would be established for war against Japan.

Nevada spent the balance of 1924 participating in a busy series of exercises with the fleet, including torpedo battle practice, long- and short-range battle practices, defense against torpedo attack by destroyers, and antiaircraft practice. The ship's log for June 11, 1924, illustrates a typical long-range battle practice run:

1019 took battle formation #1, hoisted battle flags.

1021 sighted targets broad on starboard bow.

1029 on signal went to general quarters.

1110 on signal commenced firing main and secondary battery.

1120 ceased firing.

The practice was a carefully scripted affair completed in just over an hour.

A week later *Nevada* served as the practice target for submarine battle practice. At 1057 on June 19, a torpedo fired from *S-33* hit her abreast the stack, and two hours later one hit on the port side. The torpedo hits pointed out a problem: even when the crew knew that submarines were setting up to fire at them, it was difficult to spot an incoming torpedo in time to maneuver the ship to safety.

Casualties of a different type occurred on June 23 when *Nevada*'s health inspectors declared 2,850 pounds of emergency rations unfit and ordered them thrown overboard. Fortunately, *Nevada* was on her way to the Puget Sound Navy Yard for six weeks of overhaul and a change of guns, and she could pick up new supplies while in port.

Following her time in the yard, but while still in the Seattle area, *Nevada* barely avoided disaster in a close encounter with SS *Admiral Rodgers*. Captain Luby threw both engines into reverse, and *Nevada* missed colliding with *Admiral Rogers* by *one foot*. A similar event occurred in October when an unidentified steamer crossed the battle line and *Arizona*, *Pennsylvania*, and *Nevada* had to back full to avoid colliding with the ship, which steamed on, apparently oblivious to the problems she was causing.

Nearly every cruise had one or two injuries, from fingers caught in the complex loading machinery of the main turrets to failures in diving apparatus. Diver J. O. Lloyd was hauled to the surface unconscious on February 17, 1923, following a routine inspection of the ship's propellers. Crewmembers quickly cut off his suit and rendered first aid, saving Lloyd's life. On May 5, 1923, a 14-inch shell weighing 1,400 pounds fell on Turret Captain 1st Class T. J. Connors. He was lucky to escape with contusions on his hip.

Nor were Sailors immune to the ills of everyday life. On February 21, 1925, Chief Quartermaster C. H. Ogden collapsed after climbing the ladder to the signal bridge, complaining of shortness of breath and intense pain in his chest and extremities. Clearly suffering a major heart attack, he was transferred to the hospital ship USS *Relief* with "diagnosis undetermined."

The Washington Naval Treaty had done much to dampen prospects for war between the United States and Japan, but the Navy still needed to demonstrate a capability to dash across the Pacific to retake the Philippines in the event diplomacy failed. The question was where to go for such a demonstration. A cruise to Japan was out of the question, a visit to the Philippines or Guam only slightly less so. The Navy's solution was a cruise to Australia and New Zealand in the summer of 1925. Along the way the fleet would conduct Grand Joint Army-Navy Exercise 3, another simulation of capturing an advanced base in the western Pacific.

The Battle Fleet left San Pedro at 0930 on March 2, 1925, just as the Scouting Fleet was making its way up from the Panama Canal. The two fleets engaged in mock battles on March 11, the ninth birthday of *Nevada*'s commissioning. This mammoth undertaking involved 145 ships and 45,000 men and simulated each aspect of a major naval engagement—scouting, approach, and battle—using real ships dealing with actual weather at sea.

After stops at San Diego and San Pedro the fleet proceeded to San Francisco and a gala reception. Thousands of spectators lined Market Street for a Navy parade complete with ships' bands and precision marching. Sailors in uniform enjoyed free rides on cable cars, free admission to theaters, and invitations to private homes.

On April 15 more than seventy-five ships left San Francisco bound for Hawaii and Grand Joint Army-Navy Exercise 3. The exercise was the largest transoceanic maneuver the U.S. Navy had ever conducted and marked the first time since the Great War that the bulk of the fleet, including most of the heavy units, crossed an ocean.[7] Previous fleet problems had been held in Central America or the Caribbean; Grand Joint Army-Navy Exercise 3 was the first to be held in the central Pacific.

To commemorate the start of their long journey, many *Nevada* crewmembers had their heads shaved and posed for souvenir photographs in front of the ship's massive 14-inch guns. One of the stated purposes for the cruise was for Sailors to "see the world." Recruitment and retention were constant concerns for the Navy, and cruises such as this one did much to compensate for the monotony of training missions.

The true function of what came to be known as the Great Cruise was hardly a secret, and its announcement elicited angry responses from Tokyo. Nationalist

Many of the crew had their heads shaved prior to the Great Cruise. *Beach*, The Great Cruise of 1925

factions in the Diet called it provocative, and the prime minister made a speech condemning the cruise as a clear threat to Japan. (He was correct—the cruise was meant as a deterrent to Japanese aggression.) The U.S. Navy Public Affairs Office did its best to calm the situation. Commander of Battleships Vice Adm. Henry Wiley hosted a reception for Japanese naval units while the U.S. fleet was in San Francisco, apparently to good effect. Soon afterward the Imperial Japanese Navy issued a statement that it was not at all bothered by the planned maneuvers. In a sense the Japanese had no choice. To publicly fret over the cruise would be to acknowledge the superiority of the U.S. Navy in the Pacific, something that was neither politically nor militarily acceptable.

Grand Joint Army-Navy Exercise 3 in Hawaiian waters simulated the recapture of the islands following an enemy (Japanese) invasion. Army units on Oahu represented the foe on land, and various small ships were drafted to represent enemy battleships, cruisers, and destroyers. A lightning attack, including an amphibious landing on April 27, succeeded in recapturing the island, although this may have been a foregone conclusion given the scenario. *Nevada* participated in shore bombardment, and three of her motorboats ferried troops ashore in the amphibious assault. (This was before the era of dedicated landing craft.) Enemy forces attacked the fleet during the landings, and *Nevada* had to defend herself against air and submarine attacks.

After the exercise, 3,800 officers met for 5 days to discuss what went right and, more important, what went wrong. The review emphasized the necessity of controlling the skies as well as the need for better communications within the fleet and between the Navy and the Army. The exercise was deemed a success, but clearly much remained to be learned about mounting a major amphibious operation thousands of miles from home.

Honolulu was just as enthusiastic about the arrival of the fleet as San Francisco had been. Hula dancers and other local performers came out to the anchored battleships, and *Nevada's* band played in town. Later the fleet made the short voyage to Lahaina Roads, a protected roadstead between the islands of Maui and Lanai, where, in between social events, the fleet conducted an extensive series of practices. One of these did not go smoothly for *Nevada*.

On May 22 one of *Nevada's* seaplanes was catapulted to practice spotting for the big guns. An explosive charge was used to literally blast the plane down the rail of the catapult and into the air, but on this occasion the plane did not achieve sufficient airspeed. One of its pontoons clipped a wave, and it crashed and quickly sank.

A study in contrasts. Capt. David Todd and Executive Officer, Cdr. William Baggaley took *Nevada* to Australia and New Zealand during the Great Cruise of 1925. *Beach,* The Great Cruise of 1925

King Neptune's court held during the Great Cruise. *Beach,* The Great Cruise of 1925

Fortunately the two-man crew was rescued by the prompt action of the destroyer USS *Hopkins.*

The fleet left Hawaii on July 1, 1925, and steamed to Pago Pago, where *Nevada* took on fuel from the tanker USS *Brazos.* The Great Cruise was to be a test of whether the fleet could steam independent of outside support, so fuel, food, spare parts, and all the other items ships required for operation were carried either by the warships themselves or by supporting vessels. The hospital ship *Relief* came along to provide medical care.

On July 6 King Neptune and his court visited the ship to commemorate crossing the equator. The ceremonies were similar to those conducted when *Nevada* steamed to Peru, with one important difference: Capt. David Todd was one of the initiates. Todd had the gruff appearance of a seasoned Sailor and had been awarded the Navy Cross during the Great War for his service as director of communications. It was somewhat embarrassing for such a senior officer to have to undergo Neptune's initiation, and Todd tried to balance being a good sport with the need to maintain command authority over his ship. The thorny problem was resolved when King Neptune let Todd off with the relatively light fine of a box of cigars.

Adm. Robert Coontz, commander in chief of the U.S. fleet, worried that 23,000 men and 46 ships would overwhelm the hospitality of any Australian city the fleet visited. To lighten the burden on his hosts, he split the fleet into two parts: *Nevada,* along with her Battleship Division Three mates *Oklahoma, Pennsylvania,* and Coontz's flagship, *Seattle*, went to Melbourne while the balance of the fleet—cruisers, destroyers, and the support ships—went to Sydney.

If San Francisco had offered a gala welcome, Melbourne's bordered on riotous. Special trains were scheduled on July 22 to bring thousands of well-wishers to points affording a view of the approaching fleet. Private boats came out to welcome the battleships, dangerously weaving in and out of the column to shout greetings to the crews. It was a challenge just to get to Princes Pier and tie up.

Nevada, Oklahoma, Pennsylvania, and *Seattle* at Prince's Pier, Melbourne, Australia. The ships were mobbed by tourists and well-wishers. *Beach,* The Great Cruise of 1925

The Navy on parade in Melbourne during the fleet's wildly popular visit. *Beach*, The Great Cruise of 1925

The Australians saw the visit as more than a port call by American warships—it was an opportunity for them to demonstrate solidarity with America as a force for good in the world. Officials competed with one another to express their affection for the United States and their gratitude for the fleet's visit. The *Melbourne Age* reported that "Australia welcomes the great American Fleet with feelings that thrill the fibers of its national being."[8] Other newspapers published poems gushing over the importance of the visit. Invitations for lunches, picnics, dinners, dances, and sightseeing trips poured onto the pier, and every Sailor had several activities to choose from. At one point American officers sorting through the invitations were concerned that they might give offense because there were simply not enough men to cover all of the offers. Lt. Charles Wheeler recalled that "one hostess called up and pleaded that we send three more officers to attend a dinner that she had planned. I told her that there were no more officers available and she said how about sending her some chief petty officers. She was desperate for some guests."[9]

The Americans reciprocated with ship tours, dances, and concerts. More than 125,000 people—a substantial fraction of Melbourne's population—visited the ships while they were tied up at Princes Pier. On August 1 more than two thousand people jammed *Nevada*'s decks for a dance, twice the number invited. The ship's Marines served as crowd control, limiting admittance to those lucky enough to have tickets, but this disciplined approach was put to the test when a woman fainted on the dock. Ever chivalrous, two Marines rushed down the gangway and carried her on board, only to find many more fainting ladies who required assistance. Other women gained entry through the simple expedient of being pulled in through portholes by welcoming Sailors. Lieutenant Wheeler, who would retire as a rear admiral, said, "It was the only time I've ever known in the Navy when we lost control of a ship."[10]

Aussie hospitality was (and is) wonderful, but it was becoming too much of a good thing.[11] It was almost with a sigh of relief that Battleship Division Three left Melbourne for New Zealand on August 6. Men on deck threw brightly colored streamers to newfound friends on the dock as the ships pulled away, and more than one handkerchief dabbed away tears for departing friends. In some cases it was more than friendship; during the sixteen-day stay there were a number of marriages between U.S. Sailors and Australian women. Admiral Coontz had advised the men to "make friendships quickly," and some obviously complied with enthusiasm. Despite all of the revelry, the behavior of the men on shore was excellent, with few incidents to mar the visit. Admiral Coontz and Captain Todd had worried that the easy access to alcohol in Australia might lead to problems, but while Sailors certainly took advantage of the situation, drunkenness was relatively infrequent.

Sad farewells as *Nevada* prepares to depart Melbourne. There were a number of marriages during the visit. *Beach*, The Great Cruise of 1925

Nevada called at Wellington, New Zealand, on August 11. Once again nearly every level of society extended a warm welcome. Dances, balls, dinners, concerts, and even wild boar hunts were organized with an intensity just a notch below what the men had experienced in Australia. The indigenous Maori people provided their own greeting and an introduction to their ancient culture. When the fleet departed on August 24 Rear Adm. T. P. Magruder, commander of the Light Cruiser Division and a former skipper of *Nevada*, said, "I doubt if in the history of a cruise by any foreign fleet there has been a reception as cordial and sincere as that which has been given to the American Fleet by the people of Australia, Tasmania and New Zealand."[12]

The fleet was back at San Pedro on September 26, 1925, having sailed nearly 16,000 miles over a 5-month period. During the cruise, *Nevada*'s crew consumed more than 600 tons of food, including 274,900 pounds of potatoes, 111,400 pounds of frozen beef, and 23,100 pounds of coffee. Aside from a small quantity of fresh vegetables brought on board in Australia, she had brought nearly all of those supplies along with her. Fleet tankers topped up her fuel, and necessary repairs were made by the ship's mechanics.

The Imperial Japanese Navy did not fail to take note of the U.S. Navy's ability to operate across the broad reaches of the Pacific, despite its earlier protestation of unconcern. Nor did Tokyo miss the fact that immediately after its return home, the fleet set out on a grueling set of practice cruises—*Nevada* sortied fifteen times in October alone. She had steamed 16,000 miles but was ready to go at a moment's notice.

After spending Christmas and New Year's at San Pedro, *Nevada* steamed north for the ministrations of the Puget Sound Navy Yard. During her time in dry dock the Hull Board conducted a detailed inspection of her hull and propellers and, aside from a few cosmetic items (a few oil leaks through seams in the armor plate), pronounced the ship in good condition.

Nevada had done well on the Great Cruise of 1925 and continued to do well in fleet maneuvers the following year, but both men and machinery were feeling the strain of constantly trying to do more with less. An inspection made at the Puget Sound Navy Yard back in October 1923 had revealed that the rotor wheels of her main turbines were dangerously out of alignment.[13] On June 17, 1924, the commander in chief of the Battle Fleet sent a strongly worded letter to the chief of the Bureau of Ordnance citing problems with the recoil mechanisms of the 14-inch guns. They were in such serious shape that he could not condone firing full-charge rounds until significant repairs were made.[14] Things would only get worse.

Funding problems forced the Navy to reduce crews, increase periods between overhauls, and ration fuel.[15] The Bureau of Engineering reported that the cost of repairs to machinery rose from $3.2 million in 1923 to $8.1 million in 1926, an increase typical for aging equipment.[16] Every ship seemed to have her own needs: *Pennsylvania* and *Idaho* had problems with their turbine engines, and boilers were a common problem throughout the fleet.

The Great Cruise was more than battleship diplomacy. *Nevada* fires a ten-gun salvo during training exercises. *Beach*, The Great Cruise of 1925

Nothing seemed to escape the Navy's drive to economize. Typewriter ribbons, for example, were not replaced until they were so faint that documents—including the official typed copy of the ship's logbook—were barely readable. Officers grumbled about pay—which had declined in purchasing power as a result of postwar inflation—but more about the steadily deteriorating condition of the fleet, which they thought might be hard-pressed to battle a capable foe.

The need to modernize the fleet was recognized as early as 1924, but Congress refused to allocate the necessary funds.[17] To make do with the resources available, the Bureau of Construction and Repair implemented a program of "self-maintenance" in which ships' crews carried out work normally done at a shipyard. Since crew salaries were already paid, they could perform the same work for the cost of the materials alone. Soon crewmembers were retubing boilers, lifting turbine casings, repairing propellers, and doing other major repairs.

Within a year Nevada was rated in excellent condition, with important caveats: "Like all older ships," the commander of Battleship Division Three wrote to the CNO, "the NEVADA shows her age and many improvements are desirable. With the exception of her boilers and the replacement of the damaged gun in number four turret, she is considered as capable of maintaining her station in the Battle Line as could be expected with material of her age and little less effectiveness, if any, than the other ships of this Division."[18]

But the crew could do only so much. In January 1927 the guns of the aft three-gun turret jammed at an elevation of 8 degrees. A repair was not arranged until the end of May, so *Nevada* had to go through Fleet Problem VII, a repeat of the amphibious invasion of Panama, short one turret.

At the conclusion of the fleet problem in March 1927 *Nevada* steamed to Annapolis, where Rear Adm. George Laws designated her the flagship of the Second Battleship Division, Scouting Fleet. The occasion was the annual midshipmen's cruise, when eager students from the Naval Academy came on board to learn their trade firsthand. Rejoining the fleet on the way south to the Canal Zone, the battle line passed in a presidential review at Hampton Roads, a short diversion from the more serious business of preparing for war.

The midshipmen gained valuable experience on the cruise. *Nevada* passed through the Panama Canal and steamed up the west coast of Central America and North America, making stops at San Diego, San Pedro, and San Francisco. Then she turned south and went back through the Canal for short-range battle practice in the Caribbean and a return to Annapolis at the end of August.

This was to be *Nevada*'s last cruise for more than two years. It was just about all she could do to limp from Annapolis to the Norfolk Navy Yard.

At sea, June 1927, a few months before modernization. By this time *Nevada* required constant attention to keep her going. *National Archives Photo Collection, RG 80, no. 460088*

Since her launch in 1914 *Nevada* had steamed tens of thousands of miles in the Atlantic and Pacific Oceans. She had conducted countless battle practices and had looked her best at diplomatic port calls in South America, Australia, and New Zealand. But much of her machinery was simply worn out. In the first eight months of 1927 the condenser on the port main engine failed at least eleven times, necessitating shutting down the engine for underway repair. The starboard condenser failed at least eight times. On three occasions both condensers failed on the same day, although not at the same time. (The condenser was a key component in the ship's steam cycle. Steam from the turbines was cooled in condensers so that it could be reinjected into the boilers. When the condensers failed, the boilers could not be supplied with sufficient fresh water.) Boiler failures caused by internal tubes blowing out were almost as common, with nine occurring during the same period, six of those in troublesome boiler 6. On April 24, 1927, both steam and electric steering failed, and the ship had to drop out of formation. Sailors in the steering compartment manned four six-foot-diameter wooden wheels, reminiscent of the helms on old sailing ships, to steer the giant by hand.

Personnel shortages—particularly in the engineering department—compounded the problem. *Nevada* carried only 50 percent of her approved complement of engineering petty officers, an alarming gap given the increasingly skittish nature of her machinery. Crew errors resulting from inadequate training were already a problem, and they got steadily worse without the leadership that only petty officers could provide.

Nevada needed more than routine maintenance. She needed a complete makeover. If the United States could not build new battleships until the early 1930s (a result of the Washington Naval Treaty's ten-year holiday on capital ship construction), then the only way to deal with creeping obsolescence was to rebuild the ships already in service. *Nevada* was going to get a second life.

6

Rebirth

The Washington Naval Treaty was quite specific on what modifications could be made to existing battleships. No change was permitted to the number or size of the main guns, armor could be changed only to improve protection against evolving air or submarine threats, and the total alterations to any given ship could add no more than three thousand tons to her original displacement.

The Navy's intent in modernizing *Nevada* and *Oklahoma* was to, as much as possible, bring them into line with the *Colorado* class, the most modern of the pre-treaty battleships. As America's first super-dreadnoughts, *Nevada* and *Oklahoma* fell into an intermediate category between old coal-burning battleships armed with 12-inch guns and reciprocating engines and the three *Colorado*s with their 16-inch guns and turboelectric drive. (First introduced on *New Mexico*, turboelectric drive consisted of a steam turbine driving a generator, which in turn powered an electric motor connected to the propellers.) Naval architects calculated that with sufficient funds, *Nevada* and *Oklahoma* could be provided with offensive punch and defensive armor similar to those of their successors, greatly enhancing their role in battle while remaining within the confines of the Washington Naval Treaty.

Key to the upgrade was increasing the range of the *Nevada* class' main armament. While the guns themselves were easily capable of lobbing shells beyond 30,000 yards, the openings in the front plates of the turrets prevented them from being elevated higher than 15 degrees, limiting their range to only 23,000 yards. It seemed a simple fix—enlarge the openings to permit a maximum elevation of 30 degrees so that the full capability of the guns could be utilized. Congress agreed and approved funds to make the modifications, only to reverse itself under pressure from Secretary of State Charles Evans Hughes. The British Admiralty, still smarting under the terms of the Washington Naval Treaty, argued that a change in maximum gun elevation was illegal, and Hughes, anxious to maintain good relations with London, accepted the argument. U.S. Navy lawyers strenuously disagreed and through sheer persistence convinced Congress to fund the modification.[1] A total of $13,150,000 was allocated for the upgrade of *Nevada* and *Oklahoma*.[2]

Even with congressional approval the ships had to wait their turn for modernization. The Navy's shipyards were busy converting six old coal-burning battleships to oil fuel while completing construction of the new aircraft carriers *Lexington* and *Saratoga*. *Nevada* arrived in Norfolk on September 14, 1927, but her actual modernization did not begin until January 2 of the following year.

Hundreds of men were transferred to other ships when *Nevada* reached Norfolk, leaving only a skeleton crew on board. After years of gunnery practice, maneuvers with the fleet, passages through the Panama Canal, and the Great Cruise, the remaining officers and men found it frustrating to sit motionless in the harbor. Discipline was a challenge at the best of times, and during periods of inactivity Sailors were remarkably innovative at getting into trouble. Making matters worse, *Nevada* was without a skipper for six months. Capt. C. S. Kempff left the ship in June 1927, and his replacement, Capt. H. H. Royall, did not arrive until January 1928. Fortunately, *Nevada* had a friend in the commandant of the Norfolk Navy Yard, Capt. David Todd, who had commanded her during the Great Cruise. Todd had great affection for his old ship and proved adept at finding ways to accelerate her rebuild.

Nevada pier-side at Norfolk Navy Yard, December 1927. After a decade of hard running, she was in need of attention. *National Archives Photo Collection, RG 80*

One thing led to another when naval architects began planning *Nevada*'s modernization. Substantial improvements in fire control were required to take advantage of the longer range of the main guns, but the relatively lightweight cage-style masts were not nearly strong enough to support the new equipment and its associated armor protection. The masts needed replacement regardless of improvements in fire control, however. When *Nevada* was on her way to Australia in 1925, the commandant of the Pearl Harbor Navy Yard wrote to the Bureau of Construction and Repair that many of the steel tubes that formed her masts were corroded. A similar warning appeared in a report from the Board of Inspection and Survey in January 1926. The board members noted that the "mast has excessive motion when ship rolling or guns firing. . . . The Board recommends that main mast be entirely rebuilt or removed from the ship."[3] The tubular cage masts creaked and swayed dangerously in heavy seas, and the shock waves from a salvo of the 14-inch guns turned them into giant tuning forks. The answer was a pair of heavy tripod masts firmly attached to the hull. These could easily support the weight of the new three-story fire control stations and would be much less prone to corrosion than the old cage design.

The Washington Naval Treaty prohibited upgrades to armor except to improve protection against torpedoes and air-delivered bombs. To defend against the former, designers added a "blister" to the sides of the ship—a thin steel shell mounted three feet out from the main hull at the second deck. As the hull turned inward, the separation increased to a maximum of six and one-half feet. The standoff would dissipate the explosive force of a torpedo, and the thinness of the blister would minimize the generation of destructive steel splinters during the blast. New bulkheads were added inside the hull for added protection.

While no one disputed the value of added protection against torpedo attack, the commander of the Scouting Fleet was concerned that increasing *Nevada*'s beam to nearly 108 feet might cause difficulty when she passed through the Panama Canal, a necessity in maintaining a two-ocean navy. Worse, the relatively thin plating of the blister could be damaged when she rubbed against docks or the locks of the Canal, or when tugs pushed against it. Engineer Edward L. Cochrane of the Bureau of Construction and Repair admitted that "some inconvenience may develop in Canal transits" but insisted that the ship would still fit. The protection value of the blister more than compensated for any problems that might be encountered in relatively infrequent Canal passages.[4] In fact, the increased beam did create a challenge in the Canal. *Nevada* had to use considerable power to overcome water resistance in the locks.[5]

Nevada's side armor was considered satisfactory protection against anticipated enemy shellfire, but her deck armor required strengthening to defend against air attack. Thicker deck armor would also enhance her ability to resist shells arriving at steep angles, important in long-range gun duels with other battleships. To save money, Commandant Todd suggested using armor plating left over from ships abandoned per the Washington Naval Treaty. The yard had nearly enough plates of the proper thickness and could confirm their quality by checking serial numbers against Navy records.[6] The bureau agreed with the scheme but insisted that every plate have an impeccable pedigree. Men with no combat duties sheltered below the armored deck during battle, and the armor could save their lives.[7]

Virtually everything in the machinery spaces warranted replacement. In particular, *Nevada*'s turbine engines were simply worn out. The problem was that new engines were expensive—even the cost of refurbishing *Nevada*'s existing turbines was estimated at $220,000. The chiefs of the Bureaus of Engineering and Construction and Repair put their heads together and came up with a clever solution that met the need and kept within the budget: take the newer turbines from *North Dakota*, which were in excellent condition, and put them in *Nevada*. The Navy had planned to convert *North Dakota* into a radio-controlled target ship, but why waste good engines on a ship slated for sinking? The government could save $100,000 by not converting *North Dakota* to a target ship, and the transfer of her engines to *Nevada* would cost only $168,865. As a bonus, *North Dakota*'s turbines would provide 20 percent more horsepower than *Nevada*'s old engines, enabling her to reach speeds close to her former maximum despite the additional drag induced by the antitorpedo blister.[8] The Secretary of the Navy quickly approved the plan.

Nevada's boilers were also worn out. When inspectors from the Board of Inspection and Survey opened them up in January 1926 they found numerous plugged tubes. The ship's engineering log noted eighteen tube failures during the previous six months, each of which took a boiler out of commission until emergency repairs could be made. The board's report recommended replacing the old boilers rather than undertaking "extensive repairs which could not be otherwise than unsatisfactory with an increasing number of tube failures." However, not all of the problems with the boilers were due to age. Maintenance by the crew was so poor that the board recommended convening a formal court of inquiry to investigate "culpable inefficiency" among engineering officers and men. The senior engineering officer had only six months' experience before coming to *Nevada* and did not have sufficient knowledge to maintain the equipment.[9]

While no one disputed the need for a new power plant, nothing could be done until Congress released the necessary funds. Commandant Todd devised a clever way to get around the delay: "The Department has decided that because the reboiling of the NEVADA must be undertaken regardless of the work of modernization, the work of reboiling might proceed in advance of the appropriation of Congress," he wrote to the chief of the Bureau of Construction and Repair. Since this "will require a considerable amount of structural changes, it was suggested that the structural material necessary for these changes should be similarly provided in advance of the authorization of funds for modernization."[10] Wisely avoiding a legal opinion on his creative approach to congressional authorization, Todd coopted the ship's crew and had them start tearing out the old equipment, augmenting them with yard workers who were idle after the early completion of *New York*'s modernization.

There had been substantial advances in boiler technology since *Nevada*'s design was fixed in 1911. Engineers calculated that the twelve Yarrow Express boilers installed at Fore River could be replaced by six modern small-tube units. As a bonus, the lower fuel consumption of the new boilers would increase *Nevada*'s cruising radius, a key factor considering the ever-present worries over war with Japan.

New propellers rounded out the makeover of *Nevada*'s machinery. The Bureau of Engineering was determined to wring every mile out of a ton of fuel by using the most efficient propeller design available. Engineers validated the new design with tests on scale models of *Oklahoma*'s hull (nearly identical with *Nevada*'s) in the Navy's model basin in Washington.[11]

Nevada got a completely new look above the main deck. The Navy had had enough complaints about hull-mounted secondary armament becoming wet and unusable in heavy seas. Some of the 5-inch guns had been removed before *Nevada* sailed for Europe in World War I. The remaining ones were now taken out, and ten of them were moved to a specially built deckhouse higher on the ship. The bridge and captain's quarters were rebuilt, and the smokestack was tilted slightly aft to make room for the new superstructure and the tripod-design foremast.

While the battleship still reigned supreme, the Navy understood the implications of Billy Mitchell sinking a battleship with air-delivered bombs. Eight 5-inch antiaircraft guns were added to *Nevada*'s battery, and additional antiaircraft machine guns were placed atop the fire control stations on each mast.[12]

There was considerable discussion about the torpedo tubes on *Nevada* and *Oklahoma*, which the new antitorpedo blister had rendered unusable. The General Board studied the problem and recommended shifting the tubes from their original position below the waterline to the main deck. Lt. Cdr. C. B. C. Carey of the Bureau of Ordnance dared to take exception with the esteemed admirals of the General Board, arguing that torpedoes on a ship's main deck were at risk of detonation by shell fragments or in a fire. Besides, torpedoes were unlikely to be a factor in engagements between battleships; not one of the twelve torpedoes British capital ships fired in the Battle of Jutland hit its target.[13] After considering Carey's memo the General Board reversed its decision and recommended removing

The gun ports on the front armor of the main turret were enlarged by drilling overlapping holes and then smoothing the surface. *National Archives Photo Collection, RG 19*

the torpedo tubes from *Nevada* and *Oklahoma*.[14]

The biggest change to *Nevada*'s offensive punch—increasing the maximum elevation of the guns from 15 degrees to 30 degrees—was even more challenging technically than it was politically. New turret armor would be prohibitively expensive, and engineers were unsure about the best way to enlarge the openings in the existing 18-inch-thick armor faceplates. The Bethlehem Steel and Carnegie Steel companies (the makers of the original armor) recommended preheating the armor to just above the boiling point of water and then using cutting torches to enlarge the openings. Grinders could then smooth the edges.[15]

Commandant Todd had reservations about the steel companies' approach. Cutting by torch would heat the armor, potentially changing its hardness from the original demanding specifications. After all the trouble taken in heat-treating the steel, why risk ruining its strength by using high-temperature torches? Todd asked around the Norfolk Navy Yard for advice and found an officer who had experience with cutting the thick armor on the ex-German battleship *Helgoland*. Further information obtained from the Bureau of Ordnance convinced Todd that torches were definitely *not* the way to go. Instead, he suggested the simple expedient of drilling closely spaced holes just inside the desired contour of the new gun ports and using industrial grinders to finish the openings.[16] The bureau was impressed with the quality of Todd's analysis and endorsed his approach.

As soon as approval was granted, yard crews got to work unbolting armor plates from the front of the turrets and positioning them on heavy timber cradles. Thirty-ton jacks maneuvered the plates into position under a drill press fitted with a $1 \, 3/_{32}$-inch-diameter bit. By overlapping the holes during the drilling, debris from drilling was ejected into the expanding cut, making the process much faster. Still, with seventy-two holes required per opening and ten openings to cut, it was a lengthy process.[17]

To more efficiently move shells from the magazines to the guns, new powder and shell hoists were installed in the main turrets and the newly positioned 5-inch guns in the superstructure. The 2-gun-turret magazines were configured to store 196 shells, and the 3-gun-turret magazines were able to store 214 shells, a total of roughly 41 10-gun salvos.[18]

The greatly increased range enabled by higher gun elevation meant that potential targets might be over the horizon, invisible even from the highest masts. Two catapults were installed, one on the quarterdeck and one atop turret 3, and three Vought O2U-3 Corsair pontoon biplanes were provided as aerial spotters.

By the end of March 1928 much of the demolition of old structures and equipment was done, including removal of the torpedo tubes.[19] By November the blister was complete, the new boilers were installed, the main engines had been transferred from *North Dakota*, and turret work was well along. Hundreds of yard workers swarmed over the ship, and the reduced crew of just over three hundred was berthed and fed in Marine barracks ashore to keep them out of the way.

Crew comfort also received attention in the modernization. As was typical in the U.S. Navy at the time she was built, *Nevada* berthed enlisted men in hammocks, many of them slung in the 5-inch gun compartments along the sides of the ship. On July 23, 1928, Commandant Todd wrote the Bureau of Construction and Repair that there was sufficient space to provide steel-pipe bunks for 1,053 men.

Partway through modernization at the Norfolk Navy Yard; both of the new tripod masts have been installed and an aircraft catapult is being constructed on the aft two-gun turret. *Naval History and Heritage Command, NH 013691*

Captain Royall and Norfolk Commandant Todd worked together to acquire steel-frame bunks for the crew. *Nevada State Museum*

Assuming a war complement of 1,440, that left only 387 to make do in hammocks. A peacetime crew of 1,269 would require only 216 men to sleep in the less commodious hammocks.[20]

The bureau replied that money was tight and it could not authorize the shift to bunks. Todd shot back that most of the work was already done—why not finish it?[21] In typical bureaucratese, the bureau responded: "It is satisfactory to the Bureau for the Yard to consider this item as not now definitely disapproved."[22]

After Todd got grudging approval to provide the crew with bunks, Captain Royall joined in and asked the bureau to provide suitable mattresses, because the ones supplied for use in hammocks were too short and too wide to fit the bunks. Assuming that his request would be approved, he also suggested that the Navy stock mattress covers in the ship's clothing and small stores so that men could buy their own.[23]

The bureau was not amused. It had allowed Todd to get away with building bunks, but it drew the line at Royall's demand for mattresses. Taking an infuriatingly logical tone, bureau manager Henry Williams wrote back, "Enlisted men are supposed to use their hammock mattresses irrespective of whether they are berthed in hammocks or standee bunks." As for the size discrepancy, he noted that the short hammock mattresses "are supplemented with a pillow which is supposed to remedy the conditions mentioned." He closed by saying that he would refer the whole matter to the commander in chief of the Battle Fleet, a not very subtle way of putting both Todd and Royall on report for attempting to end-run the system.[24]

Nothing escaped the bureau's attention when cost was involved. When Royall attempted to have the old lavatories in enlisted men's quarters—a bench seat placed atop a trough leading over the side—replaced with modern enamel toilets, the bureau disapproved. Enamel scratched easily and would soon present an unhygienic appearance. Besides, flush toilets would encourage crewmembers to use more water![25]

While denying Royall's request to improve the crew's toilets, the Bureau *did* order the installation of eight "experimental" metal lavatories in officers' country. Perhaps as payback for Royall's attempt to change the crew's arrangements, the bureau required that "the Commanding Officer should . . . submit reports, at six month intervals, covering the performance of these lavatories in service."[26]

The galley and bakery were to have a complete overhaul. One addition that was sure to delight the galley team was an automatic dishwasher/sterilizer. An industrial-size unit was required to handle 3 meals a day for more than 1,400 men, and the Navy chose one based on a conveyor system; dirty dishes entered on one side and emerged sparkling clean on the other.[27] Numerous other galley items required attention, from refinishing mess room furniture to repairing the cake mixer. The bureau politely refused Todd's suggestion that the ship's silverware be refinished, but he kept the project on his wish list and managed to fit it in by the end of the modernization.[28]

Although the galley itself was modernized, the men continued to eat in their berthing compartments. A junior member of each group was tasked with collecting food from the galley, bread from the bakery, and plates and silverware from the pantry. Tables and benches were stored up against the overhead and lowered on cables when needed.

Not everyone was happy with the new accommodations and food service. On October 26, 1928, Captain Royall fired off an indignant letter to Construction and Repair complaining that the officers' galley was two decks below his pantry. His mess attendants would have to climb two levels to bring food to his stateroom and, worse, walk a short distance outside. Royall conceded, "It is true that the pantry has a warming table, but no captain wants to be obliged to eat warmed over food." Besides, the warming table would add heat to an already hot cabin when the ship was in tropical climates. "The Commanding Officer wants to be on record as strongly opposed to this arrangement of captain's quarters on this ship."[29] For once the bureau attempted to be conciliatory. It was only a short walk across the weather deck to the captain's pantry, so it was unlikely that his food would get cold. As for the heat issue, the designers had provided "unusually good exhaust ventilation" to mitigate any discomfort while in the tropics.[30]

Captain Royall was not alone in trying to wrangle better accommodations on *Nevada*. On December 3, 1929, just as the ship was ready to leave for her postmodernization trials, the commander of Battleship Division Three asked the Bureau of Construction and Repair to install quarters suitable for a flag officer. *New York*, his usual flagship, was in the yard, and he wasn't satisfied with the inferior quarters of a mere ship commander. The CNO made a special effort to express his disapproval of the request.[31]

Nevada's date of completion was originally scheduled for April 30, 1929,[32] but by February of that year it had already slipped to June 29. By May only 76.6 percent of the work was done, and while the outer superstructure was complete, interior

Bow view, September 4, 1929, after modernization. The corroded cage masts have been replaced with modern tripod designs. *National Archives Photo Collection, RG 19*

compartments were still under construction.[33] Completion was pushed back to August 17. Some of the most important remaining work had to do with ordnance—the trunions holding the guns in the triple turrets were only half done.[34]

The story was similar to the original construction of *Nevada*—an optimistic early date of completion marred by unforeseen problems. But this time the Navy was doing the work at its own yard; there was no private contractor to blame for the delays. The good news was that the work done by the Norfolk Navy Yard came in $43,654.27 *under* budget, despite Commandant Todd and Captain Royall adding crew bunks, silverware replating, and other comforts to the work list.[35] The total for *Nevada* and *Oklahoma* came in at about $13.6 million, slightly over the original congressional allocation of $13.1 million.[36] As for the delay, Commandant Todd had already protected himself in January 1929 when he wrote to the Bureaus of Construction and Repair and Engineering complaining that late delivery of plans and a lack of draftsmen were putting his schedule at risk. He had been in the Navy a long time and knew how to play the game.

As Todd's punch list shortened, new crewmembers began to arrive on board, many from *Arizona*, recently arrived at the yard for her own major rebuild. On June 1, 1929, *Nevada* was transferred from what was essentially inactive status to Battleship Division Three of the Scouting Fleet, and on August 1 she was placed back in full commission.[37] Still to come were the sea trials—a retake of nearly all of the tests she underwent before her first commissioning, not surprising since she was essentially a new ship.

———

Despite all the care taken in her modernization, the rebuilt *Nevada* was not the equal of newer American battleships. USS *Colorado*, commissioned in 1923, displaced 32,600 tons against *Nevada*'s 27,500 tons and was 25 feet longer. Her side armor was similar to *Nevada*'s, but she had better internal protection against torpedoes and a more modern propulsion plant. A full salvo of *Colorado*'s eight 16-inch guns amounted to 16,800 pounds of armor-piercing ordnance, compared with *Nevada*'s 14,000 pounds, but more important, *Colorado*'s heavier shells could penetrate standard 13.5-inch belt armor at 20,000 yards, whereas *Nevada*'s guns could punch through the same armor only at 14,000 yards or less. In a running gunfight, *Nevada* might have to endure numerous damaging salvos from enemy ships before her own guns came into killing range.

But *Nevada* would not be fighting other *American* ships. All Japanese battleships prior to *Nagato* and *Mutsu* (completed in 1920 and 1921 respectively and armed with 16-inch guns) had 14-inch guns or smaller. More important, *Nevada*'s armor was thicker than that on Japanese ships, even *Nagato* and *Mutsu*. She would be an effective opponent to all but the newest of the empire's battleships. In configuring for battle, the U.S. Navy would put the *Colorado*s up against *Nagato* and *Mutsu*, and *Nevada* and other battleships would slug it out with the remainder of the Japanese battle line. Here *Nevada*'s thicker armor would prove its worth; she would be able to absorb more damage than her enemy counterparts and likely outlast them in an even exchange of fire. Ideally the U.S. fleet commander in such an engagement would keep the range at just the point where *Nevada*'s shells would penetrate thinner Japanese armor while her own armor would withstand enemy fire.

By September 5, 1929, there were 1,077 Sailors on board *Nevada* and a full complement of officers and Marines—she was ready for sea. Or so it seemed. At 0905 three tugs stood by to nudge the ship from the pier into the channel, and at 0920 both main engines were tested. The tugs waited patiently, but at 1032 Captain Royall canceled *Nevada*'s departure due to a failure in the always-problematic steering telemotor. Workers disassembled the unit and remade several parts overnight. *Nevada* left the pier at 1030 the next morning.

Gun trials were conducted at the Navy's range at Dahlgren, Virginia. The ship moored at a set of buoys off Piney Point Lighthouse and fired at a predefined location near Smith Point 31,500 yards away. To avoid hitting land, the gun directors were instructed to fire "somewhat to the left," a remarkably imprecise instruction given the specificity of most Navy procedures.[38] One pilot shot was permitted before five full salvos. The shells contained brightly colored dyes so that the splashes from individual turrets could be distinguished from one another.[39] The objective of the tests was to study shell dispersion—the tightness of a salvo pattern—at extreme range. A secondary objective was to set the air pressure in the counter-recoil mechanisms of the guns when firing at maximum elevation. This was the first time that *Nevada*'s 14-inch guns had been fired at ranges beyond about 20,000 yards.[40]

In addition to the long-range gunnery tests, ten-gun salvos were fired with the guns at 0 degree elevation, the configuration most stressful to the ship's structure. Damage was relatively minor: a sprung door in the captain's pantry, some shattered portholes, and minor issues with the ship's boats.

For her machinery and performance trials *Nevada* returned to the Navy's measured mile off Rockland, Maine. As in the builder's trials in 1915, the Navy laid down very specific requirements for the tests, starting with total displacement. The Washington Naval Treaty decreed that modifications to a capital ship could add no more than 3,000 tons to her displacement, and since *Nevada* was commissioned at 27,500 tons, she would do her second set of trials at *exactly* 30,500 tons.[41] The bureau mandated that the draft of the ship would be 28 feet, 8 inches. Obviously someone miscalculated because Captain Royall promptly wrote back that *Nevada* could not get to the specified displacement and draft unless he unloaded one thousand tons of

Nevada was to go out on September 5, 1929, but faulty steering gear caused a day's delay. *National Archives Photo Collection, RG 19*

Tugs help *Nevada* get under way, September 6, 1929. *National Archives Photo Collection, RG 19*

Nevada before and after modernization. With new engines and superstructure, she was almost a new ship. *(top) National Archives Photo Collection, RG 19, (bottom) National Archives Photo Collection, RG 80, no. 1021382*

fuel and ammunition, a process that could take eight days and might leave the ship with insufficient fuel to conduct the trials and return to Boston.[42] Without admitting any mistake, the bureau instructed *Nevada* to conduct trials with the ammunition and fuel on board, the excuse being that *normal* displacement was 30,500 tons and that the ship just happened to have extra material on board.

Performance trials got under way at 0616 on Wednesday, October 26, 1929. The weather was clear with a moderate chop on the sea, acceptable for test runs of the ship's new hull profile and power plant. In 20 standardization runs on the measured mile *Nevada* reached a respectable top speed of 20.38 knots, only 0.12 knots slower than her 1916 specifications despite the added water resistance associated with the antitorpedo blister. The new boilers and turbines were paying off.

Over the next several days the board's inspectors put *Nevada* through her paces. On Thursday morning she conducted a four-hour economy trial at fifteen knots using four of her six boilers. In the afternoon it was the same but at full power with all boilers on line. *Nevada* burned more than eighteen tons of fuel per hour at full speed. However, the boilers smoked excessively at any speed above nineteen knots, indicating a poor air-to-fuel ratio in the burners.[43]

After the full-power trial, course was set for the Virginia Capes, where a third four-hour trial was conducted, this one at ten knots with less than four tons of fuel consumed per hour. Next came punishing reversing tests. *Nevada* worked her way up to full speed, and Captain Royall ordered full reverse. During the 2 minutes and 45 seconds it took the ship to stop she covered 745 yards. From full speed astern it took 1 minute 45 seconds to stop over a distance of 266 yards.

The trials were a success, but just as in the original runs in 1915–16, various small problems surfaced with the new machinery. A feed pump blew a gasket, a condenser in the dynamo room sprung a leak, and a fuel pump malfunctioned. On the positive side, the new engines performed brilliantly. At 10 knots *Nevada* could steam 8,950 miles using her original engines, but with the *North Dakota* transplants she could go 13,530 miles. At near full speed she could now push 6,140 miles compared with only 2,780 miles with her original equipment. In terms of mileage, at the economical speed of 10 knots *Nevada* covered about 4.5 miles per ton of fuel, or about 50 *feet* per gallon. Fuel efficiency was a relative matter.

While the machinery performed well, the board was less impressed with the men operating it. The report noted that "the Engineer's force were not yet sufficiently efficient to obtain the results that should have been expected on the fuel consumption trials."[44] Captain Royall had work to do.

A broken deck lug on one of the guns in turret 3 delayed *Nevada*'s return to the fleet until January 4, 1930—two and a half years after entering the yard. It was high time to get back to sea.

7

Fleet Problems

After leaving the Norfolk Navy Yard *Nevada* steamed south for winter gunnery practice at Guantanamo Bay, joining *Oklahoma* and *Arizona* to form Battleship Division Three of the Scouting Fleet. Despite the success of the postmodernization trials, Captain Royall's pride in his newly rebuilt ship quickly evaporated as one problem after another cropped up. Even before leaving port the bridge crew noticed that steering was sluggish, especially at slow speeds. Up to 35 degrees of rudder was required to keep *Nevada* on course at 9 knots, depending on wind direction and velocity; below 6 knots the ship was almost uncontrollable in all but the calmest conditions.[1] Even a routine turn required considerable skill on the part of the helmsman to assess what corrective steering was required, based on wind conditions, to true up on the new course. Sister ship *Oklahoma* reported that with rudder amidships the ship would steam in circles in even a moderate wind, an alarming prospect if the steering gear should fail during battle.[2]

Exacerbating the steering problems was the ever-present trouble with the telemotor system controlling the rudder. Within a week of leaving the yard both the steam and electrical steering systems failed, forcing Captain Royall to hoist the breakdown flag.

While the ship herself was having teething problems, so too was her crew. Many of the officers and enlisted men were new to *Nevada*, and the few who had served prior to her rebuild were out of practice. One of Royall's greatest challenges was to mold a thousand individuals into a coherent and coordinated fighting machine.

The dangers of being out of practice were demonstrated in a particularly grisly manner on February 16 off Guantanamo Bay. During a routine catapult launch of plane 3/6, Lt. Walther G. Maser, the senior aviator on board, stepped in front of the catapult's exhaust just after giving the order to fire. The blast from the high-explosive charge that propelled the plane into the air decapitated Maser and blew his body overboard, leaving only a part of his skull on the deck. Boats lowered from *Nevada*, *Oklahoma*, *Texas*, and *New York* searched for the body without success. Two days later all hands were mustered aft on the quarterdeck for a memorial service.

The mourning period was short—thirty minutes later *Nevada* was under way for more gunnery exercises.

———

The Navy conducted two fleet problems in 1930, each simulating the defense of the Caribbean against an attack by a coalition of European powers. During the Battle of Navassa Island, Navy planes incapacitated two aircraft carriers within twenty minutes, a portent to the stunning U.S. victory at Midway a dozen years in the future. The ability of aircraft to play such a decisive role in battle led Vice Adm. W. C. Cole to recommend the creation of dedicated task forces of swift aircraft carriers screened by fast cruisers and destroyers.[3] Other senior officers in the fleet supported his recommendations, which would be adopted with brilliant success in the coming war.

A more genteel engagement took place off Hampton Roads in May when the fleet conducted a mock battle for the benefit of President Herbert Hoover. In the best traditions of the Navy, a grand procession of battleships passed the presidential yacht, each rendering a twenty-one-gun salute.

———

Guns trained to starboard, March 24, 1930. Note the two spotter planes aft. *National Archives Photo Collection, RG 80, no. 63420*

Captain Royall's worries about maneuvering at low speeds were painfully realized when *Nevada* transited the Panama Canal on June 10, 1930. In Culebra Reach, on the Atlantic side, the rudder stuck at 17.5 degrees after the order was given to place it amidships. Royall ordered an immediate shift from steam to electric steering, hard right rudder, and full reverse on the port engine. Collision Quarters was sounded, and the starboard anchor was let go as an additional measure to slow the ship. When she finally stopped, *Nevada* was perpendicular to the channel, her bow pointed toward the bank, with 165 fathoms of anchor chain trailing behind her.

The agony was not over. With a Panama Canal pilot on the bridge, *Nevada* collided with the dock as she entered Pedro Miguel locks, damaging the blister plating on her starboard bow. Less than two hours later the portside blister abreast the bridge hit the side of Miraflores locks. *Nevada* seemed to be bumping her way through the Canal. Even anchoring was a challenge—after she finally made it to the Pacific side of the Canal, the starboard anchor was lost. The physical damage to the ship was minimal, but Captain Royall and his crew were sorely embarrassed— few things brought down the scorn of navy men as did the perception of poor ship handling.

Insult was added to injury when a July inspection gave low marks for training and "smartness." Commander of Battleship Divisions, Battle Fleet sent a tersely worded note stating, "Decided improvement may be expected."[4]

After a quick trip to the Puget Sound Navy Yard to repair the damage sustained in passing through the Canal, *Nevada* returned to San Pedro for short-range battle practice, night battle practice, and tactical exercises with the fleet. Some of the gunnery runs were conducted on one-day sorties from San Pedro, while others were weeklong affairs with the participating ships anchoring overnight at San Nicholas Island or Santa Barbara Island to save fuel.

Many of these exercises did not involve actual firing but were intended to train officers and crew in targeting, aiming guns, or rapid loading while under way. On firing runs, a towing vessel would typically pull three or four targets resembling large billboards. Long-range battle practice targets representing large ships (cruisers and above) were 140-foot-long by 40-foot-tall constructions of wood mesh. Twenty-foot-tall targets of the same length simulated destroyers. For short-range battle practice, several targets measuring 15–25 feet square were mounted on a common sled. Hits were easily counted by the shell holes in the target, and because the noses of shells bore distinctive colors, each hit could be traced back to a specific gun on the ship. For safety's sake, battleships frequently towed targets, since a wild shot could endanger smaller ships.

Short-range battle practice focused on repelling attacks by destroyers. Night battle practice had the same objective but was more challenging because it was harder to spot where shells fell. Night tactical exercises explored the use of search-lights and star shells to illuminate the enemy, weighing the advantages and disad-vantages of each against operational objectives, weather conditions, disposition of friendly forces, and so on. Searchlights were generally superior out to about 4,000–5,000 yards, but they were beacons to attract enemy fire; star shells were useful out to 12,000–13,000 yards, but in misty weather they were little more than a glow in the sky. No perfect solution to night targeting was found prior to the introduction of radar later in the decade.

Nevada typically expended several dozen 5-inch shells in a short-range battle practice and a few dozen 5-inch star shells in a night battle practice. Antiaircraft runs could expend more than one hundred rounds of 5-inch cartridges or several thousand rounds of machine-gun ammunition. As budgets got tighter, ammuni-tion was strictly rationed, and commanders complained that firing so few rounds per gun did not accurately simulate actual battle.

Annual gunnery competitions were closely followed throughout the fleet. Scoring well meant more than just bragging rights—good shooting could yield a letter of commendation in an officer's personnel folder and twenty dollars in prize money for the successful gun crew. Yet gunnery competitions were inherently arti-ficial. To make the competition fair, an identical situation had to prevail for each ship. Targets at the end of a 1,000- or 1,500-yard tow cable could not maneuver as actual ships would, nor could they shoot back. For this reason the Navy augmented live-fire target practice with simulated fire in highly complex tactical exercises that stressed the ability to locate, engage, and destroy an enemy of unknown strength and disposition.

Keeping a turret in ammunition required nearly one hundred men, all of whom had to work in flawless synchrony to get off two or more rounds per minute. It was not uncommon for fingers or hands to be caught in hoists, loading trays, or other machinery. The thin silk powder bags were prone to ripping, spilling powder in the turret or one of the handling rooms below, a fire and explosion threat that had to be dealt with immediately. During gunnery exercises off Guantanamo Bay in 1934, an enterprising ammunition handler scooped up spilled powder from a broken bag and stuffed it into an undershirt, which he then sent up the powder hoist. The commander of the Battle Force recommended "the award of adequately impressive penalties" to prevent any such occurrence in the future.[5]

The relentless pace of activity in a turret and its underlying magazines occa-sionally led to heart-stopping incidents. On December 3, 1932, a 14-inch shell was dropped twenty feet into the number 2 handling room.[6] A similar incident occurred on August 14, 1935, when a shell was dropped thirty-five feet. While the risk of a shell exploding during such accidents was relatively low, the ammunition handlers, both above and below, must have watched in terror as the shells plummeted down.

Life in a secondary gun position was even more hectic than in the turrets. An experienced 5-inch/51-caliber gun crew consisting of ten men (not counting those in the magazine) could fire ten shells per minute. A 5-inch/25-caliber antiaircraft gun crew could fire up to twenty shells per minute. Rapid fire was important for secondary guns, whose principal mission was defense against destroyer and air attacks. With multiple targets moving at high speed, the secondary and antiaircraft batteries had to send a hail of metal outbound to disrupt or destroy attackers before they could launch their deadly torpedoes and bombs.

Gun crews were only part of a complex system for putting shells on target. At the top of her new tripod masts *Nevada* had three-story fire control stations containing sophisticated optical instruments to estimate the range, course, and speed of a target. This information was sent to the plotting room, deep in the protected area of the hull, where a mechanical computer coordinated the motion of *Nevada*, that of the target, and the expected trajectories of shells. Accurate predictions were more than sophomore physics—they required an assessment of the effect of prevailing winds, air density, erosion of the gun barrel by previous shots, smokeless powder temperature, and even the rotation of the earth. When each turret indicated that it was ready to fire or enough guns were ready to make it worthwhile to launch a salvo, an officer in the fire control station would close a switch and the guns would fire automatically when the roll of the ship brought the target into position.[7] To give the gun crews some warning, a salvo alarm was sounded a few seconds before firing.

While this type of "director fire" was the preferred means of launching salvos, ships also practiced local control of the guns, which would be required if the fire control stations were destroyed in battle. Depending on the tactical situation, commanders could order concentrated fire (several ships firing on the same target), divided fire (different guns on the same ship firing on different targets), or split salvos (not all guns in a turret firing in a given salvo).

Aiming was complicated by intentional maneuvers of the firing ship to evade fire from the enemy or to put the battle line in a better tactical position. For example, in repelling a destroyer attack *Nevada* might fire her forward group of secondary guns at the enemy vessels, execute a sharp turn to avoid torpedoes, and reengage with the aft guns.[8] Ships were expected to continue firing in a turn while ensuring that they would not inadvertently fire at friendly ships or at parts of their own ship.

Officers and men had to perform automatically and with clockwork precision as enemy shells landed around them. To sharpen their skills, *Nevada's* plotting room staff developed a unique "spotting board" to simulate actual battle conditions. The spotter sat on a rolling cart next to the board and watched the action through reverse lens binoculars. Scale models of battleships were placed in the middle of the board, and plane spotters sat in a hatchway above. The team learned how to communicate efficiently, make decisions, and respond to unexpected situations. Since shell flight time could be longer than the interval between shots, two or even three salvos might be in the air at the same time, making coordination all the more important.[9]

A full salvo from *Nevada's* main guns was a sight to behold. Coming out of the barrel at nearly a half-mile per second, the shells were big enough to be seen with the naked eye. Occasionally they would "kiss," or bump up against one another, on the way to the target. Since even such gentle nudges could affect accuracy, delay coils were installed so that the center gun in a three-gun turret fired a fraction of a second after the outer guns.

Nevada's modernization was barely completed when the Navy began thinking of replacing her. During the annual inspection of 1929, the Board of Inspection and Survey observed: "Under the provisions of the Treaty made as a result of the Conference on the Limitation of Armament at Washington, D.C. in 1921–1922, a ship may be laid down in 1933 to replace the NEVADA. On completion of such a replacement ship in 1936, the NEVADA, under the provisions of the above treaty is to be scrapped."[10] This was the first of several predictions of the demise of the Cheer Up Ship. She would outlast most of her critics, and by the time her life was over one of her nicknames would be "Old Imperishable."

Part of her longevity was due to the extreme financial pressures created by the Great Depression, which struck with its full economic fury just as *Nevada* was coming out of the Norfolk Navy Yard. With unemployment skyrocketing and bread lines stretching around city blocks, there was little enthusiasm in the nation for battleship construction.

Other countries saw things differently. Charismatic Adolf Hitler promised to halt the economic slide and erase the humiliation of Versailles, mesmerizing millions of Germans struggling to survive the depression. In Japan, the military leapt at the chance to provide a solution to the nation's ills. On September 18, 1931, the Imperial Japanese Army set off an explosion on the South Manchurian Railway, giving local troops an excuse to invade Manchuria and set up the puppet state of Manchukuo.

Even as Japanese troops marched into Manchuria, liberal politicians in Western capitals maintained their postwar dream of peace through disarmament. A naval arms limitation conference held in Geneva in 1927 came to naught after the United States and Great Britain failed to agree on limits to cruisers, but that did not stop London from hosting another conference in 1930. In the depths of the depression, Britain could ill afford another arms race and was prepared to offer significant concessions to prevent one. Preconference discussions between London and Washington involving detailed technical work by Prime Minister Ramsay MacDonald and President Herbert Hoover resolved the U.S.-U.K. cruiser issue, but Japan still objected to being held to 60 percent of parity. The United States relented to Japan's demands by delaying the construction of its own cruisers, giving Tokyo at least a temporary advantage and prolonging the illusion that peace might be achieved by arms control.

Around the time of the London conference, British diplomats floated the idea of scrapping *all* battleships. Why embark on costly programs to rebuild or replace them when airplanes and submarines were the weapons of the future? The United States refused to send its battleships to the scrapyard, and negotiators finally reached a compromise in which the "building holiday" for battleships, set to expire in 1931, was extended to 1936. For Britain, the compromise only made a bad problem worse—all of its battleships would need to be replaced within a short time of the expiration of the holiday. The U.S. Congress was only too happy to defer difficult decisions on naval funding to another day.

Tokyo rejected out of hand any further limitations on its battleships. Ultraconservative factions in the Imperial Japanese Navy, led by Admiral Kato Kanji, had bristled at the limits codified in the Washington Treaty. Immediately following the signing in 1922 Kato said, "As far as I am concerned, war with America starts now. We'll get our revenge over this!"[11] Obsessed with the notion of Japanese honor, Kato demanded nothing less than complete equality of arms, lecturing that economic competition with America would inevitably lead to war.

Kato's was hardly an isolated voice; Japan's animosity against the United States permeated all levels of society. A popular magazine for young people published an article in 1922 titled "The Future War between Japan and America." And when fifth- and sixth-graders in Tokyo were asked if war between Japan and America was likely, one student answered, "Yes, I think so. Americans are so arrogant. I'd like to show them a thing or two."[12]

None of this seemed to affect America's view of Japan as a partner in a stable and progressive world order. After the signing of the London Treaty Secretary of State Henry Stimson went so far as to call Japan "a great stabilizing force in the Far East," adding, "We have nothing to worry about Japan's superior position in the Far East; rather we believe it to be to our advantage."[13] The attack on Pearl Harbor scarcely a decade later would make such statements appear ludicrously naïve.

Ship's mascot 1st class, early 1930s. *Nevada State Museum*

Nevada's exit from the Panama Canal in June 1930 marked her return to familiar anchorages in San Pedro and Long Beach, once sleepy seaside villages on opposite sides of Los Angeles Harbor that had grown into bustling Navy towns. Sailors who were not married—and some who were—were easy prey for the many temptations facing young men away from home, including alcohol, automobiles, and women. The first two made for a lethal cocktail, and by the early 1930s automobile accidents had become one of the leading causes of death among Sailors. To counter these dangers, chief petty officers raised money to build a recreation hall for enlisted men at San Pedro. The chiefs had invested a great deal of time in molding boys into fighting men, and they didn't want to see their investment wasted.

Officers were not immune from dangers ashore. On December 20, 1930, Ens. William Shinn Gates attempted suicide by drinking poison. "I got into a jam in Los Angeles," he later told a newspaper reporter. "I smashed up another fellow's car. I got leave from the *Nevada* and came to San Francisco. Then I found I had overstayed my leave. That meant I was a deserter and would have to face a court martial, so I took poison." In fact, there was no order to arrest Gates, and the two passengers in the car he was driving were not seriously injured. He was taken to Mare Island Naval Hospital for treatment and was still listed on *Nevada*'s roster at the beginning of 1931.[14]

On average during the early 1930s, *Nevada* spent about one-third of her time at sea and the remainder in port or in a Navy yard undergoing repairs and overhaul. The crew always had something to do on the ship, from the excitement of firing full salvos of 14-inch guns to the more mundane tasks of painting and polishing. The military highlight of the year, however, was the annual fleet problem that put the reason for every other activity on the ship into sharp focus: *Nevada* was a *warship* intended to fight and win battles at sea.

Fleet Problem XII, held in 1931, pitted a "European power" against American forces defending the Panama Canal. Unlike previous scenarios, however, this one included the added complication of a "Pacific power." Both the Secretary of the

Navy and the assistant secretary attended Fleet Problem XII, and, significantly, several British warships participated, including the Royal Navy flagship HMS *Nelson*.

Nevada was in the thick of intense (simulated) fighting throughout Fleet Problem XII. Numerous encounters with attacking destroyers tested her secondary batteries, and mock air attacks gave her antiaircraft guns a workout. At 0938 on February 19 she engaged in a different type of antiaircraft defense when her main battery opened up on an enemy aircraft carrier at a range of 25,300 yards. She had only a moment to fire before enemy cruisers laid a smokescreen to cover the carrier's escape, but the event highlighted a serious deficiency in the tactics of the day: having aircraft carriers steam in formation with battleships could bring them within gun range of the opposing fleet.[15]

Nevada's role in Fleet Problem XII came to an abrupt halt on March 12 when the engine room reported excessive vibrations in the starboard low-pressure turbine. Inspection revealed that the last row of blades in the turbine was badly damaged. *Nevada* was forced to limp back to San Pedro and then to Puget Sound Navy Yard on her port engine alone. She spent two months in the yard having the turbine repaired and undergoing other overhaul work.

The April–June 1931 overhaul was her first since the modernization, an opportunity to take care of many of the mechanical deficiencies identified during her shakedown cruise and subsequent operation.[16] The damaged blister plating was repaired, and a new ammunition-handling system was installed for the 5-inch antiaircraft battery. Yard personnel and the ship's crew tackled the perennial problems with the steering telemotor, finding that at least part of the problem was that the system was dirty and poorly assembled.

As some problems were fixed, others became apparent. The commandant of the Navy Yard raised concerns about the watertight integrity of scores of compartments in the hull. Supposedly "solid" bulkheads were riddled with openings for electrical cables and ventilation shafts, many of which had poor seals. Unfortunately, there was no money to address the problem.[17] Ten years later, the attack at Pearl Harbor would graphically validate the commandant's worries over leaky compartments.

Harkening back to Captain Sims' interest in gunnery, *Nevada* was chosen to host the 1931 Secondary Battery Gunnery School, an annual event that involved personnel from across the fleet. In almost daily sorties from San Pedro the broadside batteries fired upward of two hundred rounds per day, a strain on guns and their crews alike. Another gunnery event on December 4, 1931, presaged a major future mission for the ship: shore bombardment in support of amphibious landings. The invasion site was San Clemente Island, and two of the ship's planes helped spot simulated gunfire in support of the landings.

Fleet Problem XIII, conducted in Hawaiian waters during February and March 1932, was done in conjunction with the U.S. Army, the first joint exercise since 1925. The assumption was that a Pacific power had captured the Hawaiian Islands, and that the fleet, accompanied by an Army landing force, would recapture them. The problem was a test of the Navy's ability to conduct amphibious operations over the vast reaches of the Pacific, a thinly disguised practice for taking advanced bases in the western Pacific in a future war with Japan. *Nevada* provided bombardment support for the landings using both main and secondary batteries and lent her boats for landing troops. The crew was alert to the constant threat of submarine attack, and on several occasions the secondary guns had to be diverted from ground support to warding off attacking subs. Significantly, Fleet Problem XIII also involved a carrier raid on Oahu, an eerie precursor to the Japanese attack nine years later.

Nevada missed Fleet Problem XIV, which was conducted while she was undergoing scheduled overhaul at Puget Sound in late 1932 and early 1933. As a consolation prize the galley kept the reduced crew well supplied with treats. On January 1 the Apex bakery delivered 200 pies and 150 pounds of jellyrolls. Three days later 156 pounds of cake and 150 pounds of cupcakes came on board; more pies and cakes followed, including 200 pumpkin pies on January 10. Many of the men on the ship were in their teens or just beyond, still growing and performing physically demanding work over long hours. An intake of 4,600 calories per day was not unusual, so a few pieces of pie or cake per day added little to waistlines.

There were more serious deliveries to the ship during the overhaul: the increasing danger of air attack—particularly by dive-bombers—led to the installation of eight .50-caliber machine guns, four on each of the two masts. While the 5-inch/25-caliber antiaircraft guns had proven useful against high-altitude bombers, only rapid-firing machine guns were effective against dive-bombers.

The big guns came in for their share of attention. After the modernization at Norfolk, gunnery officers had noted erratic performance of the main battery and a larger dispersion pattern than should have been achievable given the design of the guns.[18] Part of the problem was "lost motion," or looseness in the various elevation and training mechanisms, but there was a worry that the guns themselves were not properly installed. The Bureau of Ordnance objected to criticisms of its guns in a letter to the CNO: "In the opinion of this Bureau, the trouble experienced by the NEVADA can be attributed to poor workmanship on the part of the Navy Yard, Norfolk, in installing the deck lugs."[19] The commandant of Norfolk had already fired back at previous complaints about workmanship: "It would seem that any serious defects might have been discovered in the course of the many battery checks and gunnery practices incident to the vessel's service in the last four years."[20]

Whoever was at fault, the problem was fixed when the main and secondary batteries were regunned during the 1933 overhaul.

Capt. William Pye took *Nevada* out of dry dock in late February 1933, and after taking on 1,354 containers of powder for the main guns and more than 1,000 rounds for her secondary batteries, he ran her through the required post-overhaul full-speed and smoke-suppression runs. She caught up with the fleet in March for battle practice and was hit three times on the starboard side during advanced torpedo practice.

March brought greater concerns for many members of the crew. On March 10 a magnitude 6.3 earthquake hit Long Beach, damaging many homes and forcing families to sleep on their lawns. The Navy sent patrols to prevent looting, but this did not stop the worries of men far from home and helpless to assist loved ones.[21]

After a summer conducting Secondary Battery Gunnery School it was *Nevada*'s turn to conduct her own target practice with main, secondary, and antiaircraft guns. The crew of turret 3 had a banner day on September 25 when the men set a world record for short-range battle practice: twelve hits in twelve shots.

November 12, 1933, was a somber day on *Nevada*, now anchored in San Francisco Bay. Rear Adm. Ridley McLean, commander of Battleship Division Three, died suddenly of a heart attack while on board. McLean was using *Nevada* as his temporary flagship and was well known to the men of the fleet as the author

Turret 3 celebrates a world record in short-range battle practice, September 1933. Twelve hits in twelve shots. *Nevada State Museum*

of *The Bluejacket's Manual*, a practical guide for Sailors. He had served with William Sims when the latter was inspector of target practice and had commanded a battleship during World War I. At 1010 on November 13, with McLean's flag-draped coffin on deck, the ship's chaplains conducted funeral services. Men stood at attention by the rails of the fifty ships in San Francisco Bay as *Nevada*, flying the colors of Commander Battleship Division Three, steamed slowly out to sea and then to San Pedro. McLean was later buried at Arlington National Cemetery.

Fleet Problem XV, held April 19–May 12, 1934, almost didn't happen due to lack of money. The Navy's annual appropriation for that year was the lowest since 1916, but the leadership argued that practice in realistic battle situations was a top priority for the fleet, and funds were scraped together to conduct the exercise.

The scenario was a familiar one: Atlantic and Pacific powers combined forces for attacks in the Caribbean and Central America. But Fleet Problem XV was the most complex simulation yet, involving thirty-one separate actions. During one battle the American fleet lost all six of its battleships to torpedoes.[22] In a particularly fierce night attack, a destroyer came so close to *Nevada* that Capt. Adolphus Staton ordered the running lights turned on to help avoid a collision.

But the most spectacular engagement of Fleet Problem XV was *Nevada*'s solitary charge on the enemy, a maneuver that occurred during what Rear Adm. Thomas Craven, commander of Battleship Division One, described as a "fight to the finish" between opposing battle lines.[23]

The opposing fleets made contact off the coast of Mexico. The weather was fine, and visibility was excellent—a perfect day for a long-range gunfight. The battle lines approached in good order, and at 1520 the enemy opened fire. *Nevada* opened up at 1537 at a range of 24,000 yards. Sometimes she shot at her own designated target and sometimes she joined with *California* or *Maryland* in a "double concentration" on a single enemy ship. Forty-five minutes into the battle, dive-bombers attacked *Nevada*—nearly every gun on the ship was actively engaged in the battle.

Nevada began taking hits. The assistant umpire on board deemed three secondary guns out of action and ruled that damage to the smokestack reduced the ship's speed to just twelve knots. Captain Staton knew that he could not keep up with the U.S. battle line, but instead of sheering out of column *away* from the enemy, as was typical for a damaged ship, he veered *toward* the opposing battleships.[24] It was the only way that he could keep in the fight, and he counted on the element of surprise to disrupt the enemy's plans. At the very least he would attract fire otherwise intended for his compatriots, and he might even get in a few good shots of his own.

Attract enemy fire he did—while *Nevada* was closing to 9,000 yards, 3 turrets were deemed hit, and numerous secondary guns were ruled out of action. The fore and aft tops were shot away, and the bridge, signal bridge, and charthouse were all declared destroyed. But Staton kept on going, firing salvo after salvo from every gun that would bear. By the time cease-fire was called, *Nevada* was only 1,735 yards away from the enemy—point-blank range. She had "fired" 887 rounds during the battle.[25] Both sides had taken heavy losses, but when the smoke cleared the enemy was withdrawing and the United States had won the day.

It was an astonishing performance, a heroic demonstration of the very type of individual initiative that the fleet problems were designed to develop. In a real battle Staton would have sacrificed his ship, his crew, and himself for the victory of the fleet. The commander in chief wrote in an after-action report:

> In order to encourage initiative and prompt decision the Commander-in-Chief directed that . . . every commander and captain should act in accordance with the Fleet Cruising Instructions or as required by the existing situation *without awaiting instructions from superior authority* [italics in original].
>
> The decision of the Commanding Officer, USS NEVADA in fighting on the engaged side of the Battle Line meets with the entire approval of the Commander-in-Chief and sets a valuable precedent for such action in battle.[26]

Transiting the Panama Canal, April 1934. The new torpedo blister made it a tight fit. *National Archives Photo Collection, RG 80, no. 455904*

Nevada did not always rank among the top ships for gunnery. She scored so poorly in long-range battle practice in May 1934 that her commanding officer was instructed to report in writing how he was going to improve his ship's performance.[27] But when the chips were down, as they were during Fleet Problem XV and later in actual combat, *Nevada* always came through.

——

The difficulty steering at low speeds that had appeared on *Nevada*'s postmodernization shakedown cruise continued to frustrate the helmsmen and navigators. Engineers at Puget Sound studied the problem during a March 1934 overhaul and realized that the new torpedo-protection blister diverted water flow away from the rudder, reducing its ability to turn the ship. They considered various solutions, including installing dual rudders or shortening the shafts to bring the propellers forward.[28] The Bureau of Construction and Repair did its own analysis and ordered the installation of a "deadwood" section between the current rudder and the curve of the stern that would reduce turbulent flow and increase the ability of the rudder to provide positive steering.[29] It worked.

One modification during the 1934 overhaul was to prove especially important in extended fleet operations: the installation of piping and hoses to allow underway fueling of destroyers. *Nevada* carried more than two thousand tons of fuel and could easily part with enough to keep several destroyers going during extended deployments. Using battleships for fueling smaller ships made good sense because they were on the scene and were relatively stable platforms in moderate seas.

Nevada quickly recovered her excellence in gunnery. The 5-inch/51-caliber battery set a Navy record in short-range battle practice, prompting prize money for the crew and a letter of congratulations from the commander in chief of the U.S. Fleet, who noted: "This score was obtained through general excellence indicated by accurate gun pointing, rapidity of fire, no casualties, and excellent control."[30] The record score was even more impressive given the challenges *Nevada* faced in the competition—she had just come from three months in the yard, and more than two-thirds of her officers above the rank of ensign and nearly half of the secondary battery enlisted men were new to the ship.[31] Given that inexperience, the results of the practice were truly outstanding: *Nevada*'s secondary guns scored nearly 85 percent hits, and the turrets were nearly as good. Gun crews were firing more than two shots per minute from turret guns and an amazing twelve shots per minute—one every five seconds—from the secondary guns.[32]

——

As *Nevada*'s gunnery improved, international relations deteriorated. On December 29, 1934, Japan gave the required two years' notice that it was withdrawing from the Washington Naval Treaty, signaling the end of interwar arms control. Japan was its own worst enemy in mishandling the treaty system. With nationalism rising in China and the Soviet Union rapidly recovering from its revolution, Tokyo faced two strong competitors in the Far East. It could have embraced cooperative treaties with the United States and Great Britain as a balance to these challenges but instead chose to pit itself against nearly all comers. If, as Admiral Kato Kanji said, war with the United States started with the Washington Naval Treaty of 1922, defeat for Japan started with its withdrawal from that treaty at the end of 1934.

On the very same day that Japan announced its withdrawal from the Washington Naval Treaty, Adm. Joseph "Bull" Reeves, commander in chief of the U.S. Fleet, announced Fleet Problem XVI. This was to be the most complex fleet problem ever attempted—a true strategic exercise that spanned more than 5 million square miles of ocean in a triangle stretching from the west coast of North America to Hawaii to the Aleutians. As a concession to Tokyo, Reeves stipulated that the Navy would remain east of the international date line and would come no closer than two thousand miles to Japan. But the message was crystal clear: Fleet Problem XVI was a rehearsal for the coming war in the Pacific.

Japan, represented by the "Black" fleet, was assumed to have captured Midway and to have deployed its submarines to whittle down American surface forces steaming west. This was in accord with Japanese naval planning that assumed the U.S. Navy would hasten across the Pacific for a quick, decisive battle to settle the

Steaming in calm seas, August 1935, *Nevada* looked her interwar best. *National Archives Photo Collection, RG 80, no. 423349*

war. Amazingly, carriers played little role in Fleet Problem XVI, never detecting one another, let alone attacking. Admiral Kato, the fierce advocate of Japanese naval expansion and a believer in the supremacy of the battleship, could not have planned it better.

The only damage *Nevada* suffered during Fleet Problem XVI was due to tugboats. While helping her out of Berth 5 at Pearl Harbor, two overenthusiastic tugs dented her blister plating, sheering rivets and bending supporting beams. But this didn't stop *Nevada* from sortieing with the fleet or participating fully in the fleet problem. During her trip to Midway for the anticipated clash with the Japanese, she simultaneously fueled two destroyers, one on each side. With surface action, shore bombardment, and now underway refueling, *Nevada* was a true multipurpose unit of the fleet.

By the end of 1935 *Nevada* had been on duty for almost twenty years, well beyond the lifespan her creators envisioned. However, her age was more than compensated for by the dedication and hard work of her successive captains and crews, all of whom fell under the spell of the Cheer Up Ship. The Report of Material Inspection of November 1935 concluded: "In view of the exceptionally high state of preservation of the USS NEVADA and her apparently efficient operating condition, the board feels that the work involved [in overhaul] is warranted by the probable many remaining years of life and useful service of the vessel."[33] *Nevada* would serve for another decade. Many of her later officers and crew, not yet born when she was launched, would conclude that her best years were yet to come.

8

Oranges and Chrysanthemums

The United States began planning for a Pacific war in 1906. The assumption was always that Japan would overrun the Philippines, Guam, and other American possessions in the Far East, and the job of the U.S. Navy was always to recapture those possessions, destroy the Imperial Japanese Fleet, and blockade Japan. War Plan Orange, as it came to be known, went through numerous revisions over the next three decades, alternating between what plan historian Edward Miller refers to as the "thrusters," who advocated a quick "through ticket" from the West Coast to the Philippines, and the "cautionaries," who argued for a more measured approach.[1]

The U.S. Navy's lack of fortified bases in the western Pacific led to the eventual acceptance of the cautionary doctrine, which by 1934 dominated planning. Rather than a dangerous dash across the Pacific to engage the Japanese fleet in its home waters, the Navy would capture one of the Marshall Islands, most likely Eniwetok, and build a supply and service base. From there the fleet would advance along a series of island stepping-stones to Japan. In a stroke of strategic brilliance, planners recognized that the Navy need not attack every Japanese-occupied island; many could be left to "wither on the vine," deprived of supplies and reinforcements.[2] The ultimate goal was not to capture and occupy the empire but to blockade Japan until Tokyo sued for peace.

The problem with the cautionary approach was that it entailed a "long" war, one lasting two years or more. Isolationism had again taken hold in the United States, and the majority of the population was dead set against America's involvement in another foreign war.[3] Navy leadership worried that people might not have the patience to endure a long campaign.

However, reluctance to engage in foreign conflicts did not equate to lack of preparedness. Tokyo's withdrawal from the Washington Naval Treaty at the end of 1936 meant that the "holiday" on capital ship construction was over, and the necessity to create jobs for American workers had already loosened congressional purse strings for naval construction. The National Industrial Recovery Act of 1933 provided $238 million for thirty-two new ships, including two aircraft carriers, four

View from port quarter, 1930s. Engineering worked hard to reduce the amount of smoke.
National Archives Photo Collection, RG 80, no. 1021377

light cruisers, twenty destroyers, and various other vessels. The Vinson-Trammell Acts of 1934 and 1938 increased funding still more to bring the Navy up to the full strength permitted by the Washington and London treaties.[4]

<hr />

As blueprints were being drawn for the new battleships *North Carolina* and *Washington* in early 1936, *Nevada* was having her secondary battery regunned at the Puget Sound Navy Yard. Numerous small items were taken care of during the periodic overhaul, from painting the hull (done by the crew to save money) to the installation of electric drinking fountains.

From Bremerton she steamed south to participate in Fleet Problem XVII, which, while set in Central America, was actually intended to simulate a surprise attack on Hawaii. For three days (May 5–7) U.S. forces engaged in a pitched battle with attacking "Japanese" ships and aircraft.[5] *Nevada* steamed on only one engine for two of these days due to a leaky starboard condenser. Another interruption to the mock battle came on May 20 when Capt. Robert Ghormley stopped all engines and assembled the crew at division parade to receive King Neptune and his royal court. For a few hours, tradition trumped tactics.

Maneuvers during 1937 focused on meeting an enemy battle line that enjoyed superior speed—a euphemism for Japan's four fast battle cruisers. The U.S. Navy's solution was to force an encounter on parallel courses, but with the two battle lines steaming in opposite directions. When the enemy reversed direction to engage, its faster battle cruisers would be in the rear, where their speed advantage was nullified. In long-range battle practice in April 1937, Battleship Division One—including

Nevada—was directed to deploy to port when gun range reached 20,000–21,000 yards. The enemy obligingly turned around to engage, and *Nevada* commenced firing at 18,700 yards, hitting her assigned target on the sixth salvo. The practice was challenging for turret crews and plotting room alike because the turrets had to suspend fire and turn while the target crossed the bow or stern, opening up again as soon as there was a clear shot. As a further complication, firing personnel were required to wear gas masks during the exercise—the use of poison gas was still considered a viable threat.[6]

With each passing year, gunnery practices and fleet exercises felt increasingly like rehearsals for war. Hitler sent 22,000 troops into the Rhineland in 1936, drawing little more than feeble protests from the international community.[7] Japan invaded China in 1937, brushing aside similarly weak criticism. Each country knew what it wanted—dominion over a greater empire—and each was determined to use force to get it. In 1936 Japan spent nearly half its national budget on its army and navy.[8]

The U.S. State Department held out hope that diplomacy might temper Japan's ambitions in China, but Tokyo responded to such overtures with little more than brazen contempt. On December 12, 1937, Japanese planes attacked and sank the patrol boat USS *Panay* on the Yangtze River. American missions and schools were regularly bombed even though they were clearly marked by flags painted on their roofs. Japan apologized after each incident, but the attacks continued, leading one observer to note wryly, "The most dangerous spot in an air raid . . . [is] an American mission." Tokyo understood that the American population would rather withdraw from China than risk war.[9] It was an accurate perception; President Roosevelt doubted that he would get a single vote in the Senate in favor of armed intervention in China.[10]

On March 16, 1938, *Nevada* left San Pedro for Hawaii as part of Fleet Problem XIX, set again in the "Pacific Triangle" defined by the west coast of North America, Hawaii, and the Aleutians. U.S. Navy operations in the north of the triangle brought howls of protest from Tokyo, which called them "provocative" and "aggressive." (This despite Japan's rampages in China, including the sinking of *Panay*.) In a way they were right—the fleet problem was intended as a demonstration that America was fully prepared for a fight anywhere in the Pacific.

The most profound insight resulting from Fleet Problem XIX was the vulnerability of Pearl Harbor and other military installations on Oahu to air attack. At 0450 on March 29, Vice Adm. Ernest King, of the Blue (Japanese) Fleet, launched an air attack from carriers one hundred miles off Oahu that inflicted heavy damage on Pearl Harbor as well as Hickam Field and Wheeler Field.

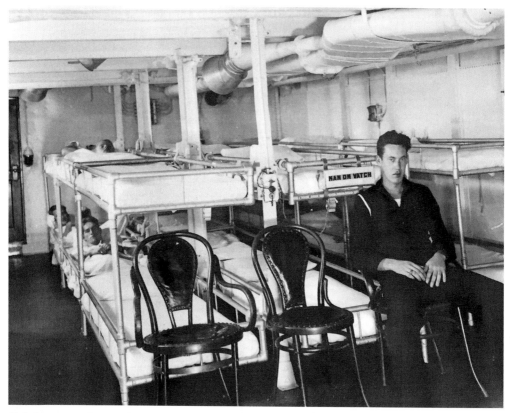

Sick bay treated everything from cut fingers to serious combat wounds. *Nevada State Museum*

Commanders on Oahu had few excuses for ignoring the danger of carrier strikes. *Nevada* had reported the presence of enemy aircraft the day before the attack, planes that could only have come from Blue carriers. Nor was King's action a spur-of-the-moment gambit. He fully intended to demonstrate the consequences of leaving Oahu relatively undefended. A Naval War College game in 1932—the significance of which was downplayed at the time—inspired his attack plan, and Fleet Problem XIII of the same year showed it was possible. Aircraft carriers were now big enough—and the aircraft that they carried capable enough—to inflict serious damage on land installations and, without much extrapolation, anchored ships.[11] Still, King's warning went unheeded; his attack was discounted as a lucky hit aided by a weather front that allowed Blue carriers to get within striking range without being detected.

Nevada spent several weeks in Hawaiian waters participating in battle maneuvers before departing for home on April 21. Failure of a condenser forced the starboard engine to be shut down partway through the cruise, a throwback to the 1920s when *Nevada*'s engineering crew scrambled to keep outdated equipment working so the ship could keep her place in the battle line.

Recovering spotter aircraft using the aft crane. The ship stopped to recover aircraft unless prevented by the tactical situation. *Nevada State Museum*

On a brighter note, *Nevada's* short-range battle practice of September 1938 was a huge success. The triple turrets scored a remarkable thirty-five hits out of thirty-six shots, with turret 4 earning the highest score ever recorded by a turret of its type. The twin turrets were almost as good with twenty-five hits out of twenty-seven shots. *Nevada* earned ten Navy "E"s and ranked second among the ten battleships that participated in the competition. In a glowing letter to the commanding officer, Commander Battleships congratulated all officers and men on their "splendid success in this important basic training for battle."[12]

With fourteen months of hard running behind her, *Nevada* desperately needed the ministrations of the Puget Sound Navy Yard. After spending the holidays at home in San Pedro she steamed north, arriving at the yard on January 22, 1939. Once again the commandant of the yard raised concerns about watertight integrity, particularly of compartments on the second and third decks. Remarkably, some compartments didn't even have watertight hatches. But the several hundred thousand dollars that would be required to fix the problem was well beyond the allocation provided by Congress, so the yard and the ship's crew did the best they could with the resources available.

Doing their best was no longer good enough, though. Despite the sustained efforts of a dedicated crew and routine overhauls, *Nevada* seemed to be reaching the end of her life. The Board of Inspection and Survey's report following a visit in October 1938 concluded:

> While no serious defects are noted, the Board was impressed with the fact that the NEVADA was in many respects obsolescent. The correction of these obsolete features to bring the vessel to a uniform standard in all departments, and to that of a first class battleship, would amount in effect to a further modernization. The Board seriously questions the advisability of piece-meal accomplishment of certain portions of the desired improvements and recommends that this policy be discontinued and that consideration be given the classifying of the NEVADA as other than a first line battleship. The above features are wholly due to age, service and design and do not imply any neglect in upkeep or operation.[13]

The good news was that *Nevada's* turbines were in very good condition. She could still reach very near her original design speed, something that her sister ship *Oklahoma* was no longer able to do with her old-fashioned reciprocating engines.

Representatives from the Bureau of Ordnance were unhappy about the maintenance of *Nevada's* main guns. It seems that the gunnery officer had taken it upon himself to allow the interior of the barrels to rust slightly rather than cleaning and oiling them after each practice. He had observed that the guns performed differently in their first salvo than in subsequent ones and attributed the difference to clean versus slightly dirty barrels. By allowing a thin layer of rust to form on the inside of the barrels he could get shells on target one salvo faster. Disregarding his logic, the bureau chief insisted, "On board ships in commission bores of guns are to be kept clean and oiled."[14]

After her overhaul and mandatory postrepair trials, *Nevada* returned to San Pedro and then, in June, to San Francisco and Seattle to pick up contingents of Navy ROTC students for a voyage to Hawaii. Routine drills conducted en route familiarized the students with the workings of a warship at sea, and while off the coast of Maui they participated in short-range battle practice. At the end of the summer the students were dropped off at their home ports and *Nevada* returned to San Pedro and the fleet.

Sailors are remarkably creative at generating excuses for coming back late from liberty or not being in the correct uniform. When Seaman 1st Class W. G. Effle walked up the gangway on September 5, 1939, dressed in civilian clothes and without a liberty card, the officer of the deck was ready for a story. Effle was, however, armed with a letter from the Venice, California, Police Department. While Effle was strolling on the Venice Pier he saw a young woman jump into the sea, an apparent suicide. Effle dove in and rescued her, losing his liberty card in the process. The police sent him back to the ship in dry clothes and with a letter explaining that he was a hero.

The seven Patten brothers, the Navy's largest serving family. Dad joined the Navy to make a complete set. *National Archives Photo Collection, RG 80, no. 28888*

Another arrival in September attracted national attention. For years, Floyd Patten, a sawmill operator in Iowa, had watched one after another of his seven sons leave home to join the Navy. By 1939 all seven of them were serving in *Nevada*'s engine room. Lonely at home, and perhaps a bit envious of his sons' adventures at sea, Patten senior enlisted with a request that he too be assigned to *Nevada*, thus creating the largest family in the fleet.[15] It was great publicity for the Navy.

The fleet was indeed a family, and its ships became homes to those who chose the service as a career. It was not unusual for a chief petty officer to remain on a ship for ten years or more, perhaps rising from seaman to chief on the same vessel. Ens. Joseph Taussig thought that some of the crusty old chiefs on *Nevada* must have come on board before he was born. Officers were obeyed and rendered due respect in public—but in private an older chief might address a young ensign as "sonny" and offer some paternal advice.[16] Smart junior officers quickly learned to think of the chiefs as resources who could make or break their first assignments.

All the ship's company treated the higher-ranking officers with deference, but the captain—the ultimate authority on the ship—was held in special reverence. "Do not refer to the captain by name," said the *Recruit's Handbook* for *West Virginia*: "He is The Captain."

New arrivals on the ship—officers and men—soon learned that getting things done often required an understanding of what at times approached a barter economy. A request might be met with, "I could help you with that if only . . . ," at which point a favor would be mentioned. Painting a compartment in sick bay might be traded for a "medicinal" allowance of alcohol, or a special request in the laundry

The *Nevada* Blue Devils band. Listening to music was a popular pastime at sea. *Nevada State Museum*

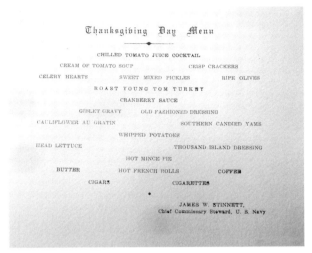

Thanksgiving Day menu, 1939. The Navy put on quite a spread. *Nevada State Museum*

might be better received if an extra dessert was offered.

Storekeepers were notorious for keeping watch over their domain. "It was difficult to ascertain whether the Government or the storekeepers paid for the gear they issued, so frugal were they in relinquishing the materials in their storeroom," one member of the ship's company recalled.[17] As a result, storekeepers developed an amazing number of "close friends." When the chips were down, every man did his duty, but in peacetime and between battles, individuals were remarkably creative at making life just a bit more comfortable.

At about the time that Seaman Effle was explaining his heroic dive into the Pacific to the officer of the deck on *Nevada*, German tanks were rolling into Poland. World War II had started. France fell in June 1940—a shock to those who had thought the French army more than a match for the Wehrmacht—and the Luftwaffe began a relentless bombing campaign against British cities.

Three days after the fall of Paris, CNO Harold Stark requested $4 billion to construct a "two ocean Navy," one that could simultaneously counter both Germany and Japan. He got the money. In September Congress passed the Burke-Wadsworth Act authorizing the first peacetime draft in American history. It was clear that the United States was headed for war—the only question was when and against whom. Winston Churchill was lobbying President Franklin Roosevelt to increase support for the war in Europe, but Japan threatened American territories in the Philippines and even Hawaii. In September 1940 the threats in the two oceans were formally linked when Japan signed the Tripartite Pact with Germany and Italy. That same month the Imperial Japanese Army marched into French Indochina.

While war was spreading across the globe, Fleet Problem XXI, held April 1–May 17, 1940, focused on the seemingly mundane issues of task force organization and convoy protection. The scenario was that Japan had attacked Hawaii and had captured outlying U.S. territories. The U.S. Fleet's task was to pursue and destroy

The ship's carpentry shops could make just about anything needed during a cruise. *Nevada State Museum*

a possibly superior enemy, especially challenging in the early phase of a war when the fleet was still deploying from the West Coast. Significantly, this was the first fleet problem that did not involve nearly every unit of the fleet. Many U.S. warships, including some battleships, were engaged in the real-world duty of escorting convoys in the Atlantic.

During the postmortem critique held before 550 officers at Pearl Harbor, Adm. James O. Richardson (a former navigator on *Nevada*) emphasized the Japanese navy's expertise at night fighting, something the U.S. Fleet had been struggling to perfect for decades. The new technology of radar would solve this problem, but only after enough units had been produced and men had been trained to make radar a routine part of tactical operations. In the meantime, the United States needed to avoid night actions whenever possible.

This was to be the last fleet problem before the onset of war, the culmination of a process that exceeded the highest expectations of its creators. In a 1965 speech Adm. Chester Nimitz would observe, "The enemy of our games was always—Japan—and the course was so thorough that after the start of World War II—nothing that happened in the Pacific was strange or unexpected."[18] Except for the atomic bomb and kamikazes, they had seen it all already.

Battleships normally returned to San Pedro after a fleet problem, but the growing tensions in the Pacific prompted President Roosevelt to keep them at Pearl Harbor. Admiral Richardson opposed the idea, arguing that Hawaii was vulnerable to attack and did not have adequate repair facilities. As the commander in chief of the Pacific Fleet he was the Navy's expert on the region and was not shy about conveying his opinions. But he went too far when he said to Roosevelt, "Mr. President, I feel that I must tell you that the senior officers of the Navy do not have the trust and confidence in the civilian leadership of this country that is essential for the prosecution of a war in the Pacific."[19] He was reassigned three months later.

CNO Stark agreed with the president. The fleet was in Hawaii, he said, "because of the deterrent effect on the Japs going into the East Indies." But Admiral Yamamoto Isoroku, who would order the Japanese attack on Pearl Harbor, saw the U.S. Fleet as a "dagger pointed at Japan's heart."[20] It was not the last time that the United States and Japan would interpret the same actions in diametrically opposite ways.

Richardson's concern about basing the fleet at Pearl Harbor was reinforced by a stunning British naval victory over the Italians. On November 11–12, 1940, the carrier HMS *Illustrious* launched a torpedo plane attack on an Italian fleet at Taranto. Despite intense antiaircraft fire, the British planes put three Italian battleships out of action. This was all the more surprising given the accepted wisdom that aerial torpedoes required a minimum water depth of one hundred feet to operate. Taranto's harbor was only seventy feet deep. Japanese planners had already begun

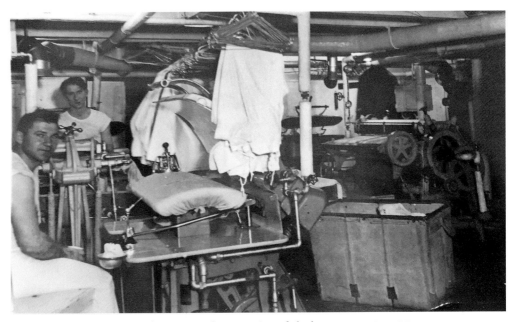

The ship's laundry routinely processed mountains of clothes. *Nevada State Museum*

Family Christmas party on the quarterdeck. Crewmembers were proud to show off their ship to friends and family. *Nevada State Museum*

to investigate—as early at 1939—how torpedoes might be employed in shallow water such as the forty-foot-deep Pearl Harbor.[21] (The solution was as simple as fitting them with wooden fins and dropping them at minimum altitude.) Taranto gave them renewed enthusiasm to apply the technique.

The vulnerability of Pearl Harbor was only part of the Navy's general concern over defending a fleet against attacking aircraft. Ships steaming in large formations could not maneuver to avoid bombs and torpedoes without risking collisions, and ships at anchor were sitting ducks. More and more antiaircraft guns were added to battleships, but Commander Battleships summarized the situation in dire terms: "It is apparent . . . that no satisfactory solution to the problem of defense against air attack has been developed."[22]

On the offensive front, the aviation divisions of battleships were among the busiest on board. Nearly every day two or three planes were catapulted into the air or, when the ship was in port, lowered over the side to take off on their own. They towed target sleeves for the ship's antiaircraft guns and spotted for the big guns during long-range target practice. Planes also performed reconnaissance missions, conducted antisubmarine patrols, and even practiced dive-bombing, although their effectiveness as offensive weapons was limited by their relatively slow speed and the fact that the crew could not see the target during the dive.[23]

Nevada spent the 1940 winter holidays at the Puget Sound Navy Yard for her periodic overhaul. Once again the ship's cooks outdid themselves in making sure that everyone still on board was well cared for. The "bean burners" disdained the dehydrated food they were forced to use at sea and exercised their culinary skills in producing massive amounts of chow. On a typical day with a full crew on board, bakers working twenty-four hours on and twenty-four hours off would produce six hundred loaves of bread. But even the bakers had multiple duties: they served another type of "loaf" with duty in the 5-inch ammunition magazine.[24]

Christmas dinner on board ship at Puget Sound was an especially lavish affair with fruit cocktail, cream of celery soup, roast young tom turkey, giblet gravy, southern dressing, and cranberry sauce. Those who wanted something other than the traditional turkey could have Virginia baked ham with candied yams and vegetables. Fruitcake, Neapolitan ice cream, and candy followed by coffee and cigars rounded out the meal.[25]

Long Beach and San Pedro were nearly deserted when *Nevada* returned from overhaul on March 1—the fleet was still in Hawaii, and only a few small vessels remained on the West Coast. Capt. Francis W. Rockwell conducted antiaircraft practice on targets towed by *Nevada*'s own planes and took on new men at San Pedro before leaving for Pearl Harbor on March 18 in company with the carrier

Lexington and a destroyer screen. No time was wasted during the transit. Every day was filled with practice at repelling destroyer attacks, tracking *Lexington* as a potential target, zigzagging to avoid submarines, and guarding against air attack. The ships arrived in Pearl Harbor on March 25, and *Nevada* was out with the Pacific Fleet the very next day.

Many of the fleet's battle exercises in Hawaiian waters simulated surface engagements with the enemy battle line. If air power failed to decide the day and a surface battle occurred, the Navy needed to be prepared. It was not unusual for ships to be out for ten days at a time, a greatly increased tempo from just a few years earlier. *Nevada*'s planes made frequent trips back to Pearl Harbor during these operations to pick up mail, sometimes in such quantity that two planes were required to carry it. Crew morale was important, and nothing kept up morale better than regular letters from home.

Despite their many tasks and the looming threat of war, Sailors still found opportunities for mischief. The ship's log contains a number of entries citing punishments issued for "gambling for money with cards" and "gambling for money with dice."

Nevada conducted Secondary Battery Gunnery School during June and July 1941, making near-daily sorties from Pearl Harbor to nearby operating areas. After a quick visit to dry dock on August 6, she joined the fleet for maneuvers and then proceeded directly to Long Beach, California, logging twenty-four continuous days at sea. On August 19 the galley practiced feeding the crew at battle stations; in combat there would be no pause for meals.

The voyage to California was a favor to *Oklahoma*, which was suffering serious engine problems. *Nevada* and the destroyers USS *Dewey* and USS *Macdonough* were her escorts across the lonely Pacific. On the way the two sisters practiced aiming guns at one another, reminiscent of similar practices before America entered World War I. *Oklahoma* broke down on August 25 and then twice on August 27; on each occasion *Nevada* dutifully stopped engines to wait for repairs to be made to her sister. By August 28 the two ships were close enough to San Francisco for *Oklahoma* to finish her journey alone. *Nevada* headed south for twelve days at San Pedro before returning to Pearl Harbor.

The constant operations increased the potential for errors and accidents. On October 22 lookouts on *Nevada*, which was in column astern of *Arizona*, saw the newly repaired *Oklahoma* pass about one thousand to two thousand yards ahead, crossing from port to starboard. *Arizona* turned on her vertical searchlight to indicate her position, but it was too late. Men on the deck of *Nevada* heard *Oklahoma* and *Arizona* sound their collision alarms and then the sickening crunch of metal on metal. Captain Rockwell immediately ordered all engines stopped and lifeboats

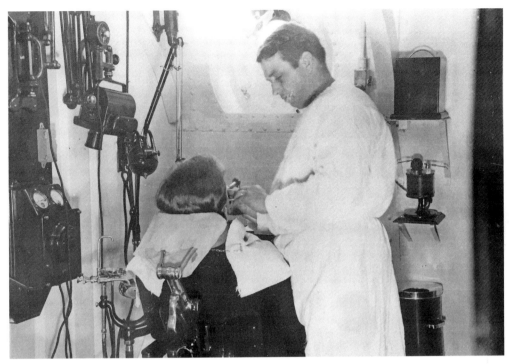

The dentist's office was not a very popular part of the ship. *Nevada State Museum*

lowered, but fortunately the damage to the colliding ships was relatively light. Both were soon under way. Capt. Edward J. Foy of *Oklahoma* was less fortunate—he was confined to port during the inquiry following the collision and later removed from command of his ship.[26]

Every time *Nevada* entered or exited Pearl Harbor she sounded Antiaircraft and Torpedo Defense Quarters and launched planes for inner air patrol. The Navy brass was certain that Japan intended to use forward-deployed submarines to whittle down the superior American fleet, and a surprise attack was always a possibility. Antiaircraft batteries and sky lookouts were manned while the ship was berthed in Pearl Harbor, a practice that would prove critical in December.

Many Navy planners still discounted the possibility of an air attack on Pearl Harbor, thinking that war would start with an attack on the Philippines or Guam. Hawaii was simply too far from Japan to be a feasible target. Just a week before the attack of December 7, when the Japanese Carrier Strike Force was already under way, Pacific Fleet Commander in Chief Adm. Husband Kimmel asked his operations officer about the chance of a surprise attack on Hawaii. The reply was a simple, "None."[27]

He could not have been more wrong. On the morning of November 26, 1941, a strike force of 57 Japanese ships including 2 battleships, 2 heavy cruisers, 11 destroyers, and 6 large aircraft carriers packed with 423 aircraft left the Kurile

Islands. On each ship's bow was the gold chrysanthemum of the Imperial Japanese Navy. Their destination was a point 275 miles north of Pearl Harbor, and their objective was the destruction of the U.S. Pacific Fleet. It was to be the "decisive battle" a generation of Japanese naval officers had dreamed of.

Nevada and *Arizona*, meanwhile, sortied from Pearl Harbor on November 29, with *Oklahoma* joining them the next day. Ostensibly the battleships were to conduct exercises in conjunction with the carrier *Enterprise*, but in fact they were creating a deception to hide the carrier's true mission—a high-speed run to deliver fighter planes to Wake Island.[28] Naval Intelligence knew that the Japanese were keeping close watch on comings and goings at Pearl Harbor, particularly of aircraft carriers. The departure of *Nevada*, *Enterprise*, and other ships was to look like any other training mission until it was too late for the Japanese to interfere.

The three battleships remained at sea as *Enterprise* made her escape, and they would have continued the charade except for a warning about Japanese submarines near Oahu. To be on the safe side, Fleet Command recalled the trio to Pearl Harbor. At 0800 on December 6, secondary and antiaircraft batteries were manned in preparation for entering port, and a short time later tugs nudged *Nevada* into Berth F-8 at Ford Island. Normally, battleships were moored in pairs, but this time *Nevada* had no partner because access to both port and starboard sides was required to exchange ammunition.

The rest of Saturday, December 6, was a quiet day on board ship. The crew mustered on stations with no absentees. At 1135 Seaman 1st Class J. C. Jones, the last man to join the ship before the onset of war, came on board with "bag, baggage, records and accounts and necessary transfer papers." First Lt. E. H. Drake, the last man to leave the ship, was detached and ordered to duty at Marine Corps Base San Diego.

Ens. Charles Merdinger later recalled the days before December 7 as "the last of the old Navy." "Life was well ordered and regular and pleasant. It was a sort of gentlemen's club, I suppose, in some ways—the junior officers' mess."[29]

That evening Lt. Gen. Walter Short, commander of the Army troops in Hawaii, saw the twinkling lights of the fleet when he was returning from dinner and remarked to a companion, "Isn't that a beautiful sight?" Somewhat ironically for the man who was responsible for defending Pearl Harbor, he added, "And what a target they would make."[30]

9

Pearl Harbor

December 7 began as a quiet, almost lazy, Sunday morning. Soft, white clouds decorated the lush greenery of the Ko'olau Mountains, and a gentle breeze ruffled the surface of Pearl Harbor. Only officers, chief petty officers, and petty officers first class were permitted to spend nights ashore, so most of the enlisted men were on board their ships. On *Nevada*, 95 percent of the men were on board, many looking forward to a day off from the hectic exercises that had occupied them for weeks on end.

Officers were free to spend nights and even weekends ashore if their duty responsibilities allowed it. Some stayed at homes they owned or rented; others luxuriated at hotels such as the Royal Hawaiian or the quaint bungalows of the Halekulani.[1] Most of the senior officers, including Capt. Francis W. Scanland and Executive Officer Harry L. Thompson, were ashore, leaving command of the ship to Lt. Cdr. Francis J. Thomas, a Naval Reservist who had joined the ship on June 22. Fortuitously, Thomas was the assistant damage control officer. His skills would prove useful later in the day.

The first sign of trouble came at 0350 when the Coast Guard cutter *Condor* sighted a submarine periscope less than two miles from the entrance to Pearl Harbor. Suspicious that a friendly submarine would be submerged outside the pre-scribed operating areas, *Condor* used a blinker light to alert the patrolling destroyer USS *Ward*. After two hours of searching, *Ward* spotted the sub headed toward the open antisubmarine net at the harbor entrance and moved in to attack it with gun-fire and depth charges. Within minutes her skipper declared the sub sunk.

Not until 0712 did anyone think to notify Fourteenth Naval District, the command center governing Hawaiian waters, of the sighting or the depth charging. As soon as the commandant, Adm. Claude C. Bloch, heard the news, he ordered the ready-duty destroyer USS *Monaghan* to sea and sent instructions to close the antisubmarine net. He also called Cdr. Vincent R. Murphy, Pacific Fleet Commander in Chief Husband Kimmel's duty officer. Murphy in turn spent a frustrating half-hour trying to get through to Admiral Kimmel's home. It seemed that the Navy operator on duty did not speak good enough English to understand what was being asked of him.

As dawn approached, Vice Admiral Nagumo Chuichi, commander of the Japanese Carrier Strike Force, increased the force's speed to twenty-four knots in a dash south toward Oahu. The force had so far escaped detection, and his scout planes indicated that the American fleet, minus its aircraft carriers, was tucked up in Pearl Harbor, apparently unaware of the impending threat.

Nagumo had originally intended to launch the strike before dawn, but worries about inexperienced pilots taking off from carriers in the dark convinced him to delay until the first glow appeared on the eastern horizon. Rough seas compounded his anxiety. The bows of the carriers were rising and falling through an arc of nearly forty feet; waves occasionally broke over the decks. Pilots would have to time their launch to coincide with a rise in the bow or risk plunging into the Pacific, perhaps suffering the ignominious fate of being run over by their own carrier. Despite the dangers, morale was excellent, especially after Nagumo broke out the very same "Z" signal flag that Admiral Togo Heihachiro had used at the epic battle of Tsushima in 1905 when the Imperial Japanese Navy had achieved a crushing victory over a Russian fleet.

Forty-three fighters were the first to make it into the air from the carriers' packed decks, followed by 49 high-level bombers, 51 dive-bombers, and 40 torpedo planes. At 0620 the last plane was aloft and the signal was given for this first wave of 183 aircraft to head toward Oahu. Only 2 of the original 185 planes planned for the first wave failed to launch successfully.

Aviation crews scrambled to bring up the second wave of aircraft, but it was not until 0715 that launches began. Thirty-six fighters, 54 high-level bombers, and 78 dive-bombers rose into the sky with clockwork precision, only 1 of the dive-bombers aborting due to engine trouble. Within 90 minutes the total force of 350 planes was aloft, including 79 fighters, 103 high-level bombers, 128 dive-bombers, and 40 torpedo planes.[2]

At 0702 two Army privates manning an experimental radar station at the north end of Oahu spotted what appeared to be a massive fleet of incoming planes. They called in their observation, but the duty officer at Fort Shafter immediately dismissed it. The Army was expecting a flight of B-17s from the West Coast, he told them, so the blips were nothing to worry about. The enlisted men thought that the *number* of blips was unusually large for a flight of friendly planes, but it was already past their time to shut down, so they closed the site and went to breakfast.

A more convincing indicator of an air attack occurred at 0748 when leading elements of the Japanese force hit the seaplane base at picturesque Kaneohe Bay. Shocked duty officers made frantic calls to Bellows Field and Hickam Field, but no one would believe that the base was actually under attack. The Japanese had a field day strafing and bombing the Navy's long-range reconnaissance planes; by the time they were through not a single operational plane was left.

Five minutes later attack force commander Fuchida Mitsuo radioed Admiral Nagumo, "Tora, tora, tora!" a prearranged signal indicating that the force had achieved complete surprise. Due to the vagaries of radio propagation, Fuchida's signal was also picked up by Admiral Yamamoto's flagship *Nagato* in distant Japan. The Japanese high command was delighted. So far their plan was working.

At 0755, less than ten minutes after the attack on Kaneohe, a Japanese dive-bomber passed within six hundred feet of Rear Adm. William Furlong on the mine-layer USS *Oglala*. A second later a bomb hit the seaplane ramp on Ford Island. Furlong recognized the markings on the aircraft—this was no accidental bombing by a U.S. Army plane—and immediately ordered General Quarters. Consistent with the established policy, he instituted the Emergency Sortie Plan and instructed all ships in the harbor to head to sea.[3] At 0758 Rear Adm. Patrick Bellinger radioed all ships: AIR RAID ON PEARL HARBOR X THIS IS NOT DRILL.

On *Nevada*, most of the crew had just finished breakfast. Some men had wandered back to their bunks, hoping to catch up on some sleep. Four played catch on the aft deck, where chaplains were setting up for morning services. The ship's organist was repairing a sticking key on his portable organ prior to the start of hymns.[4]

Ensign Taussig's watch as officer of the deck and acting air defense officer was due to begin at 0800, and as he came on deck he was fretting about what size flag should be flown at morning colors.[5] These things needed to be done right, especially since *Nevada*'s twenty-three-piece band was assembling to play the national anthem. Taussig told an enlisted man to run forward and ask men on *Arizona*, moored just a few dozen yards forward of *Nevada*, what size flag they were using. But as the seconds ticked down to 0800, a more serious issue threatened to disrupt the ceremony. On the other side of Pearl Harbor planes were maneuvering at low altitude and there were rumbles of muffled explosions. Was it an unscheduled practice by the Army? Odd for a Sunday morning, but just the kind of thing the top brass might dream up to keep people on their toes. In any event, there was morning colors to execute, and the conductor's baton came down at precisely 0800.

Just as the band launched into the national anthem and the flag was raised, Taussig noticed a plane approaching the anchored battleships. To his astonishment, it dropped a torpedo. But only when he saw the red circles on the plane's wings, and certainly after the blast of the torpedo hitting the side of a battleship moored ahead of *Nevada*, did he realize that the fleet was under attack.

Events then took on a breathtaking pace. After completing a torpedo run on *Arizona*, a Japanese plane banked over *Nevada*'s quarterdeck, its rear gunner firing down on the assembled musicians and Marine guard. No one was hit, but the just-raised flag was shredded. The band continued to play the Star Spangled Banner. Bandmaster Oden McMillian picked up the pace, but no one seemed to know the correct procedure when the national anthem was interrupted by the start of a war. After the last note sounded, the musicians carefully packed up their instruments before running to their duty stations.

Ensign Taussig pulled the alarm bell and shouted into the public-address system, "All hands, General Quarters. Air raid! This is no drill!"[6] The ship's bugler tried to interpose himself between Taussig and the microphone, but the ensign thought this a waste of time under the circumstances; he grabbed the bugle and threw it overboard.[7] He then sprinted up six ladders to his duty station in the starboard antiaircraft director. The first thing he saw when he looked in the gun director was a Japanese plane squarely in the sights. Moments later he was hit in the left leg by a projectile, which proceeded onward through the ballistic computer. Though seriously wounded, Taussig refused to leave his station and continued to direct fire while lying on the deck.[8]

Nevada was ready for war. There were more than enough men on board to man all of the antiaircraft guns, including six of the nine officers in charge of the gun crews. Captain Scanland had previously decided that General Quarters would be sounded during an air attack rather than Air Defense. This would set condition Zed—close all watertight doors—ensuring maximum watertight integrity. Within seconds of Ensign Taussig's alarm the hull resounded with the clang of hatches slamming shut.

Just before the attack started, the 5-inch antiaircraft gunners had begun their daily fire control check. All firing circuits were cut in, compressed air was supplied to the rammers, and the gyros were spun up to speed—the guns were ready to fire. Twenty-five rounds of ammunition were close by in a ready box. The antiaircraft machine guns were similarly supplied. The .50-caliber guns had 7,000 (forward) and 8,000 (aft) rounds at their positions; the two .30-caliber machine guns located aloft on the searchlight platforms had 850 rounds each.[9]

The captain's orderly usually kept the keys for ammunition boxes, but on this Sunday morning the ready box temperatures were being taken, so all of them were unlocked except those for the .50-caliber machine guns. Rather than wait for keys to be sent up for those, crewmembers simply knocked the locks off with a sledgehammer.

Twenty-five rounds of 5-inch ammunition would last just over a minute at the well-rehearsed firing rate of twenty rounds per minute. Without a steady stream of fresh ammunition from the magazines below it would be a short battle.[10] *Nevada*'s crew met the challenge and kept the ammunition coming throughout the fight.

———

The Japanese attack occurred in two waves. The first, lasting from 0755 to 0825, consisted of torpedo planes and dive-bombers. An unintentional fifteen-minute lull in the attack provided much-needed time for American gun crews to replenish ammunition and get ready for follow-on attacks. It was time well spent: the second wave brought twenty-five minutes of high-altitude bombing and a further thirty minutes of dive-bombing. By 0940 the air attack was essentially over, and Fuchida was rounding up stray planes to return to the carriers.

The attackers found that "surprise" was a relative term at Pearl Harbor. Within five minutes of the start of the attack they came under withering antiaircraft fire. Losses were relatively light among the planes in the first wave, but the second wave had a tougher time. Fuchida deemed the American fleet "well prepared for battle" and thought that Japanese ships would not have done as well in a similar situation.[11]

Weeks before, gun crews had been authorized to shoot when under attack, without waiting for permission from officers or any other authority.[12] *Nevada*'s gun crews saw no reason to question the order once bombs began to fall. Two .30-caliber guns, continuously manned while in port, opened up on the first plane that came within range. It was 0802. Seconds later machine gunners poured shells into the fuselage and wings of another plane that promptly turned and crashed within one hundred yards of the port quarter. It was an important kill because the second plane had not yet dropped its torpedo. A minute later the .50-caliber and 5-inch guns went into action.

At 0803, even before officers could reach the bridge, Chief Quartermaster Robert Sedberry instructed the engine room to make all preparations to get under way. The sooner *Nevada* was able to maneuver, the better able she would be to avoid bombs and torpedoes.

Nevada's gunners fired at any plane that came within range, but they were not always successful. Minutes into the attack one Japanese "Kate" managed to drop its torpedo just a few hundred yards off the port bow. Men on deck watched the torpedo streak toward the hull and felt the ship shudder under its impact. Later inspection would reveal that the blast had ripped a sixteen-by-twenty-seven-foot hole in the bow.[13] *Nevada* began to list to port.

The 5-inch gun crews prevented a second torpedo from being launched when they scored a direct hit on an oncoming plane. Observers reported that the aircraft simply disintegrated, possibly because the 5-inch shell detonated the torpedo's warhead.

To complicate matters, a crane maneuvering a garbage hopper over the port side had broken down, partially obscuring the fire of one of the 5-inch antiaircraft guns. This was maddening to the crew, who could see high-altitude bombers approaching on both bows. All of the remaining guns shifted to the new targets, including the .50-caliber machine guns, which had little chance of inflicting damage at such heights. But the crew attributed the hail of fire from the ship's guns as a factor in confounding the aim of Japanese bombers, because while several bombs fell close by, none hit the ship.

To help correct the increasing list to port, Damage Control counterflooded four compartments on the starboard side. Even though *Nevada* was "buttoned up" below the waterline (standard practice while in port), Lieutenant Commander Thomas did not want to take the chance of capsizing an unbalanced ship.

While *Nevada* was fighting for her life, *Arizona* was losing hers. The Japanese knew that U.S. battleships had thick deck armor—in some cases several layers of steel protected vital spaces belowdecks—and they countered by putting fins on armor-piercing shells to drop from planes. At 0808 one such bomb dropped from high altitude hit next to *Arizona*'s number 2 turret and penetrated to the magazine. The resulting explosion blew the battleship in half and killed more than a thousand men,

Arizona has just exploded and *Nevada* is struggling to raise steam for departure. *Naval History and Heritage Command, NH 50932*

including Capt. Franklin Van Valkenburgh and Rear Adm. Isaac Kidd. Dozens of men on *Nevada*'s bow were blown overboard by the blast. USS *Vestal*, a repair ship moored outboard of *Arizona*, caught fire and immediately began to maneuver clear of her doomed berth-mate.

Nevada suffered only minor structural damage from the explosion, but another danger soon became apparent: burning oil was gushing from *Arizona*'s ruptured fuel tanks. Not even a heavily armored battleship would long survive in a sea of burning oil. *Nevada* needed to put distance between herself and *Arizona*, and the sooner the better. Fires were lit under boilers 1, 3, 4, and 5. Boiler 2 was already in service to power auxiliary systems, and boiler 6 was in pieces, undergoing overhaul. The engine room crew used every trick they knew to raise enough steam to move the ship, knowing that her survival was in their hands.

While the logbook indicates that only one boiler was generating steam at the time of the attack, it appears that Ensign Taussig had ordered a second boiler lit during his watch the night before. He was concerned that one boiler had been operating continuously for several days, and he wanted to annoy the engineering officer by ordering the extra work of starting up another one. Ensign Taussig's action, combined with the extraordinary work of the engine room crew, helped to save *Nevada*.

The smoke from fires on *Arizona* and other damaged ships had one advantage—it shielded *Nevada* from a round of high-altitude bombing. Commander Fuchida had previously chosen *Nevada* as his prime target, but when clouds and smoke obscured the ship he switched to *Maryland*. (*Nevada*'s logbook states that bombs struck her before she got under way, but photos taken as she was passing the battle line show no bomb damage. The official damage report states that bombs did not hit the ship until she was near the end of the line of moored battleships.)

The wisdom of counterflooding starboard compartments to stop the list to port got a sad endorsement when *Oklahoma*, which had taken multiple torpedo hits, slowly rolled over on her port side and capsized. She didn't have a chance; most of her watertight doors, including those in her antitorpedo blister, were open in preparation for an inspection the following day. When the tops of the blisters dipped below the surface, water poured in. *Oklahoma*'s gun crews couldn't even shoot back because vital parts of their guns were in the armory for cleaning.[14]

The men on the surrounding ships were stunned at the sight, unable to conceive that a battleship could capsize, obscenely exposing her bottom to sunlight. It was especially shocking to old-timers on *Nevada*, who had sailed with *Oklahoma* on many occasions and had heard stories of joint operations in the last war.

The surprise was universal. After Commander Murphy finally got through to Admiral Kimmel at his home, the commander in chief ran out to his yard to witness

Japanese planes bombing his beloved battleships. Neighbors gathered around him, equally incredulous that this could be happening. Mrs. John Earle, wife of Admiral Bloch's chief of staff, murmured "Looks like they've got the *Oklahoma*."[15] Later, while Kimmel was watching the continuing attack from his office window, a spent machine gun bullet broke the glass and hit him in the chest. "It would have been more merciful if it had killed me," he subsequently said.[16]

———

There was no time on *Nevada* to follow the usual procedure of singling up lines prior to departure. Chief Boatswain Edwin Hill led a detail of ten men down the gangway and dove into the water. Swimming for all they were worth, they reached the quay and disconnected the numerous cables and lines securing the ship in place. At 0820 Hill and his men—not about to be left behind as their ship sailed into danger—swam back to the ship.

Normally it would take four tugs to maneuver a battleship out of her berth, but there was no possibility of that now. Hill's team, now back on board, cast off the remaining lines, and Lieutenant Commander Thomas ordered Sedberry to move the ship away from the quay. At 0840 the port engine was backed one-third, and then both engines were backed full. The boilers were only just coming up to pressure, and the heavy load absorbed almost all the steam they were producing. Engineering reduced the flow to all nonessential auxiliary systems, and the engine room crew held in the automatic low-pressure trips on the dynamos. Steam pressure held steady at about 150 pounds per square inch, and the rapidly heating boilers took over the heavy load.

Slowly the 30,000 tons of *Nevada* backed out of her berth, just nudging a dredging pipe astern. Lacking rudder control at low speed, Thomas ordered the starboard engine ahead and the port engine astern, turning the ship so that she would clear the burning *Arizona*. Then he rang up full ahead and *Nevada* started down the channel. Sedberry, following the instructions of acting navigator Lt. Lawrence Ruff, did a masterful job at the wheel, threading the ship between the shore and another dredging pipe, all the while keeping a wary eye out for Japanese planes.

Fearing that there might be mines south of *Nevada*'s berth, shore authorities ordered Thomas to take the ship around the north end of Ford Island. But by the time he received the message the ship was already committed to the direct route to the sea. There was no room to turn around, and Sedberry steered south.

Nevada passed so close to *Arizona* that one officer thought he could light a cigarette from the fires. Antiaircraft gun crews were afraid that the heat might ignite the shells stored near the guns, so they shielded the ready boxes with their bodies or played fire hoses on them to keep them cool. Meanwhile, the guns continued to hammer away at the swarming Japanese planes.

Under way at Pearl Harbor! *Nevada* steams south under intense air attack. *National Archives Photo Collection, RG 80, no. 013638*

Amid the shock and carnage of that morning, with *Oklahoma* capsized and *Arizona*'s superstructure a twisted mass of burning metal, *Nevada*'s colors streamed proudly from her stern as she passed along the battle line. (There had been no time to transfer the flag from the stern to the mast, as is required when a ship gets under way.) Men on other ships took cheer from the Cheer Up Ship, and hundreds would remember the scene as the most inspiring moment of the battle. "I had never seen anything so gallant," Ted Mason of *California* later wrote. "I choked with emotion as she came bravely on."[17] Mason and other observers were sure that *Nevada* had been hit by bombs as well as a torpedo, but the damage they saw was actually the result of *Arizona*'s explosion and other near misses.

There was little that *Nevada*'s crew could do for the men on the other battleships, but they could help those desperately struggling in the water. As the ship slowly moved down the harbor, men on deck threw lines to those they could reach. Once on the ship, many of those men immediately jumped to help man antiaircraft guns, getting back into the fight.

Fuchida's switch from *Nevada* to *Maryland* brought only a brief reprieve—his original target was now clear of smoke, and a moving battleship was too tempting a prize to pass up. He figured that if he could sink *Nevada* in the entrance to Pearl Harbor he could bottle up the ships inside and prevent new arrivals from using the base. Planes en route to attack *Pennsylvania* in dry dock diverted to *Nevada*, and she quickly became target number one for the entire bombing force.

Nevada was already a familiar target for the Japanese bombardiers. During their practice for the attack they had dropped dummy bombs on an outline of the ship painted on the ground.[18] Now so many bombs fell near *Nevada* during her dash to the sea that the splashes occasionally obscured her from view.

At this, the worst possible time, *Nevada*'s starboard antiaircraft shell conveyor system broke down, stopping the supply of shells to the 5-inch guns. Undeterred, the crew immediately set up a human supply chain, passing shells by hand so that the guns could keep up rapid fire. It was not enough—there were simply too many planes and too few guns to shoot at them.

Five bombs hit the ship in quick succession starting at 0900.[19] Three hit on the forecastle, penetrated the deck, and exploded below. One of these exited the hull on the starboard side before detonating; the explosion pressed the hull plates inward and started major flooding. Another passed through a gasoline tank and out the bottom of the ship before exploding.[20] While it did not ignite the gasoline, the breach in the gas tank released vapors that would cause problems later in the day. The third bomb penetrated to the second deck, bounced back up, and blew a large hole in the deck.

Two bombs hit the superstructure. One penetrated the port director platform in the foremast and exploded on the upper deck at the base of the stack. The other exploded above the crew's galley.

Fires immediately broke out forward and amidships. A blaze in the forecastle incinerated most of officers' country and the wardroom. Amidships, a particularly intense fire in a 5-inch gun position next to the galley was fed by powder stored near the gun. The captain's quarters were completely gutted—the damage report suggested that the large quantity of paper in the captain's office might have contributed to the severity of this fire.

While all of this was happening on deck, the "black gangs" were working frantically in the engine rooms. The bomb strike near the stack sent a pressure wave down the boiler uptakes, extinguishing the fires in all the boilers. Ventilators and air intakes sucked smoke into the engineering compartments, forcing the men to abandon them. But clean air was available from a second ventilation trunk aft, and the boiler room crews were soon able to reenter their workspaces and relight the boilers.

Smoke from the fires also entered the dynamo room that supplied critical electrical power to the ship. Warrant Officer Machinist Donald Ross ordered his men out of the area, but he stayed and continued working to keep the power on until the fumes overcame him. Rescued and resuscitated, Ross insisted on returning to his station to secure it and switch the load to the aft dynamo room. Having done that, he raced back through the ship and manned the aft dynamo, finally collapsing from heat exhaustion. For his heroism, which was a key factor in saving *Nevada*, he was awarded the Medal of Honor.

Shortly after 0900 it became apparent that *Nevada* was not going to make it out of the harbor. Commander Battleship Force ordered her not to try, and Thomas stopped the engines with the intention of anchoring near Hospital Point. Chief Boatswain Hill, the same man who had swum out to release the lines holding *Nevada* to the quay, went forward to prepare to drop anchor. As he was working, a bomb hit the forecastle, destroying the capstan that lowered the anchor and blowing Hill and an undetermined number of other men overboard. Hill was posthumously awarded the Medal of Honor for "distinguished conduct in the line of his profession, extraordinary courage, and disregard of his own safety during the attack on the Fleet in Pearl Harbor."

Machinist Donald Ross refused to leave his post in the forward dynamo room and kept vital electrical power flowing. Rescued and revived, he raced to the aft dynamo room to continue his work. He was awarded the Medal of Honor, and his ashes rest with *Nevada* today. *Naval History and Heritage Command, NH 97461*

Without functioning anchors, Lieutenant Thomas had few options to secure his ship. The bow was dangerously down and sinking lower by the moment. As damage control officer, he knew that watertight integrity was a problem; it was only a matter of time before the ship settled on the bottom. Where should he put her so that she could be repaired and refloated?

Thomas chose to intentionally ground the ship on the eastern side of the channel between the floating dry dock and channel buoy 24, starboard side to the beach and on an even keel. At least, that was where he *thought* he was. Smoke from burning ships and shore facilities was so thick that his exact location was impossible to pinpoint.

Just after the ship grounded, Captain Scanland arrived by boat, and five minutes later two harbor tugs arrived to help fight the fires. With the attack apparently abating, all personnel not manning the antiaircraft guns were ordered to man hoses forward and amidships. Casualties were assembled and transferred to the hospital ship USS *Solace* and Naval Hospital Pearl Harbor.

At about 0925, with little or no progress being made on the fires, Scanland ordered the forward magazine flooded. (The aft magazine had already been flooded by mistake as *Nevada* passed *Arizona* on her way down the channel.) The bulkheads of the magazines were hot to the touch, and even though the internal sprinkler system was augmented with fire hoses to keep the ammunition cool, Scanland wanted no repeat of *Arizona*'s explosion.

The probability of a magazine explosion was relatively low. At the time of the attack *Nevada* was midway through exchanging her main battery ammunition for a new supply of heavier shells that had greater penetrating power. All of the old shells had been removed the previous day, along with their powder charges. The ammunition handlers were exhausted at the end of this procedure, so it was decided to delay loading the new powder until Sunday. The ammunition barge carrying the powder was on its way out to *Nevada* when the Japanese planes appeared overhead.[21]

The harbor currents dislodged *Nevada* from her sandy berth, and without anchors to hold her she began to drift into the main channel. Tugs moved to the stern in hopes of pushing her back toward shore, but the current against the massive hull was simply too strong for them to counter.

Scanland tried a different strategy. With the assistance of the two tugs, he maneuvered *Nevada* stern first to the western side of the channel, off Waipio Point. Ordering full reverse at the last minute, he grounded the starboard quarter on a

Aground. A tug helps crewmen fight stubborn fires. *National Archives Photo Collection, RG 80, no. 019940*

coral shelf at 1045, bow pointed south. The ship was listing 4 degrees to starboard and continued to settle by the bow, but at least she was in shallow enough water that the main deck would remain above or near the surface, greatly simplifying later refloating.

———

With the ship stable and the attack apparently over, Scanland and Thomas took stock. *Nevada* had sustained one torpedo hit on the port bow and at least three 250-kilogram bomb hits on the forecastle forward of turret 1. One more 250-kilogram bomb hit forward of the stack in the bridge structure, and a 60-kilogram fragmentation bomb with an impact fuse had hit the boat deck above the crew galley. *Nevada* had escaped the heavy armor-piercing bombs that killed *Arizona*, but she was still a shambles.

The torpedo had struck on the port side between turrets 1 and 2, about midway between the keel and waterline. The torpedo bulkhead was pushed two feet inward over an area of about four hundred square feet. It was holding, but enough seams and joints had been opened to slowly flood the surrounding compartments. Two of the bombs that hit the forecastle opened other holes in the hull, adding to the flooding started by the torpedo hit.

The bombs amidships started major fires that destroyed much of the superstructure. The stack was peppered with bomb fragments, and two of the broadside gun casemates were burned out, along with the crew's galley and the captain's quarters. As Captain Scanland poked through the wreckage of his stateroom he found a ceremonial sword behind a charred bureau. "My Mother and Dad gave me this sword when I graduated from the Naval Academy many years ago," he said quietly. Chief Jack Haley had tears in his eyes—*Nevada* had been his first and only ship, his home for more than twelve years, and it pained him to see her sitting helpless on the bottom of the harbor.[22]

Most tragic was the loss of life. An accurate count would have to wait until the fires were out and all compartments could be searched, but the preliminary tally was twenty-nine men killed, one hundred wounded, and seventeen missing. Divers were put over the side every thirty feet along the length of the ship to see if any men were trapped in air bubbles belowdecks. The divers hit the hull with five-pound hammers and listened for a response. None came. *Nevada* had flooded slowly enough that everyone belowdecks was able to escape.[23]

In return for the damage she received, *Nevada*'s gun crews claimed to have shot down as many as eight planes—one at the very start of the battle, four more before the ship got under way (including the direct hit on a torpedo plane by a 5-inch shell), and three dive-bombers that attacked while the ship was grounded

The fires are finally out, and recovery work can begin. *National Archives Photo Collection, RG 80, no. 32539*

off Hospital Point. In the heat of combat, with multiple ships firing on the same aircraft, it was difficult to determine whose shells brought down which planes, but it seems probable that *Nevada*'s gunners shot down at least two torpedo planes and three bombers.

Gunnery officers were not able to say how many rounds *Nevada* fired at the attacking planes, because some of the shells exploded when fires broke out around the ready boxes; a simple subtraction of before and after wasn't accurate. A rough estimate suggested that 650 5-inch antiaircraft rounds and 13,000 .50-caliber machine gun rounds were fired during the course of the day.

The damage to the ship might have been much worse but for the heroism of the crew. In his action report describing the battle, Captain Scanland wrote, "The Commanding Officer finds it extremely difficult to single out individual members of the crew as deserving of special praise. Every officer and man aboard, without exception, performed his duties in a most commendable manner and without regard to personal safety."[24]

Nevertheless, some men deserved special note. Ens. T. H. Taylor, the port anti-aircraft battery officer, was wounded by shell fragments and deafened by explosions, but he continued to direct the fire of his guns. He ordered fire hoses to spray cooling water on nearby ammunition boxes, keeping them from detonating and causing further damage to the ship. Boatswain's Mate 1st Class Adolfo Solar opened fire on Japanese planes on his own initiative, without waiting for orders, and kept up a continuous hail of bullets until he was killed by a shell splinter. Every man on *Nevada* had a role to play on that fateful day, from those in the boiler rooms who raised steam in a record forty minutes to the bridge crew who steered the ship through a channel filled with burning oil. All across Pearl Harbor there was a dedication to country, ships, and shipmates that would, in the coming years, win the war for the United States.

Nevada continued to settle through the afternoon, the starboard list increasing to 8 degrees. By 1300 the forward dynamos had to be secured due to flooding, and by 1400 water was over the floor plates of the number 1 boiler room. One by one the boiler rooms had to be abandoned, ending with hastily reassembled boiler 6, which was farthest aft and on the high side of the list.

Firefighting and repair parties worked tirelessly through the afternoon; no sooner were fires at one location brought under control than new ones broke out somewhere else. Everything was burning: paper, clothing, paint, and the oil leaking from damaged fuel tanks. At one point in the afternoon a muffled explosion rattled the forecastle, apparently the ignition of gasoline vapors released from the fuel tank pierced by a Japanese bomb. These fires were particularly difficult to extinguish, and flare-ups continued into Monday. So great was the damage produced by fires and gasoline explosions that it was difficult to assess the more limited destruction caused by the bombs themselves.

By midafternoon the men were exhausted—they had been fighting the Japanese and scrambling to keep their ship afloat for five hours straight. They needed food,

The forward deck was pushed up when a bomb exploded below. *National Archives Photo Collection, RG 80, no. 013635*

Rear Adm. William R. Furlong inspects the damage. There was considerable skepticism that *Nevada* would ever sail again. *National Archives Photo Collection, RG 80, no. 323800*

water, and a few minutes' rest to recuperate from the shock of the attack. The galley was wrecked, so food was brought on board from the cruiser USS *Helena*.

Just before 1600 the colors were dropped to half-mast and the dead were removed from the ship. There was no time for grief. Fires were still burning, the ship continued to sink, and rumors of more Japanese attacks abounded. Marines were sent ashore to guard the land approach to *Nevada* in response to fears of sabotage or invasion. Trigger-happy crewmembers fired on the Marines and just about anything or anyone else that moved. *Nevada*'s antiaircraft guns opened fire on three unidentified planes, hitting none of them. Elsewhere in Pearl Harbor, ships and shore guns shot down friendly planes trying to land on Ford Island. Nerves were taut, and the unwritten order of the day was to shoot first and ask questions later.

When the sun came up on Monday, *Nevada* was drawing forty-four feet of water forward and twenty feet aft, compared with thirty-one feet in normal circumstances. The tugs *Turkey* and *Rail* assisted in pumping, a hopeless task given the numerous leaks throughout the ship, but they at least slowed the rate of sinking so that compartments could be inspected before they filled with water. New fires that broke out on the signal bridge and the forecastle were promptly extinguished. When the generators failed completely at 1300, *Turkey* took over the electrical load. Boats arrived with ammunition for the antiaircraft guns and food for the crew. The ship's force carried out diving operations to assess the damage underwater, the first step toward getting *Nevada* back in the war.

Despite her sorry appearance, the Navy's official report categorized *Nevada*'s damage as "relatively superficial."[25] The ship's vital machinery—boilers and engines—was undamaged, and most of the guns were still operational. Fires had caused considerable damage, more than the original bombs in some cases, but *Nevada* sank, quite simply, because of a lack of watertight integrity.

Pearl Harbor was a disaster, but it could have been much worse. If the Japanese had caught the fleet at sea without adequate air cover, the entire battle line might have been sunk in deep water, an irretrievable loss to the United States in men and ships. As it turned out, six of the eight battleships at Pearl Harbor on December 7 would be salvaged to provide valuable service in the war. Only *Arizona* and *Oklahoma* were total losses. The three cruisers that were hit were back in service by February 1942. All of the other ships —three destroyers, the minelayer *Oglala*, the repair ship *Vestal*, and the seaplane tender *Curtiss*—returned to service in one form or another.

The human losses were more serious. A total of 2,335 servicemen were killed in the attack, triple the number lost in the Spanish-American War and World War I combined. An additional 1,143 men were wounded.[26] Japanese losses were

Bomb damage to the crew's galley made a complete refit necessary. *National Archives Photo Collection, RG 80*

relatively light. Twenty-nine Japanese planes failed to return from the attack, and another 111 were damaged, some severely.[27] Fifty-five Japanese airmen and nine submariners were killed.

Some historians have speculated that critical fuel, ammunition, and repair facilities might have been the target of a third wave of attackers, a case Fuchida Mitsuo bolstered in his memoirs.[28] By the time the first two attack waves returned to their carriers, however, it was too late in the day to recover, rearm, and relaunch them.[29] The aircrews were exhausted after many hours in the air, and the ships in the attacking force were low on fuel. In addition, there was the possibility that planes from the absent American carriers might find the fleet. Imperial Navy planners carefully considered the priority of targets and put shore installations and repair ships well down the list.

Pearl Harbor was a tactical success for the Japanese but a strategic failure. Tactically, the attack damaged the Pacific Fleet and delayed America's response to Japan's aggression in the Far East. But the surprise attack fired the determination of the American people for a fight that would end only with the total defeat of Japan. The Navy's response to Pearl Harbor would be relentless and complete—not a single one of the fifty-seven Japanese ships involved in the Pearl Harbor attack would survive the war.[30] "Never in modern history," wrote naval historian Samuel Eliot Morison, "was a war begun with so smashing a victory by one side, and never in recorded history did the initial victor pay so dearly for his calculated treachery."[31]

10

Back in the Fight

Within hours of the attack on Pearl Harbor, CNO Harold Stark ordered all U.S. naval forces to "execute unrestricted air and submarine warfare against Japan."[1] A formal declaration of war would come the following day after President Roosevelt addressed a joint session of Congress, but Stark didn't need a piece of paper to tell him he was at war.

With two battleships lost and six others damaged, Stark was forced to change the near-term strategy in the Pacific. War Plan Rainbow Five—the most recent version of Plan Orange—would still govern the general conduct of the naval conflict, but its full implementation would have to wait until damaged ships were repaired and new ones became available.

Top priority was given to fixing the ships that could be returned to service in the shortest time. *Pennsylvania*, in dry dock at the time of the attack, had taken little damage, as had *Tennessee* and *Maryland*, both of which were moored inboard of other ships, giving them protection from torpedoes. All three battleships left Pearl Harbor on December 20 bound for Mare Island and Puget Sound for repairs. With *Colorado* just emerging from overhaul and *Idaho*, *New Mexico*, and *Mississippi* on their way to the Pacific from the Atlantic Fleet, the United States would soon have a powerful surface force to defend the West Coast and support carrier operations.

The remaining battleships at Pearl Harbor presented a spectrum of challenges. When Fleet Maintenance Officer Cdr. David H. Clark first stepped on board *Nevada* he thought it unlikely that she could be refloated. And even if that were possible, she would need extensive repairs to make her battle ready. Adm. Chester W. Nimitz, newly appointed commander in chief of the Pacific Fleet, voiced a similar opinion during his own visit. The ship was a sad sight—a mass of wreckage above the waterline with an unknown amount of damage below. Plus, she was more than twenty-five years old—ancient considering the rapid development of naval technology.

Yet *Nevada* might still play a part in the war. Given the location of the torpedo and bomb hits, it was likely that her engineering plant was intact. And she still carried ten 14-inch guns that could be useful in bombardment missions or even surface engagements against weaker opponents. It was worth a try.

In the meantime, *Nevada* had an immediately available asset: her men. Divers, engineers, and a bevy of helping hands were needed to start her recovery, but other skills, from cooks to turret crews, were urgently required elsewhere in the fleet. By Monday afternoon all but about three hundred men had been reassigned. *Nevada's* antiaircraft gun crews remained on board. No one knew where the Japanese fleet was or whether another attack was coming. Every available gun, on every available ship, was trained on the sky.

While engineers pondered how to refloat her, *Nevada* continued to settle into the mud of Pearl Harbor. At 0030 on December 9 her stern slipped off the coral shelf on which Captain Scanland had perched it. The draft aft rapidly increased to thirty-four feet, and the list dropped to about 2 degrees. She had finally hit bottom.

Raising *Nevada* would require knowledge, determination, and a healthy dose of optimism. The Navy assigned Emile Genereaux, a salvage expert recently recruited to the Naval Reserve, to the task. Genereaux immediately set about gathering a team of trusted assistants who would soon come under the spell of the Cheer Up Ship.[2] It made little difference to them when, on December 29, CINCPAC ordered *Nevada* placed in "commission in ordinary," a form of reserve status. She was still a commissioned battleship, and she *would* sail again.

Divers began to survey the damage on the very afternoon of the attack. It was pitch black underwater because of the oil and other materials leaking from the ship, so the divers had only their sense of touch to gather information. Lowered over the side to a prescribed depth, they moved hand over hand along the hull, facing constant danger from jagged pieces of metal, currents produced by water entering the hull, and tangled air hoses. Navy divers made more than five hundred dives on *Nevada* during the initial salvage operations, each one of them a feat of heroism.

In the midst of the challenge to refloat the ship, Navy life went on. On December 17 Fireman 3rd Class M. L. Lehman reported on board after being absent without leave since November 6. With a war on, he wanted to do his duty. Since the brig was underwater, he was made a prisoner at large and given a summary court-martial. The following day his sentence of a bad conduct discharge was remitted provided he maintained a good record for the next six months. Men who knew the ship were scarce, and he was soon back at work with his shipmates.

Talent was scarce in all ranks. On December 15 all hands were gathered aft to witness a change of command: Captain Scanland was ordered to report as commanding officer of the cruiser USS *Astoria*, and Cdr. Harry Thompson, the executive officer, took over as *Nevada's* CO.

Salvage work proceeded seven days a week, with only the nightly blackout halting work topside. Even Christmas Day began with the usual routine. The ship's log for that day notes: "0635 Commenced salvage operations, diving operations, and cleaning up ship."

The obvious challenge to refloating *Nevada* was patching the holes in her hull and pumping out the water. Engineers calculated that 10,400 tons of water would have to be pumped out, a daunting but not insuperable task. If enough holes could be plugged so that the pumps removed water faster than it flowed in, *Nevada* would lift off the bottom and tugs could move her across the channel into Dry Dock 2. Once she was high and dry, more substantial repairs could be made.

The holes created by the bombs were relatively small—wooden patches could cover them. The exit hole from one of the bombs that hit the forecastle was covered on December 19, and other patches were fabricated and installed on problem areas identified by the divers' hand-by-hand inspection of the hull.

More challenging was the massive breach created by the torpedo that had penetrated the antitorpedo blister and outer hull. The explosion had bent huge pieces of metal outward, and divers had to cut them away before a patch could be fitted. Since the hull had settled into the mud, the surrounding harbor bottom had to be dredged just to assess the damage. Nothing, it seemed, was going to be easy.

Nevada entering dry dock on February 18, 1942. Down at the bow, listing, and a mess, she would live to fight again. *Naval History and Heritage Command, NH 83056*

To design the patch to cover the torpedo damage, salvage crews crawled over the capsized *Oklahoma*, *Nevada*'s sister ship, measuring the curve of her hull. Engineers fabricated a fifty-foot-long by thirty-two-foot-tall wooden structure and, on January 9, carefully lowered it over *Nevada*'s side. But the big patch was unwieldy to maneuver in the pitch-black water, and after weeks of trying, Genereaux's team decided to give up and rely on rapid pumping to keep the ship afloat long enough to reach dry dock. Divers, including hastily trained members of the ship's crew, felt their way down passageways to close watertight hatches, seal drains, cover portholes, and otherwise prevent the passage of water from one part of the ship to another.[3]

Slowly the water level began to recede, revealing a mess of staggering proportions. Rotten food was mixed with tons of wet furniture, clothing, and paper to create a situation that the Navy's official damage report characterized as "better imagined than described."[4] Crewmembers used high-pressure hoses to spray a hot caustic solution on oil-covered bulkheads, decks, and overheads, but ultimately every item and every surface had to be wiped down by hand.

The dangers of the work were put in stark perspective when, on February 7, two men died and several others were injured after inhaling hydrogen sulfide gas produced by decaying organic matter. While the salvage crews had noticed the rotten egg smell associated with hydrogen sulfide, they did not know that the gas could be fatal if inhaled in sufficient concentration. Improved ventilation measures were immediately instituted to prevent future occurrences.[5]

On February 13, two months and a week after the attack, the continuous pumping achieved its goal and *Nevada* lifted gently off the bottom. Five days later tugs arrived to move her across the channel to Dry Dock 2. Admiral Nimitz, who was initially skeptical about *Nevada*'s salvage, was on hand to witness the event and congratulate the salvage team. The Cheer Up Ship was the first of those sunk at Pearl Harbor to be refloated, a source of encouragement to her own crew as well as those on the other battleships that had taken a pounding on December 7.

Now that the ship was empty of water, a more accurate assessment of the damage was possible. Part of the mess that had challenged the crew—the ubiquitous presence of fuel oil—turned out to be a blessing in disguise because the oil had protected metal parts from corrosion while they were immersed in saltwater. All of the vital machinery, including the main engines, dynamos, and electrical motors, was salvable, a tremendous factor in deciding what to do with the ship.

Navy Yard workers replaced the temporary wooden patches on the hull with metal ones and rebuilt the affected portion of the antitorpedo blister. The starboard propeller and shaft, damaged during the second grounding, were fixed, as was the rudder. Inside, the gasoline tank and some other structures damaged by bombs were permanently mended, and machinery was disassembled, cleaned of oil, and put back into operation. No attempt was made to deal with the wrecked superstructure beyond getting the galley functional. Top priority was to get *Nevada* out of Pearl Harbor and into a stateside yard for a thorough overhaul.

"With a new coat of war paint on the exterior, the ship is now beginning to look like her old self," Ens. C. W. Jenkins wrote in the war diary on April 3.[6] But the improvements were more than cosmetic: the next day the ship was ready to feed the crew, and two days later men began to come back on board for berthing. After months of living in temporary quarters ashore, it was good to be home.

Damage to the starboard side. The first task was to remove the twisted metal, making way for permanent repairs. *National Archives Photo Collection, RG 80*

Raised from Pearl Harbor, *Nevada* leaves for Puget Sound and her second modernization. *National Archives Photo Collection, RG 80, no. 64768*

At some point during the refloating process *Nevada* acquired a new nickname. In addition to the Cheer Up Ship, men began to affectionately refer to her as "the Old Maru." Yes, she was old, but she was big and strong and she instilled a sense of confidence in all who sailed in her.

Admiral Nimitz visited the ship on April 7 to present medals for heroism demonstrated during the December 7 attack. "If a ship has personality and a soul," he said in a brief speech on the quarterdeck, "and I am convinced that she has, what a proud moment this must be for this gallant ship, whose sons are well represented in the list of honors about to be awarded."[7] It was the first time since the attack that the officers and men of the Cheer Up Ship had appeared together in dress whites, and it was a fine feeling indeed. Seven *Nevada* men received Navy Crosses (six more Navy Crosses were awarded after the ceremony for a total of thirteen). Eleven days later Admiral Nimitz, on behalf of President Roosevelt, presented the Medal of Honor to Donald K. Ross, who had almost singlehandedly kept the dynamos running during the attack. Chief Boatswain Edwin Hill was awarded the Medal of Honor posthumously for his role in getting the ship under way.

On April 22, 1942, *Nevada* left Pearl Harbor bound for Puget Sound Navy Yard in convoy with four merchant ships and six warships. Steaming regally down the channel, she looked every bit the fighting ship. Three new scout planes were on board, and all of her guns were fully operational. She certainly needed work, but *Nevada* was ready for action.

It was a jubilant time for the crewmembers who had remained on board during the exhausting cleaning and refloating, but there was to be no rest on the way to Bremerton. Captain Thompson ordered a series of exercises, including 5-inch gunnery practice on a target spar towed by USS *Pyro*. Navy bride Peggy Hughes Ryan, a homeward-bound passenger on the steamship *H. F. Alexander*, hoped that the gunners were good shots. *Pyro* was an ammunition ship and was a bit too close for comfort.[8]

Resources were scarce at the start of the war, and some in the Bureau of Ships (successor to the Bureau of Construction and Repair) questioned how much time and effort should be devoted to fixing a twenty-five-year-old battleship. One option was to return her to the same condition she was in before the attack. Others argued that with a relatively small investment *Nevada* could be upgraded to be as modern a vessel as her basic design made possible. The CNO made the decision: *Nevada* was to have a significant overhaul to enable her to function as a useful member of the fleet.[9]

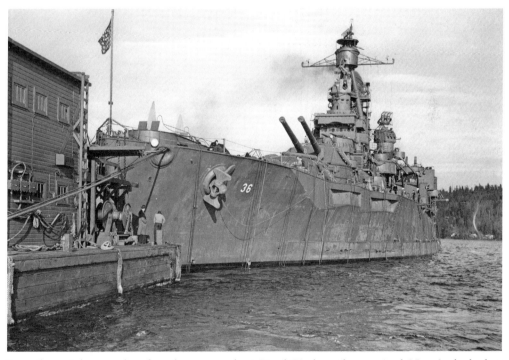

Less than eight months after she was sunk at Pearl Harbor, the repaired *Nevada* docked at Puget Sound. *National Archives Photo Collection, RG 80, no. 242142*

The three faces of the Cheer Up Ship: (*top*) the original design, 1927; (*middle*) after modernization, 1930s; (*bottom*) after repairs, 1943. *National Archives Photo Collection, RG 19; RG 80, nos. 1021382, 583043*

Detailed design work had started while *Nevada* was still resting in the mud of Pearl Harbor, and the initial plans were ready by the time she arrived at Puget Sound. First, her wrecked superstructure was stripped off and replaced by a much more compact design. Since it was unlikely that *Nevada* would be slugging it out in surface actions with other battleships, her heavily armored conning tower was removed and replaced by an open bridge and an enclosed steering station. As an additional weight-saving measure, main battery ammunition was reduced to ninety rounds per gun.

The weight saved was put into a significant upgrade of *Nevada's* secondary armament. Having learned the lesson of Pearl Harbor, and expecting any future battles to be heavily influenced, if not decided, by air power, the designers gave *Nevada* a massive array of antiaircraft guns. Her 5-inch/25-caliber batteries were removed and replaced with eight mounts, each containing twin 5-inch/38-caliber guns. Additional air defenses consisted of eight 40-millimeter quad gun mounts and forty-one 20-millimeter Oerlikon machine guns. Nearly every available space on the deck and superstructure was fitted with antiaircraft guns, an addition the crew would appreciate during Japanese kamikaze attacks later in the war.

Nevada old-timers hardly recognized her new silhouette. The mainmast was shorter, and the smoke pipe was canted aft to prevent smoke from fouling the bridge. The catapult on turret 3 was gone, leaving only the one on the quarterdeck; two planes would be sufficient for future scouting and spotting missions.

Equal in importance to her new guns and airplanes, *Nevada* received the latest in radar equipment. No longer would lookouts have to peer through dark and gloom in search of attackers or targets. Aircraft and surface vessels would now be "visible" in plenty of time to prepare for them.

The urgency to get the ship back to sea stimulated ingenuity. When yard workers couldn't find enough copper to complete repairs on the main electrical switchboard they resorted to the next best thing: solid silver. It wasn't a question of price—there simply wasn't any copper available, and the U.S. Treasury had tons of silver sitting in vaults. *Nevada* had the most valuable electrical switchboard in the U.S. (and likely any other) Navy.

The Cheer Up Ship was originally designed to carry around one thousand men, but the need for increased armament, better fire control, and additional personnel to assist in damage control brought her wartime complement to more than two thousand. These extra men required berthing, food service, and fresh water and put a considerable strain on the ship's limited infrastructure.

The attack on Pearl Harbor was the first of a series of rapid blows delivered to the Allied powers. After heroic defenses, Wake Island and the Philippines fell to the

Japanese onslaught, as did Guam, Singapore, and the Dutch East Indies. At sea, Japanese aircraft sank the British battle cruisers HMS *Repulse* and HMS *Prince of Wales*, a blow to Allied sea power in the Pacific and an indicator of the changing nature of sea warfare. A scratched-together fleet of American, British, Dutch, and Australian ships attempted to stem the Japanese advance by blocking the South Java Sea, but they were too weak to stand up against Japan's superior forces. It seemed that Admiral Nagumo's carriers, which had not received a scratch for all the damage they inflicted, were invincible.

That perception was about to change.

The Japanese knew that they had only a short time to secure their territorial gains before the industrial might of the United States released a juggernaut of men, planes, and ships into the Pacific. What they did not anticipate was how training, determination, and boldness would enable the U.S. Navy to take the initiative even with the limited resources it had on hand. Vice Adm. William Halsey's carrier group centered on *Enterprise* raided the Marshall Islands in February 1942, and on April 18 sixteen B-25 bombers took off from USS *Hornet* and bombed Tokyo. Neither attack did much physical damage, but both scored a huge morale victory for the Americans and put the Japanese on notice that their defensive perimeter and even their home islands were not immune from attack.

Nimitz's big break came in the spring of 1942 when Navy code breakers deciphered a Japanese dispatch describing a forthcoming operation: Admiral Yamamoto was planning an attack on Midway Island in the hope of drawing the entire Pacific Fleet out for the longed-for decisive battle. He was committing a major part of his carrier forces to the operation, along with a battleship support group.

Yamamoto got his decisive battle at Midway, but it turned out to be a resounding victory for the Americans. By the time it was over, four Japanese carriers were on the bottom, at the cost of only one American carrier. Even more devastating over the long term, Japan lost hundreds of experienced aviation mechanics, armorers, and flight deck personnel who could not be quickly replaced. It was a defeat from which the Japanese would never recover.

———

Nevada's Puget Sound overhaul took just eight months, about one-third the time of her 1928–30 rebuild at Norfolk. On December 7, 1942—exactly one year after she was sunk at Pearl Harbor—she was under way to change berths. Two days later she was at sea firing test shots from her new 5-inch and 40-millimeter guns. In speed trials, she gingerly worked up to full power but had to back off when a reduction gear in one of the main engines overheated. A few days in the yard fixed the problem, and the next week she was making 19.3 knots—not bad for an old battleship raised from the dead.

Nevada was ready to fight, and Admiral Nimitz already had a mission picked out for her: provide bombardment support for the recovery of two of the Aleutian Islands the Japanese had captured the previous year. Part of Admiral Yamamoto's Midway strategy was a diversionary move north into the Aleutians, a frozen chain spanning the gap between Alaska and the Soviet Union. With luck, the Americans might split their forces to address this second threat, increasing the probability of a Japanese victory at Midway. (Some historians speculate that Yamamoto was in fact reluctant to divert forces to the Aleutians, perhaps fearing the Americans would not take the bait.)[10]

Warned by the code breakers, Nimitz did not take the bait. As the carriers battled it out in the central Pacific, a small Japanese invasion force landed on uninhabited Attu and Kiska. They were low-value targets—Attu consisted of 345 square miles of frozen mountains and mud, and Kiska was less than one-third that size—but the Japanese thought that holding them might deter the United States from using the Aleutians as a northern route to attack Japan.

While the islands had little strategic value, many Americans objected to U.S. territory remaining in Japanese hands, and the Navy was under pressure to get them back. By spring of 1943 Nimitz thought that he finally had sufficient resources to send a force northward, and he ordered *Nevada* to get ready to help retake the islands.

First, however, Capt. Howard Kingman, who had relieved Commander Thompson as CO on August 25, had to get his men into fighting shape. Many of them had joined the ship since her departure from Pearl Harbor, and quite a few were new recruits fresh from civilian life.

Christmas Eve 1942 found *Nevada* steaming south from Puget Sound firing her main battery in gunnery exercises. She anchored in Los Angeles Harbor on Christmas Day and over the coming weeks returned to her old stomping grounds off the coast of Southern California for target practice and other training.

Gone were the peacetime days of Monday through Friday at sea with weekends in port. Kingman packed as much as he could into every hour of training: defense against torpedo attacks, day spotting practice, antiaircraft practice, and to cap things off, night battle practice. Land-based planes and destroyers conducted simulated torpedo attacks on the ship, and in anticipation of future missions, *Nevada* pounded San Clemente Island with her main and secondary batteries to hone the crew's skill at shore bombardment. When Capt. Willard A. Kitts relieved Kingman on January 25, the routine hardly missed a beat.

On April 7 *Nevada* weighed anchor and proceeded north with the battleship USS *Idaho* and four screening vessels, together forming Task Group 16.12. To a

Snow and ice make walking on the deck treacherous; operating in the Aleutians, March 1943.
National Archives Photo Collection, RG 80, no. 220773

shore-bound observer it looked like any other training sortie, but this time the ship would be at sea for more than two months.

Every attempt had been made to keep the force's destination a secret. Cold-weather gear was hidden away, and officers conspicuously studied maps of the North Atlantic and even Argentina. Medics talked about the dangers of tropical diseases. But after only a few days of steaming the crew could tell that they were not headed toward either the Panama Canal or the South Pacific.

On April 16 the task force anchored in Kuluk Bay, Adak Island, almost midway between the westernmost tip of the Alaskan mainland and Japanese-held Attu. The constant threat of Japanese air attack kept everyone on edge. Engine Control was ordered to be ready to get under way at an hour's notice, and every twenty minutes the turbines were turned over for one minute.

Task Group 16.12 departed Adak on April 17 and crossed the 180th meridian the next day. The ships were moving into enemy waters, only four hundred miles from the Japanese naval base at Paramushiro and closer to Japan than any U.S. battleship had been since the start of the war. Sonar contacts led Captain Kitts to ring up maximum speed to foil possible torpedo attacks. Submarines were known to be in the area, and battleships were prime targets.

The weather was dreadful. Main turret crews had to elevate their guns to avoid having muzzle bags ripped off by waves breaking over the bow, and at times green water washed over the forward 40-millimeter gun mounts. But there was no holing up belowdecks to ride out the storm: there were destroyers to fuel, provisions to transfer to the smaller escorts, and constant lookout duty. Weapons had to be test-fired in the frigid conditions and aircraft maintained for flight. For men on deck it was miserable duty—snow squalls frequently reduced visibility to zero, and ice caked every gun, cable, and handrail. Being washed overboard was tantamount to a death sentence; the water temperature was 28°F, and the air temperature was only a few degrees above that. Fog seemed perpetual, limiting air operations and causing several collisions among the smaller vessels of the task force. But the fog also shielded the force from enemy aircraft, so the Americans got the better part of the weather bargain. Even when seas were calm, the fog dampened noise and created an eerie atmosphere.

Nevada's ever-finicky steering acted up once again. This was particularly worrisome because the maps available to the navigator were hopelessly inaccurate. Several times Kitts ordered full astern as the fathometer indicated rapidly decreasing water depth, sometimes ten fathoms or less. Rocky pinnacles were visible above the water, so others certainly lurked below the surface, waiting to tear a gash in the hull.

On May 1 *Nevada*, *Idaho*, and their escorts put into Cold Bay to link up with *Pennsylvania*. The armada now comprised three battleships and twenty-four other ships, a sizable U.S. force for anywhere in the Pacific at that time. Task Force 51 left Cold Bay on May 4, and landings started on May 11 at Holtz Bay, on the northeast part of Attu. *Pennsylvania*, *Idaho*, and their escorts provided fire support and were the target of at least two torpedo attacks by Japanese submarines. There was little opposition on land, however, and 1,500 men were ashore by the end of the day.

Nevada, serving as Adm. Francis Rockwell's flagship, was assigned to support the invasion at Massacre Bay, on the southern portion of the island. She was the heavy firepower behind a group of three transports, the biggest concentration of troops in the invasion. General Quarters was sounded at 0715 on May 12, and thirty-one minutes later *Nevada*'s main battery opened up on Japanese shore positions. Her two planes were catapulted aloft to spot the fall of shells.

Off Attu, May 1943. Bitter cold and near-constant fog made for a difficult voyage. *National Archives Photo Collection, RG 80, no. 77069*

Fog delayed the landing. Anxious Army personnel paced the deck, worried that the longer they waited the better prepared the defenders would be to repel them. By midday there were no signs of improvement in the weather, so it was decided to go forward with the invasion.

The landing was difficult. The rough sea capsized one landing craft and pushed another onto the rocks. Since the invasion at Massacre Bay was conducted under the full view of Japanese positions, *Nevada*'s supporting fire seemed a godsend in securing the beachhead. The main and secondary batteries laid down a barrage on the ridges above the bay, where the Japanese had retreated prior to the invasion. The enemy was dug in, but the high-explosive shells took their toll. Lt. Hubert Long reported that "dead Japanese, hunks of artillery, pieces of guns, and arms and legs rolled down out of the fog on the mountain."[11] But the Japanese still managed to hurl shells down on the Americans, making what was thought to be a secure beachhead anything but secure. With the on-again, off-again schedule, *Nevada*'s 14-inch battery engaged on four separate occasions during the day.

On May 11 and 12 the bombarding ships steamed at moderate speed in deep water in case they needed to evade submarines or aircraft attacks, but on the morning of the thirteenth Admiral Rockwell ordered *Nevada* close inshore. He wanted to be *right there*, close to those directing the fire and positioned to address a target in the shortest possible time.

Not everyone agreed with Rockwell's tactics. One bridge officer dutifully reminded the admiral that rocky pinnacles and enemy submarines were a very real danger to the ship. Shouldn't they withdraw to deeper water where there was more room to maneuver? Rockwell would have none of it. "Screw the torpedoes! Slow speed ahead,"[12] he barked. *Nevada*'s remarkable luck held when, a short time later, the destroyers USS *Farragut* and USS *Edwards* attacked a submarine that may have launched torpedoes at her. The torpedoes missed, if they were indeed launched, and the destroyers sank the submarine.

The battleships loosed a terrific storm of ordnance over three days, almost emptying their magazines, and on May 14 they turned toward Adak to reload. Admiral Rockwell was less enthusiastic about *Nevada* remaining in submarine-infested waters without ammunition to contribute to the fight. Bad weather kept Japanese torpedo bombers on the ground at Paramushiro, but had it cleared and the shoals and rocky pinnacles hemmed in the battleships, the result could have been a disaster.

New Mexico and *Mississippi*, two of the battleships CNO Stark transferred from the Atlantic to the Pacific after Pearl Harbor, joined the formation on May 22, expanding the task force to five battleships plus escorts. If Admiral Yamamoto decided to send reinforcements to the Aleutians, the U.S. Navy was more than ready to give them a hot reception. But the Japanese commander in chief refused requests to send a heavy surface force to the area—his top priority was to hold Guadalcanal and other points in the South Pacific.

By this time the 2,630 Japanese soldiers on Attu were in a desperate situation—their numbers were dwindling and supplies were short. Conversely, the Americans were being reinforced daily by a flood of men and materiel. Rather than wait for the certain end, 1,000 Japanese troops executed a banzai charge on the American lines. It didn't start out as a suicide attack, but rather as a gambit to capture U.S. artillery and supplies. And it might have worked but for the quick initiative of Brig. Gen. Archibald Arnold. Waving his pistol, Arnold rallied his troops and directed their fire onto the charging Japanese. By the end of the day U.S. forces had killed half of the attackers; the remainder committed suicide. A weaker charge the next day ended with the same result. The battle for Attu was over.

Attu was, for its size, one of the bloodiest battles of the Pacific theater. The Japanese defenders were almost completely wiped out, and U.S. casualties numbered 50 percent more than the original number of Japanese troops on the island. It was an important battle for *Nevada*, the first of many times that her commanding officer would ignore potential danger to get in close for bombardment support. Captain Kitts would receive the Legion of Merit for his role in the Attu campaign.

The recovery of Kiska seemed to be following a similar path. Relentless bombing by Army planes was followed by bombardment from *New Mexico* and *Mississippi*. But it was a waste of ordnance. On July 28 Japanese cruisers and destroyers made a dash to the island and removed more than 5,000 troops. When 34,000 Americans landed, they found the island deserted.

Bow-on off San Francisco, July 1, 1943, on her way to the North Atlantic for convoy escort duty. *National Archives Photo Collection, RG 80, no. 74450*

With Attu and Kiska secure and no surface forces to fight, *Nevada* was ordered south to San Francisco. She passed under the welcoming Golden Gate Bridge on the morning of June 17, having been at sea for seventy-two days. For two weeks the ship was pampered at the Bethlehem Steel Ship Yard while her crew took in the pleasures of San Francisco. By now these men were no "Market Street Commandos" but hardened seamen who had endured the rigors of sustained Arctic operations. They had no way to know that their time in the Aleutians was but a foretaste of what they would soon see in the North Atlantic. Once out of the shipyard *Nevada* was immediately ordered to report for convoy escort duty.

She left San Francisco Bay for the Panama Canal on July 1 and passed her former home port of San Pedro without even stopping. It was a disappointment for the crew—for all they knew, they wouldn't get back to California for many months, if ever.

Accompanying *Nevada* on the journey to the East Coast was the new escort carrier USS *Croatan*. The trip quickly turned into a training opportunity for both ships—pilots from *Croatan* used *Nevada* as a target for simulated attacks, and antiaircraft gunners on *Nevada* had plentiful aircraft to aim at courtesy of *Croatan*.

A long line of ships were waiting their turn to go through the Canal when the task force arrived, but *Nevada* and *Croatan* jumped the queue, hardly pausing before transiting to Cristobal. Once in the Atlantic the danger changed in name only—German submarines replaced Japanese submarines as the principal threat. Lookouts on *Nevada* sighted a periscope on July 16, and the 5-inch gun crews put two rounds on it. The same thing happened the following day, but in this case the "periscope" turned out to be a floating barrel, later sunk by machine-gun fire from the escort USS *Baldwin*. When lookouts reported yet another "periscope," *Nevada*'s own 5-inch battery addressed it in short order.

The task force steamed up the coast to Norfolk, where *Nevada* paused for installation of new evaporators to increase her supply of fresh water, a boon to crewmen accustomed to scrimping on water. She also took on a new skipper: Capt. Powell M. Rhea. It was a homecoming of sorts for Rhea, who had served as engineering officer in *Nevada* from 1929 to 1932. During the last war he had escorted convoys to Europe, so he was also familiar with the vagaries of the North Atlantic. After assuming command, Rhea took his new charge into Chesapeake Bay for gunnery practice involving all calibers of guns. *Nevada* was back at sea on September 2, operating under secret orders to proceed at once to Gravesend Bay, New York, for convoy escort duty.

Aggressive antisubmarine measures by the Allies had greatly reduced losses from U-boats, but convoys carrying thousands of troops across the Atlantic still needed protection from German surface forces that might break through the

Change-of-command ceremony, July 21, 1943. Capt. Powell M. Rhea returns to the ship on which he previously served as engineering officer. *National Archives Photo Collection, RG 80, no. 74172*

British blockade. *Nevada* fit the bill nicely. She outgunned anything the Germans could send against her, and her relatively modest cruising speed was comparable to the pace of a convoy—typically ten to fifteen knots.

Barely a day after arriving at Gravesend Bay she was under way with Task Force 27, the covering force for convoy UT-2 en route to the United Kingdom. UT-2 started out with twenty ships steaming in eight columns, but within twenty-four hours mechanical problems forced three of them to turn back. Thirteen destroyers prowled the perimeter of the formation, searching for submarines, shepherding strays back into the fold, and occasionally escorting the lame back to port. Land was sighted on September 14, and the merchantmen scattered to their assigned ports while *Nevada* anchored in Belfast Lough, Ireland.

There was hardly time to catch a glimpse of the Irish coast before *Nevada* picked up convoy TU-2 for the trip back to the United States. On September 28, after an uneventful voyage, *Nevada* tied up to North Jetty at the Boston Navy Yard. She had been at sea for nine months with only a few hurried days in yards at San Francisco and Norfolk to take care of urgent repairs. Men and machines would have a much-needed break until the end of November.

A week of refresher training at the Navy's operational areas in Casco Bay, Maine, preceded *Nevada*'s return to escort duty. It was a comprehensive course, with all calibers of guns exercised along with the aviation unit. Even practice firing could be dangerous. Two days out of Boston, a firing cutout mechanism that was supposed to prevent a gun from firing when pointed inboard at the ship failed on one of the 40-millimeter guns. Four men were injured when four projectiles hit the open bridge. It could have been worse; the Bofors gun fired automatically at a rate of two shells per second, and four guns were attached to a single mount.

Convoy UT-5 departed New York on December 5 with *Nevada* providing the heavy support. Once on the other side she returned to her usual berth in Belfast Lough until a return convoy of twenty-seven ships and twelve escorts was ready to depart on December 20. It was to be anything but a pleasant crossing.

Three days into the voyage, *U-471*, mistaking *Nevada* for a lowly cruiser, fired a torpedo into the center of the convoy. The torpedo missed the rich field of ships, and the submarine was unable to line up for another shot before land-based B-24 bombers scared it off.[13]

But submarines would be the least of the convoy's troubles. The seas picked up on Christmas Eve, and by Christmas night winds were clocked at sixty knots. Captain Rhea ordered speed reduced to ten knots in deference to the empty merchantmen, but it was almost impossible to keep order in the convoy. As the day

Rough weather in the North Atlantic, March 26, 1944. *National Archives Photo Collection, RG 80, no. 220791*

progressed the ships scattered over a ten-mile patch of ocean, and nearly every vessel suffered storm damage.

Even *Nevada*, at 30,000 tons, was not immune from the storm. On Christmas night heavy seas carried away two motor whaleboats along with numerous life rafts and deck gear. The shackles holding aircraft number 11 to its catapult broke loose, and the plane went over the side, carrying its highly secret IFF (Identification Friend or Foe) equipment with it. In enemy hands, the IFF would allow an aircraft to appear as friendly until it was close enough to attack a ship. The loss of even a single unit was a serious issue.

The storm began to abate somewhat on the twenty-sixth, but by then topside was a shambles. The second aircraft was washed overboard at 0410, again carrying IFF equipment. The only consolation was that both planes were so beat up by wind and waves that neither was likely to float long enough for the enemy to recover it. In any event, the seas were far too rough to order destroyers to mount a comprehensive search-and-destroy mission on the planes. They were too busy herding errant merchantmen back into the protective embrace of the convoy while keeping an ear out for submarine sonar contacts.

Nevada got back to Boston on New Year's Eve and was put on the "limited availability" list pending repair of the storm damage. She didn't return to active duty until February 8. But this time there was no week of refresher training—5-inch antiaircraft gun practice was conducted while *Nevada* was steaming from Boston to Gravesend Bay to meet up with eastbound convoy UT-8.

On the first day out Captain Rhea was frustrated that USS *Barnett*, one of his convoy charges, could make a best speed of only fourteen knots, one knot below Rhea's assigned speed of fifteen knots. Accumulated over days of steaming, the difference could affect the schedule of air coverage and surface rendezvouses. There were twenty-five troop transports in UT-8 carrying thousands of men bound for Britain, so this was no time to be flexible in procedures. On the positive side, UT-8 had two escort carriers to provide air coverage. If German submarines were to show up, at least there was a way to fight back, preferably at a distance from the main convoy.

After a smooth return journey and a quick stop in dry dock at the Boston Navy Yard, *Nevada* was under way again on March 21 for Casco Bay to conduct gunnery training and engine trials. In a full-power run the next day she reached 19.7 knots.

The challenge then shifted from high-speed dashes to creeping up to a buoy. When on bombardment duty the ship would need to moor in a precise location so as not to interfere with landing craft and other vessels. It was important to get it right, and Rear Adm. Carleton Bryant came on board on March 23 to personally observe the crew's mooring skills.

Captain Rhea, bundled up against the cold, on the bridge, March 26, 1944. *National Archives Photo Collection, RG 80, no. 220774*

Target practice initially focused on antiaircraft defense using the 20-millimeter and 40-millimeter automatic guns and the 5-inch antiaircraft batteries. Ammunition was no longer carefully rationed to cut training costs, and on March 22 alone the 20-millimeter guns expended 2,841 rounds and the 40-millimeter guns shot 548 rounds. Five-inch guns could run through more than a hundred shells in a single practice session.

The main battery was not forgotten, nor was the use of the secondary battery for surface action. Day spotting practice was followed at dusk by night spotting practice, which used radar to direct rounds to the target raft. Night illumination was a special concern, and during some practice sessions, gunners expended more than one hundred rounds of star shells.

The real focus of training started on March 29 when *Nevada* and her escorts approached Seal Island for bombardment practice. The destroyer escort USS *Loy* was positioned about a mile offshore to simulate a shore fire-control party, and one of *Nevada*'s own planes was used for air spotting. The main battery opened up on designated shore targets at 26,000 yards, firing 20 rounds in 15 minutes before the ship turned around for another run. The secondary batteries went into action when the ship closed to 15,000 yards. They fired shells designed to burst 50 feet above ground level, the optimal height for inflicting casualties in troop

A correspondent is transferred to *Nevada* while she is under way, March 26, 1944. Not a pleasant way to come on board! *National Archives Photo Collection, RG 80, no. 220784*

concentrations. Including morning antiaircraft practice, every type of gun on the ship got to fire at a target.

Further confirmation that shore bombardment was to be a key mission came when the ship returned to Boston in early April. While she was moored at North Jetty, 515 14-inch armor-piercing projectiles were removed from the magazines and replaced with 578 high-explosive rounds. These "high-capacity" rounds contained 105 pounds of high explosive compared with the 34 pounds in an armor-piercing round and were intended for softer targets. Over the course of a week the crew also loaded 2,400 rounds of 5-inch munitions and 305 rounds of illumination projectiles.

Nevada had one more day of shore bombardment practice in Casco Bay before receiving orders to prepare for "extended service," presumably in Europe. She sailed with *Arkansas* on April 18 as part of Task Force 27.8 under Rear Adm. Morton L. Deyo. *Texas* joined the group shortly afterward. *Nevada* was about to play her part in the greatest amphibious invasion in history: D-Day.

11

The Atlantic
D-Day and Southern France

Ernest King, CNO, was reluctant to allocate ships to Operation Neptune, the naval component of the invasion of France. He had his hands full in the Pacific and thought that the Royal Navy, right on the doorstep of Europe, should handle fire support for the landings. Rear Adm. John L. Hall, in command of the American 11th Amphibious Force, had another opinion. For his troops to have any chance of success, the "Atlantic Wall"—a massive array of steel, concrete, and barbed wire guarding the coastline of France—had to be broken. Artillery emplacements, some many miles inland, had to be eliminated lest they shower the beaches with deadly accurate fire. The reinforcements the Germans had deployed at key spots had to be held in check long enough for the invaders to establish a defensible beachhead. Air power might take out artillery and hold reinforcements at bay, but only the precision fire of large-caliber naval guns could knock holes in the Atlantic Wall itself. If American soldiers were to be committed to the fight, then American ships should be in there too. King finally relented and allocated three old battleships (*Nevada*, *Texas*, and *Arkansas*), three cruisers, and thirty-four destroyers to support the D-Day invasion.[1]

Landings were planned at five locations between Le Havre and the Cherbourg peninsula: the Americans would come ashore at Omaha Beach and Utah Beach, and the British and Canadians at Gold, Juno, and Sword Beaches. An armada of nearly 7,000 vessels—including almost 700 warships—was amassed to carry the 150,000-man invasion force, provide bombardment support, and sweep for mines.[2] Overhead, 2,200 bombers were set to attack key targets on the beaches and inland.

After returning to her familiar anchorage at Belfast Lough, *Nevada* underwent a grueling training regimen focused on improving bombardment accuracy and responding to directions from shore and air observers. She quickly proved herself more than ready for the mission: in practice shoots off the coast of Scotland on May 10, main battery gun crews scored 11 direct hits out of 16 shots at a range of 24,000 yards; a day later they scored 9 direct hits out of 16 single-gun shots at the same range.

Crew relaxing on deck, May 30, 1944. Life would soon get very busy. *National Archives Photo Collection, RG 80, no. 252278*

Despite, or perhaps because of, the pressure to bring the ship to a peak of performance, there were mishaps. On returning to port on May 10, Captain Rhea was inching *Nevada* between a British aircraft carrier and a sandbank at Greenock, Scotland. With the ship creeping along at five knots, he put the rudder over and . . . nothing happened. Momentum carried the ship forward until a gentle lurch indicated that she had run aground. Rhea immediately ordered both engines back full emergency, without effect. Tugs were called in to pull on the bow, but *Nevada* remained stuck. Finally, a line was put over to the cruiser USS *Tuscaloosa*, and with her help and *Nevada*'s engines back full, *Nevada* slipped off the sandbar. So far so good, but with full astern she was making rapid progress on the British carrier behind her. Rhea ordered ahead one-third, ahead two-thirds, ahead standard, and then, "All ahead full emergency!" with full right rudder. She passed the carrier "close aboard to port," but there was no collision. *Nevada* suffered no damage in the incident beyond the pride of the bridge crew.

Equally embarrassing, though less public, was a 0200 call to Lt. Cdr. Walter Buckley of the Engineering Department. The forward diesel generator room was flooding. He rushed down from his stateroom and was greeted by eight feet of water—and not a single person in sight. The man in charge had gone off for a cup of coffee. Buckley was livid: his ship might sink as a result of enemy action, but certainly not because people weren't paying attention! The Sailor responsible for the flooding soon found himself in a much less comfortable assignment.[3]

On May 28 Admiral Bertram Ramsay, the British commander of the Allied Naval Expeditionary Force, signaled, "Carry out Operation NEPTUNE." The landings were planned for June 5, but much needed to be done before soldiers waded ashore. Minesweepers were among the earliest to leave port, along with slower vessels that would take days to make the crossing. *Nevada* left her mooring in Belfast Lough on May 30, but poor visibility forced her to return to her anchorage. Since the invasion plan had already been briefed to the crew, the ship was "sealed" to prevent anyone from going ashore with information that could compromise the time and place of the landings.

Listening to the ship's band, May 30, 1944; one of the last concerts before D-Day. *National Archives Photo Collection, RG 80, no. 252274*

Sweeping the deck, May 30, 1944. Rhea wanted the ship to be at her best for the invasion of France. *National Archives Photo Collection, RG 80*

Unnamed officer reading a letter from Adm. Alan G. Kirk telling of the upcoming invasion of France, June 2, 1944. *National Archives Photo Collection, RG 80, no. 252288*

Nevada finally departed Belfast Lough at 0222 on Saturday, June 3. She made her way to "Piccadilly Circus," a circular area in the English Channel through which all ships and boats approaching Normandy would pass, and from there steamed through mine-swept channels toward the continent. The weather was dismal, and the smaller ships in the group had a tough time keeping station. Crewmembers wondered how the great armada was going to make the crossing in such conditions. The most reliable weather predictions indicated continued high winds and heavy seas well beyond what landing craft could handle. Supreme Allied Commander Gen. Dwight Eisenhower was forced to conclude that the invasion could not take place as planned on June 5. Captain Rhea received a dispatch postponing H hour until 0630 on June 6 and, reversing course, steamed up and down swept channels in the Irish Sea, killing time to conform to the new schedule.

Despite the delay, the invasion was an occasion worth commemorating. Admiral Ramsay sent out a special order of the day to all officers and men of the U.S. and Royal navies: "It is our privilege to take part in the greatest amphibious operation in history. . . . The hopes and prayers of the free world and of the enslaved people of Europe will be with us and we cannot fail them. . . . I count on every man to do his utmost to ensure the success of this great enterprise. . . . Good luck and God Speed."[4]

General Eisenhower arranged for a prerecorded message to be played on the public-address systems of all ships. It ended with, "Good luck! And let us all beseech the blessing of Almighty God on this great and noble undertaking."[5]

At 0725 on June 5 the bombardment group split into two components—one heading for Omaha Beach and the other toward Utah Beach. *Nevada*, along with USS *Quincy*, USS *Tuscaloosa*, and HMS *Black Prince* formed up at Utah Fire Support Area One along with the destroyers USS *Fitch*, USS *Corry*, and USS *Hobson*. All were under the command of Rear Adm. Morton Deyo. As the fleet approached the French coast under fading light, men on deck watched flashes from guns and bombs on shore.

The pathway to the ships' assigned positions was supposed to have been marked by colored "dan" buoys dropped by minesweepers—red on the starboard side of the swept channel and white on the port side. Some of the buoys were not lit, though, and currents had dragged others well outside their intended locations. Using radar as a guide, *Nevada* led her cruiser entourage into position 11,000 yards offshore; the destroyers took up positions 6,000 yards inshore. There was too little room for the big ship to maneuver in the narrow swept channel, so when she reached her assigned position at 0442, Captain Rhea ordered anchors dropped. As the column of ships came to rest, waves of bombers and fighters roared overhead and the sound

Attendance at religious services increased as battle approached. Catholic Mass on June 2, 1944. *National Archives Photo Collection, RG 80, no. 252302*

of bombs echoed from shore. Paratroopers and glider troops had already landed on the continent to secure vital causeways across the lowlands that would enable troops to advance later in the day.

Men on deck had a ringside seat as bombs hit German installations and enemy antiaircraft fire knocked down Allied planes. But most on the ship—including those in the main turrets—could not tell what was happening beyond their narrow duty stations. A sudden jolt might mean that the ship had been hit and shipmates killed, or it might be recoil from a salvo from *Nevada*'s own guns. Captain Rhea left communication channels open so the crew could hear how the battle was progressing.[6]

The men topside had a better idea of what was happening, but they were also far more vulnerable to German artillery and aircraft than those belowdecks. The main turrets could survive just about anything the Germans could dish out, but the 5-inch mounts and the antiaircraft guns were vulnerable, as were lookouts, the bridge crew, and many others.

It was a time of anticipation, of apprehension, but not really of fear. The crew had been trained to perfection to do their jobs, but no book, lecture, or exercise could prepare them for one of the greatest battles in history. They felt a determination to succeed against any odds and a kinship with the soldiers who would land the next morning. They vowed not to let them down.

While the Allies would enjoy local superiority at the point of the invasion, that superiority would quickly evaporate if German reinforcements moved up from the rear or if German artillery demolished the beachheads. Aerial reconnaissance had revealed twenty-eight German coastal artillery batteries covering the Utah beaches. The 110 guns contained in those emplacements ranged from relatively light 75-millimeter cannon to 170-millimeter naval guns. Another eighteen batteries—including one containing four 210-millimeter guns in two protected casemates—were located well inland but still within range of the beaches. Rear Admiral Deyo and Major Gen. Lawton "Lightning Joe" Collins, commander of the invading VII Corps, had prioritized the ships' targets to minimize the threat to the landing troops. For the first fifty minutes the big ships would target inland artillery batteries. They would then shift to the landing zone itself, blowing holes in the Atlantic Wall and knocking out gun emplacements that had a direct line of fire on the beaches. Finally, they would address targets of opportunity called in by land, sea, and air spotters.

Three groups of spotters identified targets and spotted the fall of shells. The ships' own planes, slow and easy targets for German antiaircraft batteries, had been

Captain Rhea wishes the crew good luck on D-Day. *National Archives Photo Collection, RG 80, no. 252308*

Nevada's big guns open up on June 6, 1944. The gun crews quickly demonstrated remarkable accuracy at extreme ranges. *National Archives Photo Collection, RG 80, no. 252415*

removed prior to the invasion. Two British Spitfires were assigned to each target set and were in constant radio contact with the bombardment force. Lookouts on board ship were effective for spotting targets visible from the mast tops, including the critical Atlantic Wall. Finally, eighteen shore fire control parties (SFCPs) provided an on-the-ground perspective, which proved especially important as the front advanced and stubborn obstacles were identified. One of the SFCPs hosted *Nevada*'s Radarman 3rd Class Leo Palumbo, who served as a knowledgeable liaison between land and sea. Palumbo was wounded while directing fire and received a Purple Heart when he returned on board.

The Germans picked up the invasion fleet on radar at 0309, but shore batteries waited until 0505 to open fire.[7] The destroyers *Corry* and *Fitch*, closest to land, were their first targets. The British light cruiser *Black Prince* replied with her 5-inch guns, which in turn attracted the Germans to her position. The gun duel between bombarding ships and shore batteries had begun.

At 0536 Rear Admiral Deyo decided to open fire, fourteen minutes ahead of schedule. The Germans clearly knew that his ships were there, and the longer he waited the more likely that they would find the right range and inflict damage. Another component of the plan that quickly went by the wayside was to have the ships anchor and fire from fixed positions. That was fine in theory, but the currents proved too strong for *Nevada* to maintain her firing orientation, even with the engines' help. Rhea raised anchor and steamed slowly near *Nevada's* assigned position, keeping the port batteries trained on the shore.

Getting under way proved a wise move because at 0542 the Germans began firing on the largest ship in the formation—*Nevada*. They managed to straddle her on their first salvo; the closest shell splashes were only four hundred yards away. Three minutes later another shore battery scored a direct hit on a landing craft one thousand yards astern.

It was getting to be a dangerous neighborhood, but *Nevada* would quickly return the favor. At 0547 she opened up with her secondary battery on prearranged targets on the beach. The main battery sent 4 rounds 17,100 yards inland; 9 minutes later *Nevada* sent 16 rounds toward a second target as directed by air spotters.

With H hour rapidly approaching, *Nevada* shifted her guns from inland targets to the shoreline. Beginning at 0616, her 14-inch guns fired forty-one armor-piercing rounds at the concrete seawall and twelve high-capacity shells at obstacles on the beaches. With the shore only 12,000 yards away, *Nevada's* guns were firing almost horizontally, and soldiers in the small landing craft swore that they could feel the draft from the giant shells as they passed just a few yards overhead.[8] At the very least the men could see the faint red glow that marked the shells' passage.[9]

One minute before H hour, with twenty landing craft only yards from the beach, Rhea shifted the main battery back to inland artillery positions. The secondary battery continued firing at the shoreline even after the first men stormed ashore, only stopping at two minutes past H hour. By this time *Nevada* had expended an

D-Day invasion armada as seen from *Nevada*. Men in the boats could hear *Nevada's* shells whistling overhead. *National Archives Photo Collection, RG 80, no. 52408*

astonishing 1,440 rounds of 5-inch ammunition. The guns were so hot from the rapid firing that the paint peeled off their barrels and sea spray hissed as it hit the metal. Shell casings, normally recovered for reuse, were simply thrown over the side to avoid fouling the motion of the mounts.[10]

The work in the turrets and on the 5-inch mounts was exhausting, all the more so because the men knew that a single misstep could spell disaster. Five-inch shells weighed fifty-five pounds, and with shells coming up the hoists at a relentless rate, it was a matter of endurance to grab each one and accurately load it into the gun's breech. Powder charges weighed less—twenty-eight pounds—but had to be handled carefully lest they rip and spill their contents on the deck, a potential disaster if a hot piece of shrapnel landed in the spill. The months of training paid off; the men went through the necessary motions almost automatically but with grim determination. Every shell fired made a soldier's job easier, maybe spelling the difference between life and death. While at Normandy, mounts 2 and 4 set a fleet gunnery record for rapid fire by shooting at the astonishing rate of three hundred rounds each over a period of twenty-five minutes.

Gun crews in the main turrets had the advantage of rammers that pushed shells into the breech, but the men worked in cramped spaces with hardly room to turn around, all the while surrounded by machinery in constant motion. Older men remembered a 1924 accident on *Mississippi* when hot remnants from a previous shot ignited a powder bag being inserted into the breech. All forty-five men in the turret were killed. Turret captains' principal challenge was to balance rapidity of fire with safety, never easy but even more difficult under battle conditions.

Gunners didn't even have time to catch their breath as the first soldiers hit the shoreline; one minute after the secondary batteries ceased shooting on the beach they opened fire with a barrage of 1,253 rounds on targets flanking the invasion site. These shots were directed by the ship's own spotters. The 5-inch guns continued firing until 0810 and then stood by, awaiting instructions from SFCPs. The main guns commenced firing at 0718, shooting intermittently as directed by air spotters until 1014, when their assigned target was deemed destroyed.

At 0900 one of the SFCPs reported that the seawall on Red Beach was broken in four places with holes big enough for tanks to drive through. *Nevada* had done her job well in preparing a path for the troops.

In addition to destroying targets of interest, the bombarding ships had a secondary effect of considerable value to the landing troops: they forced German artillery to shift fire from the beaches and approaching landing craft to the big ships offshore. That was good for the troops but a problem for the ships: *Tuscaloosa* narrowly escaped a German salvo when shells landed close astern.

On several occasions Rhea checked fire when the results of *Nevada*'s shooting could not be verified. Some of the air spot planes were shot down, and radio contact with SFCPs was sometimes lost. Smoke impeded the ship's spotters, and inland targets were not visible at all from the water. At other times the effects of shooting were obvious. At 1603 the main battery sent high-capacity rounds into an enemy artillery position, and all firing from that battery ceased. The same thing happened an hour later when shell splashes erupted near a destroyer. *Nevada* responded with ten rounds of 14-inch high-capacity shells, and the splashes stopped.

As the battle progressed, firing shifted from preassigned targets to those identified by SFCPs. One of the spotting parties included Lt. Richard Nash and PFC Vernon Stanley, dropped by transport planes near Sainte-Mère-Église four hours into the invasion. They later told B. J. McQuaid of the *Chicago Daily News*:

> We worked out our first problem a few hours after we got down. A column of German tanks was driving in toward Ste. Mere Eglise from the west. Our paratroopers, who had taken the town and were holding it, had no support from the rear because they did not join up until the following day with troopers coming from the beaches.
>
> The tanks would have cost us our grip on the town. But we had the good old *Nevada* on the other end of our line and in a matter of seconds we had given her the coordinates and she was on the target.[11]

Nevada opened up at 2129 with eighteen rounds of high-capacity 14-inch ordnance, and the ground spotter reported, "Mission successful cease firing." Seven minutes later *Nevada* sent another eighteen high-capacity 14-inch shells into a German troop concentration to the northwest of town. The SFCP radioed moments later, "Mission highly successful, check firing, new target."[12] Maj. Gen. Matthew Ridgway, commander of the 82nd Airborne Division, radioed his personal thanks and congratulations to *Nevada* for her good shooting. Good shooting indeed—the targets were twelve miles away from *Nevada*, well out of sight of the ship's spotters.

By midnight of the first day nearly 160,000 troops had landed on the Normandy beaches, about half of them American, the rest British and Canadian. *Nevada* had fired 69 rounds of armor-piercing 14-inch shells, 268 rounds of high-capacity 14-inch shells, and 2,693 rounds of 5-inch ordnance. She ended the day at anchor, waiting for what might come next.

She didn't have long to wait: at 0400 on June 7 *Texas* and *Augusta* broadcast a guided missile warning. The Germans were using radio-controlled bombs directed by planes orbiting at high altitude. *Nevada* and the surrounding ships immediately started jamming the control signals, and no ships were hit. At 0602 she was under

Some 40-millimeter gunners catch a few moments of rest, June 7, 1944. *National Archives Photo Collection, RG 80, no. 252455*

way toward her assigned bombardment position. Those who could, snatched a few hours of sleep—the lucky ones in bunks and the less fortunate wherever they could find an out-of-the-way corner. Others knew they should rest but were too keyed up to close their eyes.

As the troops moved inland, targeting ranges increased. At 0721 *Nevada* fired on a preassigned target at 21,070 yards and a half-hour later at another one at 18,820 yards. The second target was a hardened casemate containing long-range heavy guns. Air spotters reported that *Nevada* scored a direct hit, knocking out the guns. Other shells from the ship put less-well-defended artillery pieces out of action.

At 0951 gun crews took aim at the most distant target they would engage during the invasion—30,650 yards, or almost 17.5 miles, away. Using guidance from air spotters, the main turrets fired 26 rounds of high-capacity 14-inch shells and were credited with a direct hit on a gun in a hardened casemate and several other hits in the immediate area.

Not all targets were big artillery pieces or troop concentrations. Sometimes a lowly mortar would hold up advancing U.S. troops. Three minutes after *Nevada* opened fire on one such location, shore parties reported the mortar silenced and American troops advancing.

The same routine was repeated throughout the invasion. Air spotters or SFCPs called in a target, *Nevada* opened fire, and the target was reported destroyed. The years of practice were paying off—the only limitations to the destruction of any target within *Nevada*'s range were the accuracy of spotting and the rate of fire of her guns. Targets were "serviced" on a near-production-line basis. W. S. Wyatt, who later edited *Nevada*'s cruise book, called her gunnery at Normandy "the kind of performance which gunnery officers dream about."[13] By the end of June 7 she had fired nearly two-thirds of her initial inventory of main and secondary ammunition.

June 8 saw *Nevada* back in action against five separate artillery batteries, some protected by hardened casemates. Following an urgent call from an SFCP, she opened up on a large tank concentration of ninety tanks and twenty support vehicles. Turret crews began lobbing 14-inch high-capacity shells into the area and broke up the formation. Not content with scattering vehicles that could later attack U.S. troops, *Nevada* rapidly retargeted roads leading from the assembly point and destroyed still more tanks. "You really splattered them," air spot reported. Not a single tank or truck escaped *Nevada*'s accurate fire.

The Germans knew who was hitting them and tried to balance the immediate tactical needs of the ground battle with eliminating the source of the bombardment. At 0830 on June 7, shells splashed 1,500 yards off *Nevada*'s port quarter. The ship would have replied, from annoyance if not in self-defense, but the source of the attack could not be identified. Captain Rhea just ignored it—his plate was already full with a list of high-priority targets whose locations he *did* know.

In near desperation the defenders tried other tactics. On the morning of June 8 German E-boats attacked *Nevada*'s screening ships, and more radio-controlled bombs fell from the skies, one of which hit the destroyer USS *Meredith*. At 0800 the destroyer USS *Glennon* hit a mine; within minutes she was down by the stern and sinking. Fifty minutes later another mine blew the destroyer escort USS *Rich* in half.

Topside, men heard shell fragments from a German gun clatter across the deck—the enemy had the range, and it was only a matter of luck whether they would score a hit. But luck was with *Nevada*; German shells landed all around but none actually made contact with the ship. Ninety minutes later the men had the pleasure of hearing that naval gunfire had destroyed the gun that had fired on them.[14]

By the end of June 8, *Nevada*'s magazines—and those of many of the other bombarding ships—were nearly empty. During the three days of the bombardment she had fired her main batteries in 42 separate missions and her secondary battery in 12, expending 926 rounds of 14-inch and 3,491 rounds of 5-inch ammunition; only

44 armor-piercing 14-inch rounds and 25 high-capacity 14-inch rounds were left on board. At 1551 she departed for Plymouth for rearming, ending nearly eighty straight hours at General Quarters.[15] The men were exhausted and even the adrenalin rush of battle was wearing thin. A hot meal and a flat bunk were top priorities for everyone not on duty.

Nevada wasted no time in port. She moored at 0522, and by 0544 two ammunition lighters were secured to the port quarter and a fuel barge was alongside. Over the next 24 hours she would load 189 rounds of armor-piercing 14-inch, 742 rounds of high-capacity 14-inch, and 3,600 rounds of 5-inch ammunition. To feed her thirsty engines she took on 209,020 gallons of fuel.

Nevada started back to Utah Beach at 0814 on June 10 and dropped anchor there at 2049. The neighborhood had not improved in her absence. German E-boats were reported in the vicinity, and guided bombs were falling all around, one landing within a thousand yards of *Nevada*. Shells from a shore battery landed five hundred yards away. Gun crews opened fire on shore batteries at 0700 and hit other sites throughout the day. There were fewer targets to fire at as the troops advanced, and *Nevada* expended only forty-six 14-inch shells and fifty 5-inch rounds that day.

Two days later, air spotters identified a hardened gun emplacement that had been firing on minesweepers and other ships of the bombardment force. *Nevada*

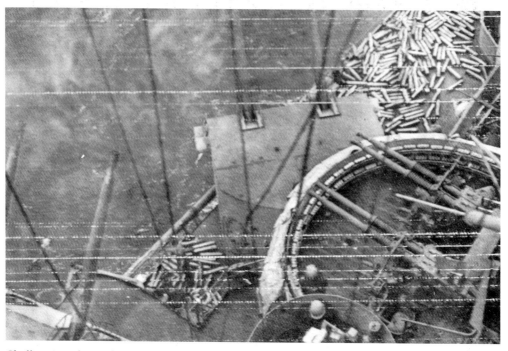

Shell casings litter the deck, June 9, 1944, the residue of intense firing on German positions. *National Archives Photo Collection, RG 80, no. 59415*

Captain Rhea and Executive Officer Yeager seem pleased with *Nevada's* contribution to the invasion of France, June 12, 1944. *National Archives Photo Collection, RG 80, no. 59418*

scored three direct hits and put the guns out of action. The surviving members of the German gun crew fled to a cement building, which follow-on shots promptly destroyed. Finally, the headquarters building of the installation was taken out. When *Nevada* was finished no activity remained at the site.

The invasion of Utah Beach was a resounding success, but nearby Omaha Beach was a different story. Shore defenses were piled layer upon layer at Omaha, and only the determined efforts of underwater demolition teams (UDTs) managed to clear a path for the landing craft. Even with the underwater obstructions removed, however, withering fire from German shore batteries decimated the approaching boats and machine guns swept the flat beaches. Only by the utmost heroism was a beachhead established and forward movement sustained.

At 1640 on June 13 *Nevada* moved the short distance from Utah to Omaha and anchored close to *Texas.* She fired her last salvos of this phase of the Normandy invasion at 0714 on June 15, scoring seven direct hits on a battery of 88-millimeter guns. Air spot wanted her to continue firing on other targets, but Captain Rhea

Passing ammunition off southern France, August 1944. *National Archives Photo Collection, RG 80, no. 256190*

received orders not to shoot unless it was an emergency. It was a case of too much of a good thing—the Navy was pleased that it was able to help make the invasion a success, but heavy use of the guns was beginning to take its toll on gun barrels.

The Germans had not given up on the bombardment force. Charles Moldenhauer recorded in his diary for June 16: "[Around midnight] the fireworks started again, with much, much shooting at German planes, which are bombing behind our front lines. Three German planes flew over the ship. Shrapnel from our beach AA guns landed all over the ship. We didn't fire at the planes. It seems like they just cruise over us, hoping to draw our gunfire and get our exact position. We didn't fire, although the temptation was great."[16]

On Saturday, June 18, Battleship Division Five departed for Plymouth and then Portsmouth, England. *Nevada*'s war diary reported simply: "All quiet on the Western Front." It was just as well she left; one of the worst June storms in decades hit the invasion area later that day—not the time to be operating in shallow waters.

Demands for more bombardment support continued to arrive at Allied naval headquarters, and on June 24 the bombardment group again set course for Normandy, only to be recalled sixteen minutes later when the operation was canceled. Ship commanders were hastily called to *Tuscaloosa* to be briefed on a higher-priority mission: the capture of the port of Cherbourg. Supplies had been pouring onto the invasion beaches, but the throughput was too low to support the number of men ashore. *Nevada*—along with *Texas*, *Arkansas*, four cruisers, and eleven destroyers—was under way early the following morning, arriving off Cherbourg before dawn on the twenty-fifth.[17]

The original intention was for *Nevada* to destroy several of the heaviest—and longest-range—gun batteries defending the port, enabling cruisers and destroyers to get in close enough to carry out their own bombardment assignments. This seemingly vital mission was canceled, however, for fear of hitting friendly ground forces. *Nevada* lay to for hours awaiting calls for fire support. Finally, at 1158, an SFCP radioed the ship to prepare to fire on eight 88-millimeter guns. But before *Nevada*'s gun director could push the button to fire, German shore batteries began their own bombardment. An enemy salvo landed a thousand yards ahead of *Nevada*, and more large-caliber shells fell among the cruisers, minesweepers, and other craft.

Within minutes a second salvo landed about a thousand yards off *Nevada*'s port bow—it seemed only a matter of time before the German guns near Querqueville would have the ship's bearing and range. That time came at 1218. A salvo straddled *Nevada*, the closest shell landing just one hundred yards from the starboard quarter and others splashing off the bow. Captain Rhea began to steer clear of his accompanying minesweepers and other escorts to give *Nevada* room to maneuver and avoid a direct hit by the next enemy salvo. Escorts laid down a thick smoke screen to obscure these course changes, but three more enemy shells straddled the ship at 1222. Men on deck suspected that there were other near misses—they could hear the shells screaming overhead—but smoke and mist (some of it from the splashes themselves) obscured their view. Poor visibility also hindered *Nevada* from getting free of the other ships—for a time she was navigating by radar alone, and well outside the approved swept channels. Rhea gambled that the risk of hitting a mine was less than that of being hit by shells.

While *Nevada* was being attacked she continued to dish out punishment of her own. A battery of eight 88-millimeter guns was quickly destroyed by a combination of 14-inch and 5-inch shells. At 1228 shore spotters reported that *Nevada*'s fire on a fortified site was "digging them out in nice big holes." Five minutes later the Germans ran up a white flag, but the Army was taking no chances. Previous German "surrenders" had been tricks to lure Americans out in the open, making them easy targets. *Nevada* kept firing.

Meanwhile, things were getting distinctly uncomfortable for the Cheer Up Ship. Salvo after salvo churned up the water around her. One shell landed just fifty yards astern and another even closer, perhaps twenty-five yards away. A third splashed so close aboard that "it is a miracle how it passed over without hitting ship. Burst threw shrapnel and water over turret No. 4."[18] Men on deck were drenched from the columns of water sent up by the impacts. Statistically, *Nevada should* have been hit, but she seemed to be leading a charmed life. Despite their best efforts, German gunners simply could not make contact.

A break came at 1327 when air spotters located the offending battery. Rhea informed the SFCPs that he would need to suspend shelling of artillery emplacements in order to target the batteries firing on *Nevada* and other support ships. He opened up with eighteen rounds of 14-inch high-capacity shells, with uncertain results. So many ships were firing at the German guns that air spotters could not distinguish which shells came from individual ships. A second plane radioed new targeting information and *Nevada* opened fire, but apparently she was firing at the wrong gun emplacement because salvos continued to straddle the ship. A few minutes later an air spotter saw the muzzle flashes of other guns he thought might be firing on the ships. Within seconds Captain Rhea had shells flying toward coordinates 26,650 yards away. Still the salvos kept coming. A large-caliber shell burst 25 feet off the port quarter, another less than 100 yards off the starboard bow. Shrapnel from the explosions rained on deck, but there was no damage or casualties.

Nevada was now barreling through the water at 20.4 knots—a full knot faster than the *maximum* speed achieved in prewar trials and just a tenth of a knot below her original 1916 specifications. The engine room crew knew that the ship was in the fight of her life and spared no effort to send the maximum amount of steam to both engines. They might not have been loading shells into guns or estimating ranges to targets, but they were just as engaged in the battle. They applied every little trick they knew, every little adjustment of valves and fuel to wring out another tenth of a knot.

Air spotters reported yet another suspect gun, and *Nevada* opened fire, achieving a hit on her third salvo. Good shooting, but again at the wrong target. At 1520 a pilot reported that he had *definitely* identified the gun that was firing at *Nevada*. Rhea sent six rounds of 14-inch high-capacity shells at the emplacement, which consisted of four 170-millimeter guns in casemates 26,300 yards away, and was preparing to fire again when he was ordered to retire. The area was simply too hot, and the trial-and-error approach to finding the right German guns wasn't working. *Nevada* formed up with *Tuscaloosa* and *Quincy* and made her way out of the fire support area. By 1945 they were back at Portland Harbor.

It seemed a miracle that, after being straddled twenty-seven times by enemy fire, *Nevada* "sustained no personnel casualties or materiel damage as a result of enemy fire during the bombardment of Cherbourg."[19] A new nickname, "Old

Imperishable," was coined to describe her incredible luck at evading enemy fire. During the Cherbourg operation she fired 112 rounds of 14-inch high-capacity and 958 rounds of 5-inch common shells, destroying several German gun emplacements in the process. It was certainly one of the more unusual—and one-sided—artillery duels of the war.

After fueling and provisioning at Portland on June 29, *Nevada* headed back to her anchorage at Belfast Lough. It was a very short stop. Before the men could get up a good game of baseball on the Fourth of July she was under way for the Mediterranean Sea in company with Task Group 120.6. Operation Anvil—the invasion of southern France—would land troops at three locations west of Cannes, and a fourth assault would be made inland by paratroops. The idea was to force the Germans to fight on two fronts in France in addition to their massive effort against the Soviets.

———

The Mediterranean was new territory for *Nevada*, which had spent most of her life in the great Atlantic and the Pacific Oceans. She arrived at Oran, Algeria, on July 10 and was reassigned to Task Force 86. She took on fuel and ammunition along with new paperwork governing operations in the Mediterranean.

A program of intense training at Taranto, Italy, preceded Anvil. These exercises were intended to weld together the multiple nationalities (U.S., British, French, and Polish) that would take part in the operation, integrating disparate methods of command. *Nevada* left Oran on Tuesday, July 18, and arrived in Taranto on Friday, mooring to buoys inside an antitorpedo net. The Germans were known to have torpedo boats in the area, and the Navy was taking no chances that a marauding E-boat might get a lucky shot at her. Crewmembers got a break from their nearly continuous action when swimming call was announced on the public-address system. A swim in the beautiful blue Mediterranean was just what they needed.

As an indication of the type of targets she would be addressing in her next assignment, *Nevada* traded 161 rounds of 14-inch high-capacity ammunition for the same number of armor-piercing rounds from *Texas*. The Germans were dug in along the coast, and *Nevada*'s job was to dig them out.

Battleship Unit 85.12.1 of Gun Fire Support Group 85.12, Task Force 85 of the Western Naval Task Force, departed Mar Grande, Taranto, on August 11 bound for France via Oran, Sardinia, and Corsica. Steaming in formation were *Texas*, *Philadelphia*, *Nevada*, and the French cruisers *Georges Leygues* and *Montcalm*. The column later rendezvoused with *Arkansas*, HMS *Ramillies*, and the French battleship *Lorraine*, creating a powerful bombardment force of five battleships and assorted cruisers and destroyers.

Nevada arrived at her assigned position at 0450 on August 15. Radio operators quickly made contact with their counterparts in the air who would direct fire, and at 0650 the ship commenced a prearranged bombardment pattern. Firing was stopped after only two salvos, however, because smoke was so thick on the ground that air spotters could not locate the fall of *Nevada*'s shells. No matter, the gun crews knew where they were shooting, and they quickly resumed laying down a pattern of devastating four- and five-gun salvos. H hour was 0800, but *Nevada* continued firing at inland targets until 0805, expending 106 rounds of 14-inch high-capacity ammunition. When the smoke and haze cleared, observers reported that her fire had been "most accurate and effective."[20] The invasion was so successful that there was little need for further bombardment support, and *Nevada* and *Lorraine* were ordered to Corsica to rearm and refuel for the next phase of the operation.

After a few days' rest at Propriano, Corsica, *Nevada*, *Texas*, and escorts were under way for Toulon. As they arrived on Saturday, August 19, they came face-to-face with a German submarine exiting Toulon Harbor, a threat that the cruiser *Augusta* promptly eliminated.

Nevada had been designed to fight in a line of battle against enemy battleships, but the advent of air power seemed to have dashed that possibility forever. At Toulon, however, she got to do the next best thing. At 1616 Captain Rhea opened fire on the French battleship *Strasbourg*, range 29,000 yards. The invading Germans had seized *Strasbourg*, which boasted eight 13-inch guns in two quadruple turrets, and converted her to a floating gun platform to defend Toulon Harbor. Within a few minutes, 14-inch salvos from *Nevada* were straddling *Strasbourg*, and at 1656 the spotter reported a direct hit. "Air Spot reported STRASBURG [sic] listing heavily and useless." It had taken 125 rounds of armor-piercing ammunition to achieve one hit, but that hit was enough. *Nevada* had sunk an enemy battleship.

The bombardment ships retired for the night but returned the next morning to fire on targets of opportunity. At 0901 *Nevada* opened up on an artillery emplacement that was firing on American troops. Eleven minutes later the emplacement was silent. Her next target was a set of six coast-defense guns spaced fifty feet apart on Cap Sicié. Seven direct hits destroyed all six guns.

Just as in Normandy, the German defenders wanted to get their own back on the bombarding ships. When large-caliber shells landed three hundred yards astern of *Nevada*, the ship's gun directors immediately asked her air spotter to identify the culprit. That was done, but the target (code name K20) was outside *Nevada*'s assigned firing area and she was forbidden to shoot. Instead, the bombardment force was ordered to turn away and retire at high speed. The crew found it frustrating to know where the fire was coming from but be unable to respond because of the dictates of naval bureaucracy.

The reprieve for the German gunners was short. August 21 dawned hazy with low clouds, but that did not stop the bombardment force from lining up on K20. *Lorraine* was to have the first crack at "Big Willie," a turret containing two naval guns that the Germans had taken from *Lorraine*'s sister ship *Provence*. *Nevada* was ordered to "stand by in case needed." *Lorraine* opened fire at 1727, but it was too late in the day to score a definitive kill. Again the ships retired to the relative safety of Corsica.

Nevada got the next opportunity to address Big Willie. As she arrived offshore on August 23, the British cruiser *Aurora* signaled, "Please give Big Willie a poke in the kisser for me. Have a grudge against him since yesterday." Rhea intended to do his best.

No sooner had *Nevada* trued up on her firing course than Big Willie opened up with a salvo that landed 500 yards to starboard. Rhea turned away to allow the escort destroyers to lay a smoke screen. Gun directors listened intently to the air spotter's report of the exact location of muzzle flashes. The Germans continued to fire. The next salvo landed 2,000 yards away, as did the following one. Finally it was *Nevada*'s turn. She commenced firing at 28,600 yards, using a combination of air spot and radar navigation. The men on deck knew that Big Willie was firing back because they could hear shell splashes even though the smoke screen blocked their view. It was, however, a one-sided exchange. Big Willie lobbed a few more shells *Nevada*'s way, but Captain Rhea sent 90 rounds of 14-inch armor-piercing ammunition in return and the German gun went silent.

The Germans were not done. A second hardened emplacement opened fire on the bombarding ships. *Nevada* replied at 28,100 yards with 85 rounds of 14-inch armor-piercing shells. Air spot reported 3 definite hits and 1 other possible hit. Nearly all of *Nevada*'s salvoes had landed within 100 yards of the target—almost perfect shooting at a range of nearly 16 miles. A short time later, after addressing another target of interest to ground forces, *Nevada* again fired on the heavy battery, but this time the results were less accurate. The near constant firing was taking its toll. "During this mission it became quite apparent that NEVADA's gun life was nearly exhausted as pattern was becoming erratic in both range and deflection." For any other ship this would have been reason to retire to a Navy yard to regun, but not *Nevada*. She remained on station and continued to pound shore installations, often landing large-caliber shells within fifty yards of the intended aim point. It was only at 1613 on August 23, when all of her armor-piercing ammunition had been exhausted, that she retired for the night.

The next day she was back, out of armor-piercing rounds but with a good supply of 14-inch high-capacity ammunition and plenty of shells for the 5-inch guns. Her assigned mission was counterbattery fire on the islands of If, Pomègues, and Ratonneau off the coast of Marseille. Special attention was to be given to guns that could interfere with minesweeping operations. *Nevada* opened fire at 0912 with fifty-five rounds of 14-inch high-capacity shells, but the air spotter reported that the pattern was large and erratic. Turret crews struggled to compensate for the worn-out guns. They were successful. After a number of salvos, air spot reported, "No guns firing on island and targets thus far fired upon damaged sufficiently to warrant no further firing."

Later in the day air spot identified another, particularly troublesome, target. The Germans had mounted a heavy gun in the side of a cliff that was immune from air and ground attack and a tough job for even the most accurate naval guns. *Nevada* was given the job and sent forty rounds of her remaining 14-inch high-capacity shells into the cliff face. One of them hit just below the gun emplacement and dropped the whole assembly into the sea. Of the four targets addressed that day, one appeared destroyed with one direct hit, one was partially destroyed, one was "well covered and out of action," and one was definitely destroyed. Good shooting for an old ship with worn-out guns.

Postwar interviews with German commanders revealed that the battleships' accuracy and rate of fire were a distinct and unpleasant surprise. Bombers could stay over their target area for only a short time, but battleships could linger for days or even weeks if required. The accuracy of naval gunfire was considerably better than air-delivered bombs, and compared with even the heaviest bombers, the magazines of battleships seemed inexhaustible.

During Operation Anvil, *Nevada* expended 361 rounds of 14-inch armor-piercing, 582 rounds of 14-inch high-capacity, and 22 rounds of 5-inch common ammunition. Her work in southern France done, she was ordered to retire to Oran to take on board her aircraft, left ashore for safekeeping during the bombardment mission.

During the stopover in Oran an incident occurred that would live long in the oral history of the ship. Recalling the exchange of ammunition between *Nevada* and *Texas* off Taranto, "some *Nevada* man referred to the USS *Texas*, in the presence of a *Texas* man, as an 'ammunition barge.'" A grudge match developed over that little remark that raged all the way from Oran to Honolulu by the way of Boston. A new chapter was written at each port the two ships happened to be in at the same time.[21]

Feuding or not, a few days later *Nevada* joined *Texas*, *Arkansas*, and other ships bound for Gibraltar and then Norfolk. Her mission in Europe had been a spectacular success, earning her the reputation of a sharpshooter who would brave the worst of enemy fire to support troops ashore.

On the way home, Executive Officer H. A. Yeager wrote a letter to all hands thanking them for their outstanding effort in European waters: "After our baptism of fire at Normandy we were a battle hardened organization and ready for anything. At Cherbourg we received the acid test. Good fortune was riding on the 'Old Maru' that Sunday afternoon and if there ever was a time we needed her it was then and there. I am proud of the way every man showed his true mettle and stood unflinchingly at his battle station. Men of the *Nevada*, in sincerest appreciation of your efforts I say to you, 'Well Done.'" [22]

A massive hurricane blocked *Nevada*'s route to Norfolk. Rather than sending her through the storm the Navy diverted her to New York, a happy turn of events for the lucky crewmembers granted liberty in the city. "New York greeted us with whistles and waterspouts!" wrote Charles Sehe on the back of a photo showing

Captain Grosskopf presiding at the distribution of silver coins from the state of Nevada. *National Archives Photo Collection, RG 80, no. 47377*

himself and three shipmates enjoying some cold beers in a tavern. *Nevada* finally tied up at the Norfolk Navy Yard on September 18 and offloaded ammunition and fuel prior to entering overhaul.

Top priority was given to replacing the worn-out barrels of the main battery. But this was no ordinary regunning. Men who had been on board during the attack at Pearl Harbor watched reverently as guns salvaged from *Arizona* were lowered into *Nevada*'s turret 1.[23] There was a special satisfaction in knowing that these barrels would soon exact their revenge on the Japanese.

Another important change made at Norfolk was that of commanding officer: on October 4 Capt. Homer "Pop" Grosskopf relieved Capt. Powell Rhea. Rhea had commanded *Nevada* in the Atlantic; Grosskopf would lead her in the Pacific. A native of Minneapolis and a former gunnery officer, Grosskopf was commissioned just three months after the ship he would now command. His goal was to make her the best shore-bombardment ship in the fleet. He would succeed brilliantly.

One of Grosskopf's first duties was rather unusual—handing out more than two thousand silver dollars awarded to the crew by E. P. Carville, governor of Nevada. The citizens of Nevada wanted to do something to recognize the contributions of the crew and thought nothing could be more suitable than some of the precious metal mined in the state.[24] The chest that had contained the coins, decorated with the Great Seal of the State of Nevada, was placed in the wardroom, and the silver dollars themselves were put to many good uses, including as belt buckles and ornaments on watch chains, necklaces, and plaques.[25]

As with all things in wartime, schedules were compressed during overhauls, and work that took months during peacetime was accomplished in a matter of weeks. The crew was granted twenty days' leave while the ship was at Norfolk, departing in two groups in early October. They fanned out across the country, using any and all means of transportation—buses, trains, and the venerable thumb out for rides. Some had not been home for many months, and the sight of a Navy uniform coming up the sidewalk brightened many a family's day.

Everyone was back on board by November 6, and *Nevada* was under way for two weeks to test her new guns. Then she headed to her old home port at San Pedro. As the ship transited the Panama Canal, Captain Grosskopf kept up a running commentary of its history over the ship's public-address system.[26]

Most of *Nevada*'s time at San Pedro was spent bringing the crew back to its usual high standards at ship handling, emergency procedures, and gunnery. There was still time, however, for some of the crew to enjoy eight days of liberty, especially important for those who had not been able to get across the country during the overhaul at Norfolk.

While in Long Beach an analog of the *Nevada-Texas* feud occurred, but this time the tables were turned. Someone from *Idaho* made a remark that *Nevada* crewmembers found offensive. A fight ensued, and men from the Old Maru swore that had the Shore Patrol not intervened, "that insult would have been forever wiped out."[27]

On December 28 *Nevada* set out with two destroyer escorts for Pearl Harbor, her first visit since her resurrection in 1942.

12

The Pacific
Iwo Jima

While *Nevada* was pounding German positions along the coast of France, the Pacific Fleet was hammering away at the defensive perimeter of Japan's Greater East Asia Co-Prosperity Sphere. American forces took Saipan in August 1944, enabling B-29 bombers to begin a ruthless bombardment of the Japanese home islands. Most of the heavy surface forces of the Imperial Japanese Navy were destroyed in the Battle of Leyte Gulf in October. That same month, Gen. Douglas MacArthur waded ashore at Leyte, keeping his promise to return to the Philippines. Slowly but inexorably the ring was tightening around Japan.

But Saipan and the Philippines were too far from Japan to serve as invasion bases—one more stepping-stone was needed. There were two options: the Bonin chain, which stretches seven hundred miles southward from Tokyo, and the Ryukyu Islands, which span the gap between Japan and Formosa. Each contained one or more islands suitable for major airfields, and the Ryukyus had harbors suitable for major naval bases. Admiral Nimitz decided to pursue both routes and ordered the taking of Iwo Jima in the Bonins and Okinawa in the Ryukyus. *Nevada* was to play a vital role in each of these endgame operations.

Pie-eating contests were popular for both spectators and participants. *Wyatt,* Cruise Book USS *Nevada*

Sailors laughing at a USO show. Any diversion from the rigors of battle was much appreciated. *Wyatt*, Cruise Book USS *Nevada*

Desperate circumstances led Japanese commanders to desperate measures, including suicide attacks by aircraft, submarines, motorboats, and even individual swimmers carrying demolition charges. Japanese aviators discovered that old wood-and-canvas planes were virtually invisible to American radar, so almost anything that could fly was a potential weapon, and pilots needed only the most rudimentary training to carry out suicide missions. Take off, fly to the target, and crash; no training in smooth landings was required. The hope was that these tactics might repeat the miracle years of 1274 and 1281, when *kamikaze* (divine winds) blew invading fleets away from Japan.

En route from San Pedro to Pearl Harbor in early 1945, every gun on *Nevada* engaged in some form of target practice—antiaircraft guns fired at sleeves towed by *Nevada*'s own planes, and automatic weapons fired at floating boxes released by accompanying destroyers, practice for destroying mines. Upon reaching Hawaiian waters, the main battery fired thirty rounds in day battle practice.

Nevada's guns were still warm when she entered Pearl Harbor and steamed down battleship row. Sailors who were on board during the attack of December 7—and some others—had tears in their eyes as tugs gently maneuvered the ship into Berth F-6, just ahead of the sunken *Arizona*. From the fantail men could see the tomb of more than one thousand Sailors and watch the swirling rainbow pattern on the water created by oil leaking from *Arizona*'s submerged fuel tanks.

Mogmog recreation area. Historian Samuel Eliot Morison wrote that one could hardly take a step without hitting a beer can. *Wyatt*, Cruise Book USS *Nevada*

Despite this somber return, *Nevada* was back in her element. Regarding target practice off Kahoolawe Lt. Edwin Swaney wrote in his diary, "Everything seemed to be a little easier now—the engines ran smoother, the guns were not as noisy, the weather improved, seas were calmer, and even the food tasted better. *Nevada* was ready for anything."[1] The Old Maru was headed to the home waters of Japan, and a thirst for revenge surged through the crew. *Nevada* departed Pearl Harbor at 0730 on January 10, en route to Ulithi in the Caroline Islands to join the Iwo Jima invasion fleet.

Additional gunnery practice, especially antiaircraft defense, followed her arrival at Ulithi on January 23. Officers and men saw these exercises less as drills than as dress rehearsals for what was to come. Ulithi was only 150 miles from the Japanese airbase on Yap, and kamikaze attacks were a constant threat. A sense of purpose in the face of danger pervaded ship and crew. Attendance at church services increased markedly as *Nevada* approached the war zone.

So too did the consumption of beer. The islet of Mogmog in the Ulithi Atoll was the rest-and-recuperation site for the forward areas, and each Sailor was allotted two cans of beer per day while on shore. Historian Samuel Eliot Morison noted that "one could hardly walk a step ashore without kicking an empty beer can."[2] Not everyone drank, and a brisk trade developed over chits that could be redeemed for extra cans, but it was still difficult for someone to collect enough chits to get drunk. Intership baseball, wrestling, and other games took men's minds off the war, if only for a few hours, and there were quiz shows and pie-eating contests for the less athletic. In another competition, prospective dance partners mobbed the small number of female nurses from hospital ships moored in the lagoon. Most men had to settle for dancing with a shipmate.

Rear Adm. B. J. Rodgers chose *Nevada* as his flagship for the Iwo Jima bombardment group and embarked on January 27. The original plan had been to invade Iwo Jima in late January, but delays in taking the Philippines pushed the date first to February 3 and then to February 19. Rear Admiral Rodgers' bombardment group, consisting of six battleships and a strong antisubmarine screen, left Ulithi for Iwo Jima on February 10. The crew had been informed of their mission several days earlier, and the junior officers' wardroom on *Nevada* was converted to the "Iwo Jima Room," its walls plastered with maps and aerial photos.

Only four and a half miles long by two and a half miles wide, Iwo Jima is shaped somewhat like a pork chop. Mount Suribachi dominates the southern end, and the northern end is marked by cliffs and highlands; in between are the only beaches suitable for amphibious landings. Since the start of the war the initial population of 1,000 farmers had been overwhelmed by the arrival of more than 20,000 Japanese soldiers. General Kuribayashi Tadamichi, the force commander,

Tablecloths, silverware, and stewards made the officers' mess a comfortable spot. *Wyatt*, Cruise Book USS *Nevada*

oversaw the creation of a network of concealed gun emplacements and tunnels designed to exact the highest price possible from invaders. He knew that he could not stop them on the beaches, so he positioned most of his troops and artillery inland, where they could make best use of the island's topography. Engineers cut tunnels deep into the slopes of Mount Suribachi and into the faces of the northern cliffs. Heavy guns were mounted on rails in these tunnels, enabling them to be fired and then quickly moved back under cover. The beaches and lowlands were saturated with a network of interlocking pillboxes and bunkers that projected only far enough aboveground to provide a narrow slit for guns. The Japanese high command hoped that the losses at Iwo Jima would be so great that the Americans would abandon plans to invade the home islands.

Rainsqualls greeted Task Force 54 on its arrival off Iwo Jima on February 16. Visibility was poor—barely a few thousand yards at times—but Rodgers was determined to get a good start on the planned three-day preinvasion bombardment. *Nevada* maneuvered to a dead stop at her firing position 12,000 yards offshore, and 7 minutes later her main battery fired the first shots of the campaign, the signal for other ships to commence firing. Turret crews were firing blind—the ship's spotters

Rear Adm. B. J. Rodgers in the foreground as the 14-inch guns prepare to fire at Iwo Jima, February 16, 1945. *National Archives Photo Collection, RG 80, no. 305280*

could not see through the rain and mist, and the ship's two spotter planes dared not fly under the three-hundred-foot overcast. But the combination of radar and the gun crews' knowledge of how their weapons performed gave them confidence that they were at least hitting close to the intended targets. Still, there was little point in wasting ammunition, so at 0719 Rear Admiral Rodgers ordered the ships to check fire.

By 0805 visibility had improved enough that the main battery could resume firing on a covered artillery position, but just ten minutes later clouds and mist again obscured the beaches, halting fire. At that point the schedule was thrown away, and the bombarding ships simply shot when they could see anything to shoot at.

When a spotter reported two "Betty" bombers taking off from an airfield in the center of the island, *Nevada* opened fire on the runway with her 5-inch battery, hoping to destroy other planes before they had the opportunity to get airborne. Again, the effects of fire were uncertain—Japanese antiaircraft fire drove off *Nevada's* spotter plane before it could assess damage.

After the guns had taken out several concealed artillery positions, Captain Grosskopf moved *Nevada* in to eight thousand yards off the beach in order to cover minesweeping operations. The diminutive minesweepers were clearing obstacles in the way of upcoming troop landings and destroying mines that the Japanese had floated out to sea. While keeping an eye on the minesweepers, *Nevada's* main battery opened up on a set of blockhouses. Air spot reported hits on and near the targets. The 5-inch battery hammered away at open artillery emplacements with airbursts. Aimers could not see the guns themselves, but the smoke from their firing betrayed their positions.

After a quick trip out to sea to recover her aircraft, *Nevada* returned to her assigned firing position. The weather had again turned bad, but Grosskopf figured it would soon clear, and when it did, he wanted to be ready. By 1402 the secondary battery was firing at antiaircraft machine guns that were giving the spotting planes trouble. Following a report of a Japanese plane taking off from Motoyama Airfield, some of guns shifted to targeting the runways.

The Japanese were not sitting on their hands. At 1058 several shells fell four hundred yards off *Nevada's* port bow, and at 1437 a small- or medium-caliber shell landed just fifteen yards off the starboard bow. Time to get going. Grosskopf rang up all ahead standard and then back two-thirds in order to stop at a new firing position. Spotters located the guns that were shooting at the ship, and the main battery fired back at them, but the spotters could not tell if they were destroyed. Either these or other Japanese guns continued to fire on *Nevada*, although their shells never got closer than five hundred yards. The Japanese even tried their luck with light automatic weapons, but these didn't have the range to reach the ship.

Communications division at work. Keeping track of messages to and from the fleet was a full-time job. *National Archives Photo Collection, RG 80, no. 355432*

At 1532 a juicier target was identified for the main battery—a Japanese ammunition dump. With the ship spotters' help, four direct hits were achieved, but no explosions resulted. Either the ammunition had been moved or *Nevada*'s 14-inch high-capacity shells could not penetrate the walls of the bunker.

To avoid being caught in constrained waters by night kamikaze attacks, the fleet retired seaward at 1730. Members of the crew not assigned to essential duties—which included antiaircraft defense—grabbed a few hours of restless sleep, one ear always cocked for kamikaze alarms.

Reveille sounded at 0400 the next morning, and the crew went to General Quarters at 0600. The two spotter planes were catapulted at 0630, and at 0650 the ship was back on station for bombardment. The main battery opened fire on four open gun emplacements, and air spot reported one direct hit and several near misses.

The next targets for the 14-inch guns—a pillbox and a blockhouse—proved more difficult. Six high-capacity rounds hit the targets with no apparent damage. Seven more rounds did no better. Grosskopf decided to close the range and moved *Nevada* to within six thousand yards of the beach. Light automatic weapons peppered the water two hundred yards off the bow but did no damage to the ship. After *Nevada* sent sixteen more rounds at the hardened targets, the spotter reported a satisfying explosion.

While the ships were blasting away at the island, underwater demolition teams (UDTs) were clearing obstacles that might impede the upcoming invasion. *Idaho*, *Tennessee*, and *Nevada* were ordered in to two thousand to three thousand yards to support them. It was one of many times during the Pacific campaign when Captain Grosskopf would order the bridge crew, "Take her in another thousand yards!" ensuring that every gun on the ship was within range of the beach.[3]

The move was deadly to the island's defenders. At point-blank range *Nevada*'s guns took apart even the hardest targets. A 5-inch gun scored a perfect hit on the door of a bunker, and a 14-inch shell severely damaged the entrance to a blockhouse. When spotters observed a group of Japanese soldiers moving about on the beach, the 40-millimeter quads opened up on them. Gun crews were at a fever pitch of readiness, apprehensive of suicide attacks and submarines but determined to play their part in avenging Pearl Harbor and bringing the war to a close. Once a target was identified, only seconds elapsed before ordnance was on its way. One of the bigger frustrations was that only those secondary guns on the shoreward side could fire; crews on the opposite side bided their time until the ship turned and it was their turn to contribute to the battle.

As the Landing Craft Infantry (LCIs) carrying the demolition teams moved closer to shore, the heavy ships were ordered to withdraw to avoid getting in their way. Captain Grosskopf decided that his position did not interfere with the operation and stayed put. The LCIs were coming under heavy fire, and Grosskopf wanted to give them as much support as he could. It was a sound decision because

Hits on Iwo Jima. *Nevada*'s pinpoint accuracy made her the "Sweetheart of the Marine Corps." *National Archives Photo Collection, RG 80, no. 303830*

Recovering a KUS2U spotter aircraft. Stopping the ship even briefly was dangerous. *National Archives Photo Collection, RG 80, no. 303871*

the Japanese mistook the UDTs for the main invasion force and responded furiously, in the process giving away the location of many of their guns.[4]

Nevada's 5-inch guns had a field day with the newly identified targets, scoring numerous hits and effectively suppressing enemy fire. When he ran out of identifiable targets Grosskopf shifted to drenching the beach with shells, creating a smoke screen for the divers clearing obstacles on the reef and inshore.

The main battery addressed tougher problems—pillboxes inland—before shifting to counterbattery fire. Alert spotters associated the flashes from four well-camouflaged guns on the crest of a cliff with shell splashes near the LCIs. *Nevada*'s main battery, along with guns from other ships, responded with a fusillade of heavy shells. In response the enemy guns diverted fire from the LCIs to the battleship that was causing so much trouble. *Nevada* was only 2,400 yards from the beach, and Japanese guns quickly got her range. One salvo landed just 200 yards off the starboard bow, followed quickly by another 150 yards off the starboard quarter.

Nevada was not the only target for the Japanese guns. While a battleship was well armored against medium-caliber fire, smaller ships were not. The destroyer USS *Leutze* was hit and her captain killed. Every one of the LCIs was hit, some of them many times. LCI-441, badly damaged, came alongside *Nevada* at 1216 to transfer five dead and twenty-two wounded, two of whom later died. Crewmembers from Old Imperishable gently pulled stretchers up over the side and carried them down to sick bay. Amid the ferocity of battle the men took tender care of the wounded, even though they were strangers from another ship. They were American Sailors in need, and that was enough.

After rendering what aid she could to the LCIs, *Nevada* moved out to 8,500 yards to recover her aircraft. The planes had been in continuous action since early morning, stopping only to refuel from USS *Williamson*. The pilots were exhausted from dodging enemy antiaircraft fire while trying to assess damage on old targets and identify new ones.

Nevada made her way south for night retirement, en route burying seven men from LCI-441. It was *Nevada*'s first burial at sea. There had been fatalities at Pearl Harbor, but those bodies had been removed for internment on shore. On this tropical evening, with the wind whipping across the open deck, crewmembers watched solemnly as one by one the seven bodies slid silently over the side to rest forever in the sea, stark reminders of the dangers ahead.

Sunday, February 18, was the last day of bombardment prior to the invasion. So far the results had fallen far short of what a similar bombardment had achieved at Normandy, when many shore batteries were silenced and huge holes were blown in the seawall. But no matter how many shells the bombarding ships sent flying toward Iwo Jima, new Japanese guns seemed to appear out of nowhere. Rear Admiral Rodgers ordered his ships to "close beach and get going."[5]

Nevada headed toward Fire Support Area 1, catapulted 2 planes for air spot, and took up station 7,000 yards offshore, using her engines to maintain position. A minute later the main battery opened fire on a blockhouse, using aircraft to spot the fall of shells. But 7,000 yards was too far away to dig out Japanese cannon, mortars, and machine guns, so Grosskopf moved in to only 2,500 yards. All the while the crew dealt with constant threats to the ship: Japanese batteries on the island, waves of kamikaze planes above, and submarines below.

Nevada with *Tennessee* and *Vicksburg* at Iwo Jima, February 19, 1945. *National Archives Photo Collection, RG 80, no. 309154*

Refueling destroyer USS *Hall* while under way. *Nevada*'s huge fuel tanks could easily replenish hungry destroyers. *National Archives Photo Collection, RG 80, no. 311875*

Even in occasional reduced visibility *Nevada*'s 14-inch guns managed to score multiple direct hits on hardened emplacements. One blew a large hole in the top of a structure, destroying whatever—and whoever—was inside. A blockhouse was completely destroyed at 0909, another damaged at 0928, and four direct hits were observed on a third shortly afterward. *Nevada*'s 5-inch guns shelled antiaircraft guns on the shore, and the 40-millimeter quads went after Japanese soldiers. Target after target was eliminated with almost assembly line efficiency.

Just before noon *Nevada*'s spotter planes landed near *Williamson* for refueling. The pilot of one plane rested only as long as it took to top off the fuel tank and get back in the air. The second plane was temporarily incapacitated by engine trouble.

At 1846 dusk was approaching—prime time for kamikazes—and *Nevada* joined up with *Idaho, Pensacola, Vicksburg,* and escorts to move to the relative safety of deep water. During the day she had expended 12 rounds of 14-inch armor-piercing shells, 223 rounds of 14-inch high-capacity shells, 338 rounds of 5-inch ammunition, and 4,442 40-millimeter rounds.

February 19, 1945, started as an ideal day for an amphibious invasion. The sky was clear and the sea was calm—optimum conditions for air and sea bombardment and for landing the invasion force. Approaching the tiny island was a mighty armada of eight hundred ships; *North Carolina* and *Washington* had joined the six older battleships already on the scene to deliver the most intense preinvasion bombardment of the war.

Nevada repeated her normal pattern—General Quarters at 0600, planes aloft at 0640, commence firing at about 0700. Her job on invasion day was to provide fire support for the landing of the Fifth Marine Division. Just as they had off the coast of France, gunners shot first at previously assigned targets and then shifted to those identified during the invasion. If air, ground, or sea spotters noted the flash of an enemy gun, it was immediately taken under fire. Standing as she was only two thousand yards off the beach, anything that could be seen from the ship could be destroyed, and plane and ground spotters made indirect fire just as deadly. So steady was the rate of fire that spotting became a challenge; all the smoke and dust being thrown into the air made it impossible to clearly see the fall of shells. The bombarding ships ceased firing just before the landing to give attacking aircraft a turn at hitting the island, then opened up again after the planes were clear.

As the Germans had at Normandy, the Japanese tried their best to silence their attackers. Shells splashed only three hundred yards off *Nevada*'s port beam—she was so close to the beach that even mortars fired on her.

The first wave of landing craft hit the beaches at 0900, the second wave nineteen minutes later. Troops and tanks struggled to advance in the soft volcanic sand and could find little or no protection from the withering Japanese fire. The Marines were having a tough time just getting across the beach, let alone much beyond it.

In the next few hours *Nevada*'s determined support of the invasion would make her "the Sweetheart of the Marine Corps."[6] At 0925 Grosskopf, watching the battle through binoculars, saw that the secondary battery was not destroying a concrete blockhouse threatening the Marines' advance. He ordered the 14-inch guns into action. High-capacity shells blew away the sand covering the target but failed to penetrate the thick concrete. Grosskopf ordered armor-piercing rounds loaded into the 14-inch guns, and subsequent salvos blew the blockhouse to pieces.

At 1020 an antiaircraft battery was reported to be "giving trouble."[7] Four minutes later *Nevada*'s secondary battery opened up with 221 rounds that resulted in a loud explosion and flames at the target site. A Japanese troop concentration was hit at about the same time. Once again the secondary gun crews worked with mechanical precision, grabbing heavy shells and powder charges from the hoists, loading them into the guns, and immediately turning around to grab the next ones. The

Nevada firing on invasion day at Iwo Jima. *National Archives Photo Collection, RG 80, no. 231961*

Landing craft at Iwo Jima, February 19, 1945. *Nevada's* gunners knew that they were paving the way for the invasion troops. *National Archives Photo Collection, RG 80*

men knew that they were within range of enemy guns, but there was no time to look up or even think of the danger.

Then there was the noise—not only for the gun crews themselves but for everyone else nearby. The blast from a 14-inch gun was almost incapacitating, but the 5-inch guns kept up a rhythm of thunderous firing that was equally wearing, one shot every few seconds. The 40-millimeter and 20-millimeter mounts added to a cacophony that made rational thought difficult and rest impossible. Some men put cotton in their ears for the limited protection it offered, but many had to wear headphones for communications, so that even that solace was denied. Prolonged exposure to gunfire permanently damaged the hearing of many crewmembers.

During long periods at action stations there was no opportunity to eat proper meals; men wolfed down sandwiches and coffee during breaks in the action. But food lost its flavor in an atmosphere reeking of cordite and the burning cork pads that were part of 5-inch ordnance.

By 1259 only seventy rounds of reduced-velocity secondary powder—used for short-range bombardment—were left on the ship. Grosskopf ceased fire with the secondary battery pending orders for high-priority targets or permission to

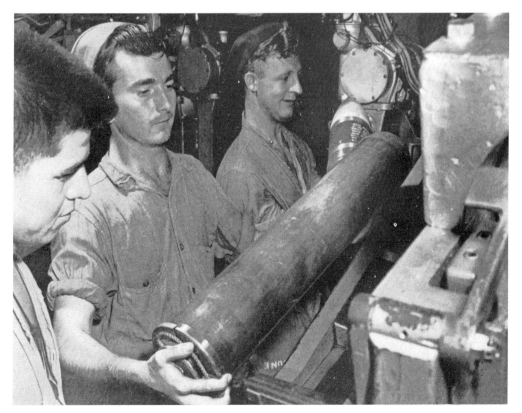

Loading a 5-inch gun was backbreaking work when hundreds of rounds were fired per day. *Wyatt*, Cruise Book USS *Nevada*

retire for rearming. But there was still plenty of main-battery ammunition, and the 14-inch guns blasted targets across the island. Even "soft" targets came to the attention of the big guns—at 1448 the guns eliminated a machine gun that was harassing advancing troops. Fourteen-inch shells were cheap compared to the life of a single Marine.

At around 1500, spotters identified an artillery piece firing from the mouth of a cave dug into a cliff face. *Nevada* fired two rounds of 14-inch high-capacity shells and scored a direct hit. The explosion blew out the side of the cliff and left the gun hanging down at a crazy angle, reminding observers of a loose tooth. Similar caves received the same treatment.

Captain Grosskopf was determined to use every gun on the ship to help the Marines onshore. Despite being straddled by small-caliber shells, he moved to within 2,000 yards of Mount Suribachi and used the 40-millimeter quads on enemy machine-gun emplacements. After 2,780 rounds the positions were neutralized.

By 1810 it was time to pick up the spotter planes and retire for the night. Under the protection of the bombarding fleet, landing craft had managed to land 30,000 troops on the beaches in a single day. But the tough fight they encountered on landing was a mere preface to the fierce battle to come; 40,000 more troops would reinforce them before the island was secured.[8]

February 20 was only marginally quieter for *Nevada*. She fired 35 rounds of 14-inch and 450 rounds of 5-inch shells at sites ranging from radar installations to ammunition dumps, with a good mixture of machine guns, mortars, and other targets thrown in for good measure. The Japanese tried firing back with large-caliber guns and managed to get within 100 yards of *Nevada*, but her famous luck held; none of the Japanese rounds scored.

At 1800 on February 21 lookouts spotted a "Zeke" kamikaze dead astern flying low over the water and heading straight for the ship. Lieutenant Swaney described what happened next:

A Japanese "Zeke" broke through the mist just above the water; and we detected it off our stern at some 8,000 yards. Air defense was sounded but we were already at battle stations where we spent most of our time during the Iwo campaign. Sky 4, the five-inch director aft of the mainmast, was assigned to take the Zeke under fire. Lt. Dave Thomas, the control officer, calmly placed the director on target, and the rangefinder operator began sending ranges to the computer. With a signal from the computer that they were on target, the two five-inch mounts on the port side were put into automatic. The computer took over until Dave gave a "commence firing" to the men in his mounts.

They shot thirty-eight rounds of five-inch projectiles in just twenty-one seconds, and the Japanese plane broke apart and fell flaming into the sea.[9]

It was the first plane *Nevada* had shot down since Pearl Harbor.

Now things got *really* intense. So many bogeys cluttered the radar screen that the forward air defense station was given permission to fire at any unidentified planes coming within 12,000 yards of the ship. There was simply no time to verify that there were no friendly planes in the mix. Antiaircraft gun crews and spotters often had to make split-second decisions. On February 22 the 40-millimeter batteries opened fire on a plane that was approaching the ship at low altitude, a classic kamikaze tactic. In this case, however, it was a friendly plane, and the gunners ceased firing after expending only twenty-three rounds.

While *Nevada* herself sustained no damage at Iwo Jima, her spotter planes were not as lucky. At 1320 on February 23, communications were lost with one of her two OS2U seaplanes just as lookouts reported a spotter plane shot down over the island. Marine regimental headquarters later radioed that the pilot, Lt. Hugh Shelden, had been killed in the crash; the observer, Capt. J. A. Friday, had survived but was seriously wounded.

February 23 also brought some good news. Sailors on *Nevada* and other ships cheered as they watched Marines raising the American flag atop Mount Suribachi; it was an emotional moment for everyone. Sailors had experienced the dangers of bombardment duty, but it paled next to the agony of the Marines who fought tooth and nail to secure every yard of the island. To see the flag raised meant that those sacrifices had not been in vain. The battle was not over, but the tide had clearly turned.

As the ground troops advanced, there were fewer targets for the bombarding ships. *Nevada* didn't fire a shot on Saturday and Sunday, February 24 and 25. The lull allowed medics time to transfer seventeen of the wounded men received from LCI-441 to the evacuation transport USS *Pinkney*. The danger had not, however, disappeared. At 2155 on the twenty-fifth an unidentified radar surface contact simply disappeared from the screen, suggesting that it was a submerging submarine.

Attacks on the ships were coming from land, sea, and air. On March 1 destroyers depth-charged submarines that were trying to line up shots on battleships. Bogeys were reported approaching the fleet, and the destroyer USS *Terry*, close inshore, reported hits by land artillery. *Nevada* laid on speed to go to her aid and transferred two medics to tend to the wounded, then moved back to her firing station two thousand yards from the beach. Grosskopf ordered the main battery to open up on some coast defense guns protected by a concrete casemate. Thirty rounds later the target

Underway transfer of ammunition. There was not always time to get to a port. *National Archives Photo Collection, RG 80, no. 353481*

was a shambles. A second casemate met a similar fate when eighteen 14-inch high-capacity rounds blew in the roof, destroying the guns inside. Nearly anything could become a target: at 1058 on March 2 two of *Nevada*'s secondary mounts opened fire on a grass shack. To no one's surprise, the target was demolished.

Ordnance was replenished on the fly. The ammunition ship USS *Lakewood Victory* came alongside on March 4 and transferred nearly three thousand rounds of 5-inch ammunition. Other vessels worked to keep the 14-inch guns supplied, delivering shells in lots of one hundred or more as time allowed. Each shell had to be hoisted to its storage location, often with a good bit of manhandling involved. It seemed that there wasn't a moment's rest for the gunners.

By March 7 the bombardment force had done about as much as it could in support of the Marines on Iwo Jima. The ships had fired more than 10,000 tons of ordnance at the tiny island, destroying everything that could be destroyed by naval gunfire. *Nevada* maneuvered to Fire Support Area 2 and transferred two thousand rounds of 5-inch ammunition to ships that could make good use of it. At 1800 Rear Admiral Rodgers ordered an easterly course, and Sailors on board *Nevada* and the other ships of the task force watched the peak of Mount Suribachi recede into the distance. Three days later the fleet pulled into Ulithi Atoll for replenishment, repairs, and, most important to the crew, some much-needed rest, recuperation, and beer.

Ulithi was brimming with supplies for the ships and troops advancing across the Pacific. By Monday, March 19, *Nevada* had taken on 700 rounds of 14-inch high-capacity shells, 400 rounds of 14-inch armor-piercing shells, more than 10,000 5-inch shells of various types, nearly 56,000 rounds of 40-millimeter shells, and more than 250,000 rounds of 20-millimeter shells. Small craft delivered fresh and frozen food, some of which had been flown in from the United States just days or even hours before. The Navy had mastered the art of logistics.

Nevada and other ships of the bombardment force did not find complete safety at Ulithi. While *Nevada* was anchored in the northern part of the atoll on March 11, lookouts watched in horror as a Japanese kamikaze crashed into the carrier USS *Randolph*. The plane had approached undetected and could well have steered for *Nevada* instead of *Randolph*. Safety was very much a relative thing.

Planners had estimated that Iwo Jima would be taken in a few days. The fierce defense mounted by General Kuribayashi turned those days into weeks. The island was not declared secure until March 16, almost a month after the first Marines landed, and mopping-up operations continued until March 26. "Uncommon valor was a common virtue," Admiral Nimitz said of the battle for Iwo Jima.

Stacked ammunition on deck was an inviting target for kamikazes. *National Archives Photo Collection, RG 80, no. 274515*

Ray Anthony's Navy Band. The musicians appear to be having as much fun as the audience. *Wyatt*, Cruise Book USS *Nevada*

A different kind of shot. *National Archives Photo Collection, RG 80, no. 312621*

Gen. Holland Smith termed February 19, the first day of the invasion, "the most savage and the most costly battle in the history of the Marine Corps." By the time it was over the Marines had lost 6,137 men. More than 20,000 Japanese died in the battle—nearly the entire defending force.[10]

The strategic value of Iwo Jima became clear in the coming months when more than 3,000 B-29 bombers made emergency landings on the island, saving up to 30,000 lives. B-29s no longer had to divert around Iwo Jima's antiaircraft defenses, and American fighters based there could accompany the bombers on their way to and from Japan, greatly reducing losses in the closing months of the war.

13

The Pacific
Okinawa

Two Jima provided an excellent fighter base and landing field for bombers, but it lacked a harbor and was too small to support the invasion of the Japanese home islands. On Wednesday, March 21, the fleet left Ulithi for its next objective: Okinawa. Only 340 miles from Japan, Okinawa was an ideal jumping-off point for the invasion of the home islands. L-day (landing day) was set for Easter Sunday, April 1.

A general apprehension permeated the fleet—if Iwo Jima was hard, what would Okinawa be like? The break at Ulithi had provided some rest—in between loading ammunition and supplies—but the attack on *Randolph* reinforced the knowledge that danger could appear at any time. Everyone understood that they were now entering the endgame and that the Japanese would fight tenaciously to defend

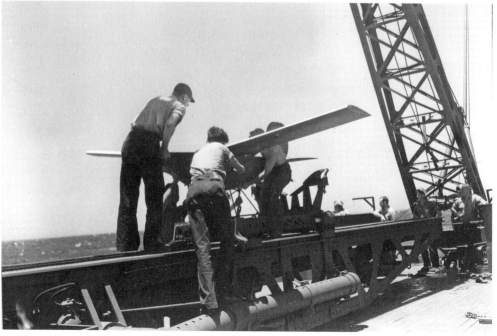

Preparing to launch a drone. These simple radio-controlled aircraft were useful for antiaircraft training. *National Archives Photo Collection, RG 80, no. 353504*

every inch of territory. As before when the ship was in a combat area, church services were well attended.

Nevada was assigned to Battleship Division Three in Task Group 54.2. The task group commander, Rear Adm. Morton Deyo, was familiar to *Nevada*'s men because he had commanded part of the bombardment forces at Normandy. Fifty-seven years old, with bushy black eyebrows, he was known as a tough officer who knew his job. He now commanded the most powerful fleet ever assembled for a Pacific invasion, including ten battleships (*Tennessee*, *Nevada*, *Idaho*, *New Mexico*, *Texas*, *New York*, *Arkansas*, *West Virginia*, *Colorado*, and *Maryland*), ten cruisers, thirty-two destroyers and destroyer escorts, and numerous other vessels.[1] No sooner were the ships out of Ulithi Atoll than they began a round of antiaircraft exercises involving drones and planes towing sleeves.

Submarines were a worry throughout the voyage to Okinawa. Destroyers reported one or more suspicious sonar contacts every day, forcing the bigger ships to make emergency turns to evade possible torpedo attacks. Not every contact turned out to be a submarine; a whale or large school of fish could produce a similar echo. Radar, sonar, and visual lookouts were constantly on edge, trying to find the right balance between crying wolf for false alarms and calling out a real threat in time to take evasive action. High winds and heavy seas worked in the fleet's favor by providing some protection from Japanese periscopes.

Okinawa appeared on the horizon on March 26. Like Iwo Jima, the island was slated to receive a carefully orchestrated preinvasion bombardment. On the approach to the island, Captain Grosskopf took command of Fire Support Unit Three, Section One, consisting of *Nevada*, *Tennessee*, and accompanying screening vessels.

The Old Maru had once again entered a bad neighborhood. Lookouts reported a submarine a mere 2,000 yards from the ship, and moments later a torpedo passed across the bow of the nearby cruiser USS *Wichita*. While the destroyer USS *Boyle* raced to drop depth charges on that sub, a second periscope was sighted only 1,500 yards away. Grosskopf changed course and rang up 17.5 knots, quickly opening the distance to 3,000 yards. Torpedoes were in the water, and every man on deck scanned the sea for their telltale wakes.

General Quarters was sounded at 1302, and the ship arrived on station at 1338. Seven minutes later the main battery opened fire on a pillbox, directed by shipboard spotters. But the bad weather complicated bombardment operations. The guns expended only twenty-four rounds in an hour of on-again, off-again shooting. When the mist cleared enough for planes to see the effect of fire, they reported near misses but no direct hits. Just before 1800 the bombardment group formed up for night retirement and the relative safety of the open sea.

The safety was, however, only *relative*. After downing a prewatch meal of peanut butter toast and coffee on March 27, Lt. (jg) O. A. Granum received word of a kamikaze attack. "I hit the PA system speaker, cut on the officers' circuit, and repeated twice the familiar 'Now all hands man your air defense stations, man your air defense stations.'" The bugler sounded Air Defense, and the General Alarm sounded. Antiaircraft guns opened up on a plane coming at *Nevada* from almost dead astern. Black puffs from 5-inch rounds filled the sky, seeming to block out the sun. The plane burst into flames and crashed. Then Granum saw a kamikaze "coming in high, through the cloud cover on the starboard bow . . . he headed for the bridge just as the five-inch opened fire. Every gun that could bear started shooting." An emergency turn was ordered to try to get the ship out of the way of the plummeting plane. Gunners exhibited nerves of steel as they calmly fired on the kamikaze, which appeared to be coming right at them. "Then through the smoke the 40's and 20's found him and started to cut him to pieces. When the scream of the plane became as loud as the chatter and rap of the guns, I assumed it was time to gather round and hold a little prayer meeting."[2]

Looking aft at the damage caused by the kamikaze attack. *National Archives Photo Collection, RG 80, no. 274487*

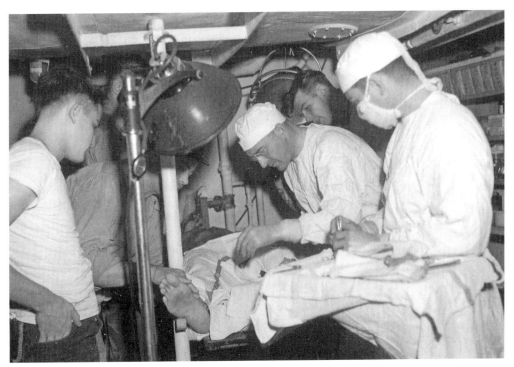

Surgeons amputating a leg, April 5, 1945. *National Archives Photo Collection, RG 80, no. 353496*

Careful transfer of wounded men after the kamikaze attack. *National Archives Photo Collection, RG 80, no. 353491*

The antiaircraft guns tore off a wing and set the plane afire, but its momentum carried the burning wreck forward. At 0622 it crashed on *Nevada*'s main deck aft, next to turret 3. Only the ship's emergency turn prevented the plane from hitting the bridge, and if only ten yards more had been gotten out of the turn, this plane too would have crashed into the sea.

Nine men were killed and forty-seven were severely wounded (two of whom would later succumb to their wounds) in the first successful attack on *Nevada* since Pearl Harbor. The injured men were gently lined up on deck, and medics quickly separated the most serious cases from more superficial wounds. Some of the casualties had been in turret 3, hit by shrapnel that had entered through openings in the faceplate. Among the dead were the 20-millimeter gun crews who kept firing until the second the plane collided with their mounts. Other gunners were badly burned but stubbornly held on to the magazines they were about to load into the guns.

The severity of some wounds demanded more medical skill than *Nevada* had on board, so an M.D. was transferred from USS *Levy* by boatswain's chair. The rough water created by both ships' bow waves made it a perilous crossing demanding close coordination between the helmsmen. During the transfer neither ship could use guns on the side facing the other, a dangerous situation given the proximity of kamikazes.

Collecting pieces of men who had been blown apart by the blast and putting them in new metal buckets was a horrible task that would haunt crewmembers for

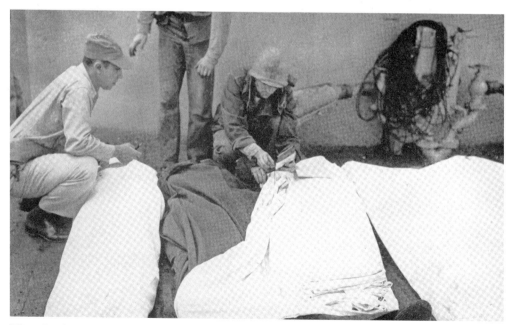

The chaplain oversees the fingerprinting of the dead following the kamikaze attack. *Wyatt, Cruise Book USS Nevada*

Flag from the kamikaze that crashed into *Nevada* on March 27, 1945. The body of the pilot is visible in the background. *National Archives Photo Collection, RG 80, no. 274500*

the rest of their lives. The stench of burnt flesh caused more than one man to gag. These fragments had moments before been shipmates and friends with lives and hopes, men who would never again see home. The ship's chaplains oversaw the fingerprinting of the dead to ensure their proper identification.[3]

The body of the Japanese pilot was found propped against the side of a hatch, missing both legs and most of his head. When intelligence officers searched his body for maps and documents they discovered that he had carefully washed and powdered his body prior to the one-way trip, and, curiously, he was wearing a parachute over his sheepskin jacket. Sailors standing over him thought, "We hate you! We hate you! [You] killed some of ours!" Lieutenant Swaney, who had been called from his station on a forward 5-inch mount to help in the recovery, shouted to a nearby photographer, "Take a picture of this s.o.b. and send it to Tokyo!"[4]

The ship itself sustained relatively light damage. Three 20-millimeter guns were demolished, and turret 3 was riddled with shrapnel from the explosion of the kamikaze's bomb, which also blew a hole in the deck, destroying the crew quarters beneath. One of *Nevada*'s two OS2U spotter planes was destroyed. But the fires were out within five minutes, and four 20-millimeter guns damaged in the attack were back in operation within half an hour. Within hours, while the wounded were still being treated, *Nevada*'s main and secondary batteries opened up on machine-gun positions on the island. The Japanese guns were firing on U.S. planes executing air strikes on the island, and air-delivered bombs didn't seem to be having any effect on them. The greater accuracy of naval gunfire did the trick.

Funeral services were held at 1615 for the ten enlisted men and one officer killed in the morning raid. All the men not on duty crowded the deck and superstructure

A somber affair: burial at sea, March 1945. *National Archives Photo Collection, RG 80, no. 305295*

to say farewell to their shipmates, each reflecting that but for fate, he might have been one of the still forms on the deck. Charles Moldenhauer of gun mount 7 fingered a small piece of metal from the kamikaze, a souvenir that he would take home and mount on a wooden plaque.[5] *Nevada's* flag flew at half-mast as each body, sewn into a canvas bag and covered with the American flag, was gently committed to the deep. Even the toughest men on board fought to hold back tears.

The remains of the Japanese pilot were afforded a similar honor. Just as the men had bowed their heads for their shipmates, they bowed them for the enemy warrior.[6] Chaplain Marion Stephenson summarized the feelings of many when he said, "While we as a nation can neither understand nor condone the strange philosophy of the Japanese kamikaze, we as soldiers and sailors can understand the devotion to duty and the unflinching disregard for personal consequences which the enemy has shown. And to God, who made us all and will judge us all, is left this man alongside our own."[7] One seaman wrote that Stephenson "taught us the relationship between fear, prayer, and a Christian attitude in battle."[8]

The wide range of targets *Nevada's* big guns addressed on Okinawa included machine-gun emplacements, antiaircraft guns, pillboxes, hardened gun casemates, an oil refinery, and planes taxiing on Kadena Airfield. But the Japanese appeared to have learned the lesson of Iwo Jima and were careful not to disclose the positions of carefully concealed guns prior to the actual invasion. General Ushijima Mitsuru knew that he could not prevent the landings, so he didn't even pretend to defend the beaches. Instead he concentrated the largest array of artillery of the Pacific war well inland, on the southern part of the island. As at Iwo Jima, the strategy was to inflict so many casualties that the Americans would either withdraw from Okinawa or at least reconsider invading the home islands.

The Japanese also modified their kamikaze tactics. U.S. Naval Intelligence estimated that two thousand to three thousand aircraft were being readied for the defense of this last stepping-stone to Japan. Rather than single planes attacking at random, the Japanese intended to overwhelm the invaders with coordinated raids of more than one hundred planes.

The Americans had adjusted their strategy as well—the fleet was now protected by a group of aircraft carriers capable of maintaining a strong combat air patrol throughout the day. These American fighters shot down more kamikazes during the battle than did ships' guns. But U.S. losses were still heavy. Destroyers serving as radar pickets suffered the most damage, but kamikazes also managed to penetrate the multiple layers of defense and hit ships within the protective circle.

Japanese ground forces were similarly more numerous than those at Iwo Jima. Planners had estimated that the Japanese had 77,000 troops dug in on Okinawa;

An LST loaded with spent casings from *Nevada*'s guns. *National Archives Photo Collection, RG 80, no. 315366*

they actually had more than 100,000. The Americans planned to attack with three Marine and four Army divisions, with one more division in reserve—172,000 combatant troops and 115,000 service troops.[9] During the amphibious phase of the operation 1,213 ships would be involved, including almost every type of vessel in the Navy.

When *Nevada* and *Tennessee* maneuvered to their firing positions on Wednesday morning, March 28, they encountered yet another threat. The Japanese were floating mines down the Bisha Gawa River, knowing that they would be swept out to sea and into the path of ships steaming up and down the coast. The cruiser USS *Birmingham* counted sixteen floating mines within four thousand yards of *Nevada*. But mines didn't interfere with Grosskopf's working over the island. The main battery opened up at 1059, firing on antiaircraft guns that were shooting at spotter planes. All of the Japanese guns were put out of action in short order.

The need to retire for the night made for an almost workaday schedule— Air Defense was set before dawn and then General Quarters. (Sometimes the ship stood down from General Quarters to allow the men to go to breakfast, with the understanding that the reprieve might be short.) By the end of the campaign the 2,500 men of *Nevada* could get to battle stations in twenty-five seconds. After the ships arrived offshore, they would bombard targets all day and then retire again for the night.

At 0400 on March 29 a bogey attempted a stern run on *Nevada*. The 5-inch guns opened fire but did not achieve a hit. Fortunately, the shell bursts alone were enough to scare away the pilot, who turned and was not seen again. Two hours later another plane crossed the stern from port to starboard under heavy fire from all calibers of antiaircraft guns. No one grumbled anymore about antiaircraft practice.

March 29, L-day (landing day) minus three, was the appointed time for the UDTs to clear obstacles near the beaches. *Nevada* moved in to seven thousand yards to give the teams maximum support. The secondary battery opened up on buildings, a railroad station, and trains on nearby tracks. After watching shells from *Nevada* hit a number of railroad cars, Captain Grosskopf was heard to comment that railroad fares on the island were likely to increase.[10]

In the afternoon the bombarding ships turned their attention to the landing beaches themselves. *Nevada* fired her main battery at the seawall, blowing holes in it to facilitate the invading troops' advance. By 1600 numerous fires raged the whole length of the beach. But the day ended with a dud—quite literally. Eleven of fifteen 5-inch shells *Nevada* fired turned out to be defective, hitting the target but not exploding. The next day *Nevada* made a quick stop at Kerama Retto, a small island near Okinawa that had been captured and turned into a forward supply base,

A comic moment at Okinawa amid the stress of combat. *National Archives Photo Collection, RG 80, no. 311738*

to replenish her depleted ammunition supplies and transfer the men wounded in the kamikaze attack to the hospital ship *Solace*.

Swarms of kamikazes attacked the fleet on the short trip back to Okinawa. Ships in the antiaircraft screen fired almost continuously until dawn. There was little sleep to be had. Constant alarms, antiaircraft fire, and the stress of knowing that kamikazes were in the neighborhood kept men awake, quietly talking to one another, waiting for what would come next.

Upon reaching her firing position 3,000 yards offshore on March 31, *Nevada* drenched the beaches with 14-inch, 5-inch, and 40-millimeter shells. Grosskopf moved in to 2,200 yards—point-blank range. A 14-inch shell made a direct hit on a "heavy installation" overlooking the beach that turned out to be an ancestral tomb. Cultural considerations had to take a backseat to the worry that the Japanese might use the ancient structures as ready-made gun emplacements. Three more tombs were hit in the afternoon.

Grosskopf then moved even closer to the beach—just 2,000 yards offshore. *Nevada*'s guns were firing as fast as their crews could load them, with new target coordinates coming in every few minutes. Almost anything that might be of value to the enemy was a legitimate target. By the end of the day *Nevada* had fired 153 rounds of 14-inch, 745 rounds of 5-inch, and 3,136 rounds of 40-millimeter shells.

L-day was exceptionally clear with only a slight haze over the island. Rear Admiral Deyo's bombardment ships took up their positions off the invasion beaches, carefully maneuvering to avoid the hundreds of landing craft assembling in multiple waves. *Nevada*'s job was to pulverize an area south of the landing beaches, preparing the way for the First Marine Division. By 0609 she was in position five thousand yards offshore; four minutes later her antiaircraft guns opened fire on an attacking Japanese plane. Shortly after 0700 Grosskopf blasted more holes in the seawall and attended to other targets inland. Many of the impacts were unobserved—the gun directors knew the location of the targets, but there were no air spotters to judge the effects of the fire.

The landings were unopposed, and men dared to hope that the bombardment had diminished the Japanese forces. By 1030 more than 50,000 soldiers and Marines were ashore. Kadena and Yontan airfields were captured so quickly that word did not get to Japanese pilots, one of whom arrived at Yontan just after the Marines took it. Hopping out of his plane, the pilot demanded fuel from the men standing around. When it dawned on him that they were U.S. Marines, he drew his pistol. The Marines promptly shot him.

To avoid hitting friendly forces, the bombarding ships ceased fire and waited for instructions from advancing SFCPs. Some targets, however, were obvious.

Nevada's 40-millimeter guns firing at Okinawa. Noise, smoke, and shell handling made this an exhausting endeavor. *National Archives Photo Collection, RG 80, no. 311740*

When observers on *Nevada* noticed a mortar firing on U.S. troops, a few shots from the 5-inch battery solved the problem.

The Japanese returned fire on the ship, landing shells within sixty to two hundred yards of the stern and the port bow. Kamikazes seemed to be everywhere, and smaller U.S. vessels were ordered to make smoke to hide the heavy ships and transports from enemy guns and planes.

There was no night retirement on L-day. The bombardment force remained in position to provide supporting fire to the troops. Without spotters there was little hope of accurate delivery at night; the intention was to harass the Japanese, disrupt their plans, and eliminate any possibility of rest. The sporadic fire was equally effective at preventing sleep on the ships offshore.

After a night of kamikaze attacks and a morning spent shelling targets on shore, *Nevada* returned to Kerama Retto to rearm and refuel. In addition to 350 rounds of 5-inch ammunition and 620,000 gallons of fuel, she took on 2 Japanese prisoners of war "for temporary safekeeping." Crewmembers crowded around to get a glimpse of them. "No more than eighteen or nineteen years of age, they appeared very humble," one observer recalled. "There certainly was no evidence of the Japanese arrogance about which we had heard so much."[11] *Nevada* had lobbed thousands of shells at German and Japanese troops, but this was the crew's first up-close view of what their enemy actually looked like. The prisoners were later transferred to USS *Mount McKinley*.

Kerama Retto was anything but a peaceful anchorage. Bogeys cluttered the radar screens all night. At 0207 on April 3 Central Command signaled that a major raid could be expected at 0230. Condition Zed (close all watertight doors) was set, and gun crews stood at the ready. All the while the men continued loading ammunition. The OS2U plane damaged in the kamikaze attack was hoisted over the side and towed to *Williamson* for repair.

Nevada was under way at 1633 and back on her firing station at 1813. Day merged into night as the battle raged on, the only difference being the slower rate of nighttime harassing fire. On April 5, for the first time in eight days, the print shop had time to get out the daily edition of the *Morning Mercury*, the ship's newssheet. The crew had a welcome break reading it over breakfast.

When *Nevada*'s 5-inch guns failed to take out some underground hangars at an airfield, the job was turned over to the main battery. The guns scored a direct hit, but ship spotters could not determine the level of damage.

Japanese guns responded with salvos of their own, shell splashes coming steadily closer to *Nevada* until they were only a hundred yards off the port beam. Grosskopf ordered radical maneuvers to throw off the aim of the enemy gunners,

Casualties from the shore battery hit. *National Archives Photo Collection, RG 80, no. 328465*

Damage in the crew compartment from shore battery hit. *Wyatt*, Cruise Book USS *Nevada*

but it was too late. The shells inched closer until, at 1742, one hit portside aft on the main deck. *Nevada*'s main battery opened up on the enemy gun, using direct fire with the ship's spotters zeroing in on muzzle flashes. It was now a gun duel. At 1746 a second shell hit *Nevada*'s starboard side, second deck. It penetrated five bulkheads and exploded in a portside compartment occupied by a damage control party of nineteen men. Two men were killed instantly and the other seventeen were wounded. Within minutes three more shells hit. The stern crane was damaged, the aft SG radar was put out of commission, and 20-millimeter mounts were destroyed. Several blister compartments were flooded. Concentrated fire by *Nevada*, other bombarding ships, and Army shore batteries eventually eliminated the Japanese gun.

Not all of the stories from *Nevada* recounted heroism under fire. During the shelling, an officer started to go down a ladder on the starboard side against the flow of men trying to climb to their battle stations. Frustrated, he drew his pistol and ordered them to make way. They did, but for the rest of the voyage the men gave him a wide berth; some even claimed that there was a "contract" on his life.[12]

Nevada continued to send harassing fire onto enemy installations even as the wounded were tended. The next morning, April 6, she left for Kerama Retto, where the bodies of the two men killed by Japanese shellfire were transferred to shore for burial.

Taking on ammunition at Kerama Retto was frustratingly slow. The cranes and booms were out of commission, so men had to shift the heavy shells by hand. With each 14-inch shell weighing in at nearly three quarters of a ton and the powder bags nearly a hundred pounds each, it was backbreaking work. And all the while the work crews were casting upward glances to check for kamikazes. Japanese planes were falling all around; had one hit *Nevada*, it would have been a disaster. The ammunition lighter finally cast off at 1550, and shortly afterward *Nevada* got under way, her decks still covered with 14-inch shells and powder cans waiting to be stowed below.

———

The Japanese were pulling out all the stops in their defense of Okinawa. Late on April 6 word came that the super-battleship *Yamato* was at sea and headed south. With her 18-inch guns she could outrange anything the U.S. Navy could send against her, and her superior speed gave her the ability to choose the time and place of a surface battle. *Yamato* was under orders to attack the American transports, beach herself on Okinawa, and add her guns and crew to the defense of the island. It was a suicide mission, but morale on the Japanese ship was high. Ensign Yoshida Mitsuru later wrote that the men "wish[ed] to repay at least a tiny fraction of our indebtedness to the emperor by fighting furiously, each man a match for thousands, and by annihilating the enemy down to his last warship and last vessel, thus restoring our momentum at one fell swoop."[13] It was bravado, but also an indication of the Japanese people's dedication and determination to fight to the last man.

A powerful force of battleships was dispatched to intercept *Yamato*, but U.S. aircraft got in the first—and final—punch. On April 7 a massive force of 280 planes pounced on *Yamato*, and within 2 hours the super-battleship rolled over and sank. Miraculously, Ensign Yoshida survived to write about the final moments of his ship.

A proud Rear Adm. B. J. Rodgers on his flagship, *Nevada*. *National Archives Photo Collection, RG 80, no. 309541*

Nevada, with her damaged number 3 turret, did not accompany the Battleship Force. She remained off Okinawa with elderly *New York*, forming a final line of defense if all else failed. But Old Imperishable was showing the strain of months of continuous combat operations. On Sunday, April 8, en route to Kerama Retto, the port engine had to be stopped due to dangerously low tolerances in the turbines. She limped into port on her starboard engine. After taking on ammunition and making temporary repairs to the ailing turbine she headed back to Okinawa. Rear Admiral Deyo wanted to send *Nevada* and *Maryland* (which had also received battle damage) back to the States for repairs but could not spare them just yet. On April 10 *Nevada*'s officer of the deck said to the crew, "Due to the fact that *Nevada* and *Maryland* will be leaving the area soon for repairs, let's get in there and give 'em hell." They did.[14]

April 12 was a long nightmare of kamikaze attacks—sixteen separate raids before dawn and sporadic activity after that. One plane passed so low over *Nevada* that a Sailor claimed he could have hit it with a rock.[15] The arrival of seven large bags of mail around midday brightened spirits, but just as the men were settling down to read their letters, Air Defense sounded. For the crews of the ships off Okinawa the war had become an endurance contest—which side could fight the longest with only hurried meals, interrupted sleep, and the constant threat of attack. Just a few months before, *Nevada* crewmembers had felt safe on the old battleship, feeling that she would somehow take care of them. Now, after the kamikaze hit and the shelling, they knew that they were in it together—ship and crew alike were vulnerable to the enemy.

Battleships and their screening cruisers and destroyers steamed in a tight formation to maximize antiaircraft protection. At 1451 *Nevada* joined other ships firing on a kamikaze headed straight toward *Tennessee*, Rear Admiral Deyo's flagship. Gunners watched in horror as the plane slammed into the battleship, narrowly missing the admiral on the bridge. Another attacker was shot down just astern of *Texas*. At times the antiaircraft fire was so intense that smoke from the guns hid the planes from view.

At 1834 *Nevada*, *Maryland*, *Colorado*, *Birmingham*, and *St. Louis* left the main formation for night firing assignments. The plan was to anchor in a fixed position and conduct overnight harassing fire, but an air attack put that plan to rest. While escorts made covering smoke, the big ships milled about, holding their fire until just before midnight.

On Friday, April 13 (April 12 in the Untied States), sad news arrived from home: President Franklin Delano Roosevelt had died at his retreat in Warm Springs, Georgia. It was a particularly heavy blow to Sailors, who for decades had seen Roosevelt as an advocate of the Navy, first as assistant secretary and later as president. He was, in the words of Samuel Eliot Morison, "their champion in peace, their leader in battle, and their guarantee of a better world after victory."[16]

Nevada's 14-inch guns open up on Okinawa, April 14, 1945. *National Archives Photo Collection, RG 80, no. 311757*

The Japanese, however, showed no respect for the death of the president. Bogeys began attacking at 0255 and kept coming through the night. *Nevada* continued shore bombardment during the attacks, breaking off at 0605 to head to Kerama Retto to offload ammunition. With turret 3 inoperative and other systems having problems, it was finally time to head east for repairs. After the transfer she headed back to Okinawa to fire illumination rounds urgently requested by an SFCP to help repel a Japanese banzai charge.

At 1935 Grosskopf was ordered to check fire—kamikazes were approaching and gun flashes would attract the planes like bees to honey—but the emergency ashore overrode these concerns, and permission was given to resume fire. Fortunately, none of the attackers made it close to the ships.

At 0819 on April 14, *Nevada*, in company with *Maryland*, *Pensacola*, fifteen transports, and seven escorts, left Okinawa and headed for home. At lunch, someone put up a leaflet dropped on the island by the Japanese citing massive losses in American carriers and battleships and promising the complete elimination of the fleet. Rather than demoralizing the men it angered them. Damage had been taken and lives lost, but the U.S. fleet remained strong and would certainly finish the job it had started.

A few hours out of Okinawa, crewmembers heard an odd noise aloft, but even the eagle-eyed lookouts couldn't see what was causing it. It was later identified as a "baka bomb"—a rocket-propelled kamikaze moving at a blistering 400–450 knots. Carried under a bomber until near its intended target, the baka was designed to be fast enough to evade American fighters and ships' antiaircraft fire; yet another thing to worry about.

After a brief stop at Guam to offload more ammunition, *Nevada* headed to Pearl Harbor. The original intention was to continue on to the West Coast, but a strike at mainland shipyards forced Grosskopf to make do with what the yard at Pearl Harbor could provide. It was a bitter disappointment for men looking forward to a stateside break long enough for them to get to see their families and sweethearts.

Morale was at a low point on the Cheer Up Ship. She and her men had been through months of hell—relentless pounding of Iwo Jima and Okinawa, kamikaze attacks, and shelling from Japanese shore batteries. Nerves were frayed, and even the determination to avenge comrades killed in battle could not completely overcome a general weariness of spirits. To address the problem, Executive Officer Yeager asked Lieutenant Swaney to organize "smokers" with boxing and wrestling matches. Crazy rules were invented for the matches, such as mounting gloves on long poles, but the men loved it. The competitions ended with a blueberry pie-eating contest, made messier and hence more amusing by having the contestants' hands tied behind them. The smokers were just what the doctor ordered—morale steadily recovered as *Nevada* approached Hawaii.

One of the most popular pastimes on board was listening to *Nevada*'s own musicians, who, when conditions permitted, played daytime concerts on the aft deck and accompaniment for nighttime movies. The ship's bands serenaded other ships when they came close, such as during refueling operations, and filled ceremonial roles when required. Musicians were among the most appreciated men on the ship, not only for their playing ability but because they also served as medics and stretcher bearers.

Trumping music and second only to movies for off-duty entertainment was card playing. Sailors could be found "from the foretop to the bilges" playing pinochle, bridge, poker, and gin rummy. While gambling for money was strictly forbidden and frequently punished, the lure of the game overcame fears of getting caught. Besides, there wasn't much else to do with cash while on board beyond buying candy and cigarettes at the ship's store or the occasional treat at the soda fountain.

Officers could retreat to the wardroom, which had many of the aspects of an exclusive gentlemen's club. Heavy leather sofas and comfortable chairs provided a place to relax while off duty, and stewards stood at the ready to refill coffee cups and

Keeping the paperwork straight. Office work in the supply department. *National Archives Photo Collection, RG 80, no. 312614*

Galley crew, April 1945. Feeding more than two thousand hungry men was a round-the-clock endeavor. *National Archives Photo Collection, RG 80, no. 312627*

provide snacks. Cards were popular among officers, too, including the occasional bet to make things more interesting. Officers might have welcomed the addition of a whiskey and soda at the end of a long day, but coffee, tea, and juice were the best they could do.

Immediately upon her arrival in Hawaiian waters *Nevada* began an intensive set of tactical exercises, including long-range battle practice with both main and secondary batteries and three types of antiaircraft drills. On April 30 she finally settled into Berth F-3 to await space in dry dock.

For the next month the crewmembers enjoyed liberty in Honolulu, sunning themselves on the beach at the Royal Hawaiian Hotel and visiting tourist spots such as the Dole Pineapple Factory. Good food was available, and there were movies at Navy recreation centers. The Red Cross hosted a picnic for eighty officers and men, and hula dancers provided amusement for the crew. Less wholesome diversions were available for a price in the seedier downtown areas. Training courses interrupted recreation for some men, but even these were a welcome break from combat.

No relaxation was evident on the ship. Yard workers labored round the clock to repair the damage caused by the kamikaze crash and the shelling off Okinawa. Pneumatic hammers resounded through the ship, and welding fumes and paint vapors ruined the tropical air and made food taste like chemicals. The engines needed attention after months of heavy use, and still more antiaircraft guns were installed.

Nevada was greeted at Pearl Harbor by Lt. Donald K. Ross, the former warrant officer machinist who was awarded the Medal of Honor for his bravery during the attack at Pearl Harbor. Ross had been commissioned an ensign in 1942. Given his pick of assignments across the Navy, he chose to return to *Nevada*. He came on board two hours after she tied up and stayed with her until her decommissioning. And then he returned one final time. After his death in 1992 his ashes were scattered over *Nevada*'s resting place in the Pacific.

Another return to the ship solved a years-old mystery. The Nevada state flag that adorned the wardroom went missing in the chaos following the attack on Pearl Harbor. Shipwright 1st Class Robert Gaynor found it in a refuse bin beside Dry Dock 2 and returned it to the ship at this, his first opportunity to come on board since the attack.[17]

Nevada finished in dry dock on May 12 and shifted to a nearby pier. Sea trials started June 1. At full power she reached 18.7 knots—almost 2 knots below what she had made during her dash away from German gunfire off Normandy, but

Officers display the *Nevada* state flag that was rescued from debris after the attack on Pearl Harbor. *National Archives Photo Collection, RG 80, no. 323798*

still respectable. The replacement guns installed in turret 3 and other new weapons were tested too, and everything worked well. On completion of sea trials she returned to Berth F-8 at Pearl Harbor, the same one she had occupied on December 7, 1941.

After a month in port the crew needed tuning up as much as the ship did. A week's work in Hawaiian training areas polished rusty skills, and on June 11 *Nevada* topped off her fuel tanks and headed west to the Marshall Islands escorted by the destroyers USS *Murray* and USS *Taylor*.

Sailor enjoying a good cigar. *National Archives Photo Collection, RG 80, no. 355433*

Jaluit Atoll was one of the Japanese bastions the drive toward Tokyo had bypassed, and *Nevada* was ordered to reduce whatever capability remained on the atoll. After first catapulting her two aircraft, she maneuvered to a firing position nine thousand yards offshore and opened fire with main and secondary batteries. If nothing else, it was good practice at shore bombardment. The Japanese responded with a few poorly aimed shots, but *Nevada*'s counterfire quickly took out the offending gun. Grosskopf moved in to four thousand yards to watch U.S. planes strafe and bomb the island before opening up again with the ship's guns.

After a brief stop at Saipan to take on aviation gasoline, *Nevada* headed back to Okinawa, rendezvousing there with *Tennessee, California, San Francisco*, and four destroyers on June 30. One night during the passage the bridge crew was startled by a radio message that began: "Hello Puppydog, come in Puppydog." Puppydog was *Nevada*'s call sign for the voyage and the accent was American, so the officer of the deck moved to respond. "Don't touch that radio!" bellowed Captain Grosskopf. After one more try the voice said quietly, "We know you are there." The caller was likely a Japanese submarine trying to get a better fix on the ship's position.[18]

A few days later *Nevada* came to the attention of another Japanese broadcaster—Tokyo Rose—who assured the crew that every ship in the task force, including theirs, would soon be sunk. *Nevada* was a favorite of Tokyo Rose, who regularly reported the ship sunk or heavily damaged. She seemed never to learn, because Old Imperishable kept popping up on her broadcasts.[19]

While *Nevada* was undergoing repairs at Pearl Harbor, the battle on and around Okinawa continued to rage. Organized resistance did not stop until June 22, by which time 32 U.S. Navy ships had been sunk and another 368 damaged. More than 4,900 Sailors were killed in the battle and almost the same number wounded in some of the most difficult months for the U.S. Navy in the entire war.

The land battle was the bloodiest of the Pacific war. More than 7,000 U.S. soldiers and Marines were killed and another 50,000 were wounded. Japanese losses were horrific: more than 100,000 killed. Mopping-up operations continued until September 7—five days after the Japanese signed surrender papers.[20]

Nevada arrived at Kerama Retto on July 2. The islands were much quieter than when she left, but still dangerous. Japanese submarines were about, and there was still the constant threat of kamikaze attack. She stayed in port only long enough to take on 264,476 gallons of fuel.

Nevada's new mission—her last of the shooting war—was to provide heavy cover for minesweeping operations in the shallow waters of the East China Sea. It was routine work, interrupted by the occasional bogey, and the crew kept busy with training and target practice. Home base was Buckner Bay, Okinawa, named to honor Lt. Gen. Simon Bolivar Buckner, who was killed in action on the island. The incessant heat made the boring work all the more unpleasant.

The crew recreation area at Buckner Bay was hardly a garden spot. Note the beer can in the foreground. *National Archives Photo Collection, RG 80, no. 339068*

Temperatures in fire rooms reached 150°F at times, testing the endurance of even the toughest men.

July 12 brought a bit of unwelcome excitement when lookouts spotted a mine dead ahead of the ship. The bridge crew reversed the engines and threw over the helm, but the momentum of 30,000 tons of steel drove *Nevada* forward. Lieutenant Swaney was in his stateroom in the forwardmost part of the ship when he noted an odd scraping sound on the hull and called the bridge to report it. His first thought on being told the cause of the noise was to request a change in accommodation, but the ship passed the mine without damage.[21]

The United States was committed to obtaining Japan's unconditional surrender—a ceasefire or armistice might only lead to a future confrontation. The challenge was to end it with minimum casualties on both sides. War Plan Rainbow Five envisioned a naval blockade to starve Japan into submission, but that could take two years or more.[22] The alternative was a land invasion with an even dearer price tag—the Army estimated that upward of 1 million American soldiers and Marines would be killed in the invasion of the home islands, an epic struggle that would likely continue into 1947.[23]

The successful test of the atomic bomb on July 16 gave President Harry S. Truman the game-changer he was looking for. On July 25 he authorized the 20th Army Air Force to begin preparations to drop two of the bombs on hitherto undamaged Japanese cities. But even the destruction of Hiroshima on August 6 and of Nagasaki three days later failed to shake the resolve of the Japanese military government; nor did the entry of the Soviet Union into the war against Japan on August 9. Admiral Onishi Takijiro declared, "If we are prepared to sacrifice 20,000,000 Japanese lives in a special attack, victory shall be ours!"[24] Emperor Hirohito saw things more clearly. He called a meeting of the government late in the evening of August 9 and insisted that peace be pursued immediately. The following day Tokyo informed the United States, Great Britain, the Soviet Union, and China that it would accept surrender

Captain Grosskopf on the bridge after the end of the war. *National Archives Photo Collection, RG 80, no. 332447*

Victory over Japan! *National Archives Photo Collection, RG 80, no. 332500*

terms with the proviso that the emperor be permitted to remain on the throne. The U.S. Navy ceased attacks at 0615 on August 15, and the war was effectively over. Surrender papers were signed on the captain's veranda of the battleship *Missouri*, anchored in Tokyo Bay, on September 2. The flag at her mast top was the same one that had flown over the Capitol on December 7, 1941.

On August 8—in between the dropping of the two atomic bombs—*Nevada* left Okinawa for Leyte Gulf in the Philippines and ten days of rest and recreation. Rest for some, anyway. An outbreak of dysentery made life unpleasant for many crewmembers. So severe was the danger of infection that guards were placed near toilets to ensure that men washed their hands after using them. Sulfa drugs were issued to everyone.

The crew knew that it was only a matter of time before the war was over, and talk turned to the role *Nevada* might play in the surrender. Some speculated that the ceremony would take place on *Nevada*, the only battleship to get under way at Pearl Harbor; at the very least she would be a proud member of the victory fleet when it steamed into Tokyo Bay. There was more than a little disappointment when the surrender was announced and *Nevada* was left at Leyte. "It was impossible for us aboard the *Nevada* to believe that our famous ship had simply

Men dancing to the ship's band on V-J Day. *National Archives Photo Collection, RG 80, no. 332588*

A comic scene as men celebrate V-J Day. *National Archives Photo Collection, RG 80, no. 332587*

been forgotten," Lieutenant Swaney later said.[25] The men consoled themselves by invoking politics as the reason—the honor of hosting the surrender was given to the battleship named after President Truman's home state: USS *Missouri*.

Morale did not improve when *Nevada* returned to Buckner Bay for antiaircraft practice and routine shipboard exercises. Men complained that there was no need for gunnery exercises, but something had to be done to keep them busy, and there was always the possibility that a rogue Japanese unit would reopen the war.

Another activity that kept the men busy was restoring *Nevada* to her full pre-war glory. As part of wartime camouflage nearly every surface of the ship had been painted a dull gray. Now that covering could be removed and the underlying brass fixtures and teakwood decks restored to like-new appearance. She was ready to go home, and the crew made sure that she looked her very best.

After riding out a typhoon on September 16, *Nevada* set course for Pearl Harbor, packed to the gunwales with soldiers and Marines headed home. She had steamed 137,027 miles and spent 389 days in combat areas since the war began and had fired more than 5,000 rounds of 14-inch and 18,000 rounds of 5-inch ammunition. Collectively, her crewmembers were awarded 2 Medals of Honor, 15 Navy Crosses, 2 Silver Stars, 10 Bronze Stars, approximately 240 Purple Hearts, 1 Air Medal, 3 Navy and Marine Corps Medals, and 2 letters of commendation from the Secretary of the Navy. More medals were to come as recommendations wound their way through the bureaucracy.

Not unexpectedly, disciplinary problems increased on the voyage east. Men were less inclined to jump in response to orders and more ready with a smart answer to a petty officer. They were going home, and derogatory comments in their record seemed unimportant. When *Nevada* arrived in Pearl Harbor on October 4, many men were detached from the ship and sent by transport to the mainland to be processed out of the Navy.

Nevada's departure from Pearl Harbor on October 9 was marked by great ceremony. A line of six battleships, from the oldest in the fleet (*Arkansas*) to one of the newest (*Iowa*), passed in review off the coast of Honolulu, crews manning the rails in dress white uniforms. It was a victory parade of tens of thousands of tons of steel manned by thousands of veteran fighters.

Anxious men watched the calendar and then the clock during the seemingly endless passage home. Finally, at 0222 on October 15, radar reported land ninety-six miles to the east. Familiar Santa Rosa and San Nicholas Islands came into sight, and *Nevada* once again rounded the San Pedro breakwater, anchoring in Berth 231. Men bid fond farewells to shipmates—some had been together for the duration—and streamed down ladders to boats that would take them to loved ones they hadn't seen in a year. It was a bittersweet day, a transition from a perilous past to an uncertain future, but overall one of rejoicing in the knowledge of a job well done.

Captain Grosskopf was one of those who left the ship, replaced by Capt. C. C. Adell. Grosskopf left with the satisfaction of knowing that he had achieved his goal of making *Nevada* one of the best fire support ships in the Navy.

———

On October 30 Captain Adell took his new charge out to sea and steered westward toward Pearl Harbor, this time as part of the Magic Carpet program to carry home soldiers and Marines. It was the first of three such round trips, one ending in Seattle and two in San Pedro. On each of them *Nevada* hosted more than one thousand returning servicemen, a tight fit made a bit easier by the smaller peacetime crew. On the second and third round trips she made remarkably short stops at Pearl Harbor, mooring in midmorning, taking on passengers for transport to the mainland, and getting under way the same afternoon. Magic Carpet was to be her last contribution to the war, but not her last to the Navy.

14

Operation Crossroads

The atomic bombing of Japan reignited a competition between the Army Air Force and the Navy that had been smoldering since Billy Mitchell's bombers sank the battleship *Ostfriesland* in 1921. Surely the atomic bomb—deliverable only by the Army's massive B-29 strategic bomber—would make slow-moving warships a thing of the past. With the expectation of rapidly declining defense budgets following the end of the war, each service frantically maneuvered to put itself in the best light.

The Army actually had more to fear from the bomb than the Navy did. Troop concentrations were "soft" targets, particularly susceptible to the heat, blast, and radiation effects of an atomic explosion. In contrast, armored warships were designed to withstand incredible punishment and keep on fighting. Plus, fleet deployments typically covered tens or hundreds of square miles—too big an area for even the new super-weapon.

The Navy decided to take the initiative and perform its own evaluation of the atomic bomb. Two days after Japan surrendered, Lewis Strauss, an aide to Secretary of the Navy James Forrestal, suggested that the Navy expose a collection of ships to one or more atomic explosions, essentially controlling the argument with the Army by defining the terms of the tests. "If such tests are not made," Strauss said, "there will be loose talk to the effect that the fleet is obsolete in the face of this new weapon and this will mitigate against appropriations to preserve a postwar Navy of the size now planned."[1]

Strauss was not alone in suggesting an atomic bomb test on ships. Representative Brian McMahon of Connecticut proposed that the bombs be used on surrendered Japanese warships, and Lt. Gen. Barney Giles, commander of the Army Strategic Air Forces, proposed the same idea to his boss, Gen. Henry H. "Hap" Arnold. The idea was gaining traction.

The Navy went further than some of its critics by suggesting that obsolete or unneeded U.S. ships be included in the tests. Admirals were less interested in showing the lethality of the weapon on foreign ships than they were in demonstrating that the U.S. Navy could survive and fight through an atomic attack.

Adm. Ernest King, commander in chief of the U.S. Fleet, called a press conference on October 27, 1945, to announce just such a test—one that would involve
between eighty and one hundred U.S. and foreign ships.

The Army shot back that it was the only branch that could deliver an atomic
bomb and proposed that Maj. Gen. Leslie Groves head up the exercise. Groves led
the wartime Manhattan Project to develop the bomb and was one of the foremost
authorities in uniform. The Joint Chiefs decided, as wise parents, that the tests
should be a *joint* Army-Navy operation involving personnel from both services.
Since most of the men and materiel would come from the Navy, the Chiefs gave
overall authority to Vice Adm. William H. P. Blandy, deputy chief of naval operations for special weapons. Maj. Gen. William Kepner of the Army Air Force would
serve as his deputy.

Blandy was at the apex of a distinguished career, a Naval Academy graduate
who had served as chief of the Bureau of Ordnance. Even more important, he was
an articulate and politically savvy officer who could be relied upon to steer the right
course in what came to be one of the most contentious events of modern times.

Among his many challenges Blandy needed a name for the operation. Figures
from Greek mythology were always popular, but he wanted something more under-
standable, something that would convey the true nature of the tests. After some
wrangling with the intelligence community, which was already using the name for
one of its own programs, he announced that the atomic bomb tests would be called
Operation Crossroads. "Sea power, airpower, and perhaps humanity itself—are at
the crossroads," he told a *New York Times* reporter.[2]

Progress was astonishingly fast, and with good reason. The postwar draw-
down of military forces meant that many talented officers were going back to
civilian life, and ships that might serve as targets were headed for the breakers.
The same thing was happening with scientists at Los Alamos Laboratory (where
the bomb was designed) who were returning to academic and research positions.
If the momentum of the Manhattan Project was to be maintained, Blandy had to
act quickly.

The idea of using only surrendered Japanese ships as the targets was quickly
amended for the simple reason that there were not enough of them, particularly
of the type that the Navy wanted to evaluate against the bomb. However, U.S. law
forbade the destruction of Navy ships unless they had officially been deemed of no
value. Blandy confirmed the confidence of the Joint Chiefs and the president when
he maneuvered Representative Carl Vinson into allowing the use of serviceable but
obsolete American ships in the target fleet.

With Vinson's go-ahead, Blandy chose four of the oldest U.S. battleships—
Arkansas, New York, Nevada, and *Pennsylvania*—along with the aircraft carrier

Saratoga to be part of a ninety-five-ship target fleet. But virtually every type of vessel in the Navy was included, from landing craft to floating dry docks.

The next question was *where* to conduct the tests. The lingering effects of radioactivity at Hiroshima and Nagasaki had surprised nuclear scientists, and Blandy wanted a remote location to avoid the possibility that fickle winds could carry a deadly debris cloud over a city. After considering locations in the Caribbean, Atlantic, and Pacific, he chose tiny Bikini Atoll in the Marshall Islands as the test site.

Bikini met all of Blandy's criteria. The atoll's lagoon provided a protected anchorage for the target ships, and the surrounding islands were big enough to accommodate the expected support teams and their equipment. Bikini was far from population centers yet close enough to a B-29 base for the delivery of the bombs. Only 162 people lived on the atoll, and after a determined sales pitch by the Navy, the governing council of the island agreed to relocate them.[3]

What had started as a simple "let's move some Japanese ships out to sea and drop an atom bomb on them" rapidly developed into the most complex scientific experiment in history, involving 242 ships, 156 aircraft, and 42,000 men. Two of the nation's nine atomic bombs were assigned to the operation, a closely held secret. Not even President Truman knew how many bombs were available at the time.

Given the secrecy surrounding everything associated with atomic weapons, the openness in planning for the experiments was astonishing. The United States was walking a tightrope, wanting to understand the military effects of the bomb while trying to convince other countries—particularly the Soviet Union—to abstain from developing their own weapons. Openness was the order of the day. Vice Admiral Blandy crisscrossed the country giving dozens of speeches about the tests. Numerous doomsday theories were being expounded in the press, including that the blasts would create mammoth tidal waves that would engulf the coast of California, that they would blow a hole in the Earth's crust allowing all of the water in the oceans to drain out, and that they might create a chain reaction in seawater that would destroy the entire planet. While not a scientist himself, Blandy's technical background at the Bureau of Ordnance helped him explain, in plain language, what the Navy intended and what was expected to happen.

Nevada completed her last Magic Carpet cruise in late 1945 and spent the beginning of 1946 in San Pedro. Captain Adell oversaw the offloading of men and equipment, a prelude to laying up or, worse, breaking up the ship. Thousands of rounds of 5-inch ammunition were transferred ashore along with tens of thousands of 40-millimeter and 20-millimeter shells. *Nevada* was stripped of much of her usable equipment. Men continued to leave the ship for processing out of the Navy. The days seemed numbered for the Cheer Up Ship.

Nevada arrives at Pearl Harbor en route to Bikini Atoll. *National Archives Photo Collection, RG 80, no. 363393*

But with February came a new lease on life, of a sort. Adell was informed that *Nevada* was to be a target ship in the recently announced atomic tests. It was a mixed blessing: a mission of global importance, but one that might well doom the grand old lady he commanded.

Adell was not alone in his thoughts for *Nevada*. Chief Steward Macaio J. Buenaflor, who enlisted in 1918, had spent seventeen of his twenty-seven years in the Navy on *Nevada*. "I am a bachelor," he sighed to an interviewer. "For many years she has been my only home. She is a good ship, a happy ship. I feel very bad." Lt. Cdr. Donald Ross spoke for other *Nevada* veterans when he said, "We hate to see her go . . . she's been a good home . . . she's had a helluva lot of hard going the past six years but she's done her duty in fine fashion."[4]

In early March Captain Adell shifted *Nevada* to Berth B-9 in Los Angeles' outer harbor to take on ammunition. The tests were to be conducted under realistic operating conditions, including having 1,500 tons of ordnance on board. Sailors who had just labored to *unload* the ship shook their heads at the wisdom of the Navy.

Ammunition was not the only thing taken on board. Four 5-inch gun mounts were removed to make way for heavy wooden crates marked "Top Secret." Inside were scientific instruments that would measure the temperature and pressure of the shock wave emanating from the blasts. *Nevada* was to become a floating laboratory. Indeed, she was to be ground zero for the first test—the aim point for the bomb. She was one of the strongest ships in the target fleet and hence an obvious choice to be closest to the explosion.

Portions of the beautiful teakwood deck were replaced with heavy steel plates that would help determine the effects of intense heat and blast on hardened steel.[5] The ship got a garish new paint job—bright orange—to make her more visible to a bomber flying at 30,000 feet. Sailors who thought the orange was merely a primer coat were dismayed to learn that their ship would retain the vivid color on her final voyage. Adding to her nicknames, *Nevada* would now be referred to as "Scarlet Fever."

The atomic tests would not require a full-crew complement, and by the first of May there were only twenty-one officers on board and a fraction of the normal peacetime crew. At 1130 she was under way for Pearl Harbor, her final voyage from beloved San Pedro. This time there were no gunnery drills, no zigzagging, and no escorts to hunt out submarines. The port condenser gave some trouble on May 6, prompting a temporary shutdown of the port engine, but the cruise was otherwise uneventful.

Arriving at Pearl Harbor on May 8, *Nevada* took on 257,000 gallons of fuel and moved to Berth F-8, her location during the attack of December 7, 1941. More ammunition was loaded along with Army equipment that would be involved in the tests. Every square inch of deck would contain some object to expose to the atom bomb. And it was not just Navy hardware: the Army wanted an opportunity to learn the effect of the new weapon on its own equipment.

Technicians examine equipment on *Nevada*'s deck that will be exposed to the first test. *National Archives Photo Collection, RG 80, no. 627424*

Nevada was under way again just before noon on May 20, steaming independently to Bikini Atoll. On May 28 she nosed up to Buoys 13 and 14 in Bikini Lagoon, joining an array of 95 target ships and another 147 support vessels containing scientists, members of the press, government representatives, and even delegations from foreign countries.

The density of ships in the target array was much greater than would be found in a fleet at sea, or even at anchor in port. The goal was to get as much scientific information as possible, not to simulate an actual combat configuration. Moored to nearby buoys were Admiral Yamamoto's former flagship *Nagato* and the light cruiser *Sakawa*. During modernization in 1928, Navy designers had fretted about *Nevada*'s ability to stand up in a running battle with the newer, more heavily gunned *Nagato*. Now both were to experience the next-generation weapon, one that some said would make surface fleets things of the past.

The American crews assigned to man the Japanese ships hated the duty, not so much because of their history but because of their design and condition. Both were filthy, bad-smelling ships that lacked proper sanitary facilities. Much more popular was the former German cruiser *Prinz Eugen*, the escort of the battleship *Bismarck* during her escape into the Atlantic in 1941. This outstanding example of naval architecture had also made her final voyage to Bikini.

Nevada was moored near old sailing mates. On either beam were the cruisers *Pensacola* and *Salt Lake City*, and just beyond lay *Arkansas*. *Pennsylvania*, the former fleet flagship, was on her starboard quarter. The Cheer Up Ship was among friends.

———

Operation Crossroads was originally intended to comprise three tests, code-named Able, Baker, and Charlie. Able would be an airburst in which the bomb would detonate at an altitude of about five hundred feet. At this height the nuclear fireball would not touch the surface, and residual radioactivity would be limited to that produced by the materials in the bomb itself.

The Baker test was designed to test the effects of an underwater explosion. A heavy steel vessel containing the bomb would be lowered to a depth of ninety feet—midway between the surface and the bottom of the lagoon. Rather than heat and pressure, the Baker explosion was expected to produce an intense underwater shock wave that would fatally damage the soft underbellies of the moored target ships.

Charlie was to be detonated in the open ocean thousands of feet below the surface. Its purpose was to test a theory that a deep underwater blast might create a shock wave strong enough and over an area wide enough to destroy an entire fleet in one go. Public reaction and political sensitivities ultimately led President Truman to cancel the Charlie test.

Each of the explosions would be produced by a "Fat Man" bomb similar to the one dropped on Nagasaki. A 10,000-pound assembly of high explosives and plutonium, Fat Man could be carried only on the largest bomber available, the B-29. It was an ungainly device with poor aerodynamic properties, a challenge for bombardiers to deliver with any accuracy. That challenge would be all too apparent in the Able test.

———

Life at Bikini Atoll was pleasant. Navy Seabees had constructed basketball courts, baseball diamonds, and other recreational facilities. Beautiful white sand beaches offered opportunities to sunbathe and swim. Everything seemed to be provided in luxurious quantity, including the beer served at two bars on the island. As the test date approached, quartermasters worried about what to do with the leftover beer. Could it remain on the island or should it be moved to the supply ships that would evacuate the atoll? Vice Admiral Blandy provided the answer: "There really isn't any problem; if I know anything about military men, there won't be any unconsumed beer."[6] There wasn't.

With Operation Crossroads estimated to cost upward of $100 million, nothing was left to chance. The Army held a competition for the best bomber crew to deliver the Able bomb. A target patch with dimensions close to those of *Nevada* was laid down on a nearby island, and bomber crews practiced dropping "pumpkins" that simulated an atomic bomb. (This was not the first time *Nevada*'s silhouette was used to train bomber pilots—the Japanese had used a similar system to train pilots for the attack on Pearl Harbor.) The winner was *Dave's Dream*, piloted by Maj. Woodrow P. Swancutt.

Everything about Operation Crossroads was supersized. The experiments were to be the most photographed events in history, consuming almost half of all the unexposed film in existence. Fast cameras capable of taking eight thousand images per second would capture the initial instant of the explosions while still, movie, and television cameras would record every aspect of the setup, explosions, and effects. The cameras were mounted on towers constructed on nearby islands and in aircraft that would circle outside the danger zone.

A huge array of scientific instruments covered every ship and island in the atoll. They ranged from complicated spectrometers that would record the optical light emanating from the atomic explosion to arrays of tin cans secured to the decks of ships. British physicist William Penney, who had assisted in the development of the bomb at Los Alamos, had proposed using cans as a cheap and effective way to measure blast pressure. The degree to which they were crushed would allow him to deduce the pressure at their location.

Support barges cluster around *Nevada* prior to the Able test. *National Archives Photo Collection, RG 80, no. 10972*

All personnel would be evacuated from the lagoon during the explosions, but *Nevada* took on a few special guests who were destined to remain on board: a collection of goats and rats that would help scientists evaluate the effects of the bomb on living creatures. All were given adequate food and water to see them through the experiments. These animals turned out to be among the most controversial aspects of Operation Crossroads, eliciting tens of thousands of protest letters from animal lovers around the world. One writer went so far as to say that since good goats were rarer than good congressmen, why not use congressmen in the tests?[7] A Sailor on *Nevada* made a personal proposal: "If those goats survive, I'm going to recommend our Chief Petty Officer for the next test."[8] Dogs were another matter entirely. So many letters expressed concern for canines that Blandy decided to forbid their use in the experiments.

A full dress rehearsal, code-named Queen Day, was scheduled for June 23, but weather forced a one-day delay. On board *Nevada*, crewmembers secured all machinery and equipment except for a diesel generator that would power a radar beacon and searchlight intended to guide the bomber to its target. Condition Zed was set.

The crew began evacuating the day before the dry run, moving to the support ship USS *George Clymer*. Captain Adell, along with a party of four officers and three enlisted men, stayed on board the night before the simulated drop to ensure that everything was ready. After turning on the radar beacon and searchlight, they left the ship at 0415. *Dave's Dream* delivered a simulated bomb right over *Nevada*, close enough for bomb fragments to land on her deck.

With the Able test scheduled for July 1, a week away, scientists and engineers scrambled over the ship to install and calibrate instruments. Photographers took hundreds of photos of the array of test objects cramming the deck, an assortment that included a Navy seaplane, an Army truck, canned goods, and samples of military uniforms. Twelve members of Congress came on board on June 29, some expecting that it would be the last time they would see *Nevada*. Secretary of the Navy James Forrestal came, as did Gen. Joseph W. Stilwell and representatives of the Joint Chiefs of Staff. Boats bringing VIPs jostled at the gangway with those evacuating the ship's crew.

Some men were reluctant to leave the ship that had become their home. Lieutenant Swaney told the story of a chief petty officer who had been on board since before the war. Prior to leaving, he knelt down on the quarterdeck and kissed his ship. "Good-bye, my friend," he said as he made his way toward the waiting boat.[9]

By the end of the day only Captain Adell, four officers, and four enlisted men remained on board. They repeated their routine of ensuring that the searchlight and radar beacon were operating before they left the ship at 0400.

July 1 dawned with a heavy cloud cover, but forecasters predicted that it would soon clear.[10] Congressmen, reporters, and Sailors lined the rails of the support fleet, now a safe ten to fifteen miles outside the lagoon. Others crowded around windows on aircraft. One airborne reporter looking down at the doomed target fleet thought, "Those proud old warriors, the *Nevada*, *Pennsylvania* and *Arkansas*, looked ominously lonely. You had a moment of pity for them."[11]

At fourteen seconds before 0900 the bombardier of *Dave's Dream* announced, "Bomb away! Bomb away! Bomb away and falling!" Forty-eight seconds passed as "Gilda," code name for the bomb, fell from its release point at 30,000 feet to the designated detonation point 520 feet above the lagoon's surface.

The atomic detonation was a disappointment to the thousands anticipating a tremendous blast that might knock them off their feet. There was a brilliant flash, but it was hardly visible through goggles mistakenly made too dark. The shock wave took almost a minute to arrive at the distant observation ships, by which time it was only a dull bump. With their goggles off, men watched the characteristic mushroom cloud of an atomic explosion, a boiling mass of red and purple that rose into the stratosphere. But they had expected more from a detonation that was the equivalent of 23,000 tons of TNT.

The Able test. *Nevada* was to be ground zero, but the bomber missed the mark. *National Archives Photo Collection, RG 80, no. 396226*

The event was a bigger disappointment than the observers realized. Despite numerous practice runs, the B-29 missed *Nevada* by 1,500–2,000 feet. Many cameras intended to record the details of the blast were pointed in the wrong direction, and numerous scientific instruments were destroyed in the explosion or went off-scale. Exhaustive analysis of the drop failed to reveal the reason for the error. Once again, *Nevada*'s charmed life was in evidence.

Radiation monitors entered the lagoon two hours after the drop to measure residual radioactivity in the water and on the target ships. All seemed within the predicted values, and Vice Admiral Blandy gave the go-ahead for reentry of the lagoon at 1430.

While the blast might have been underwhelming from a distance, the carnage in the target fleet was impressive. One press representative wrote, "The fleet looked as though it had returned from a quick trip to hell."[12] The attack transport *Gilliam*, directly under the explosion, sank immediately, as did two destroyers, another transport, and *Sakawa*. Submarine superstructures were stripped off and their periscopes bent at crazy angles. *Nagato*, within a thousand yards of the detonation, suffered less damage than any other ship that close, a tribute to her armor.

Captain Adell and a boarding party were left cooling their heels on *George Clymer* while radiation monitors determined which ships were safe to reboard. Finally, at 1335 on July 3—two days after the explosion—an inspection party left for the ship. A second party came on board soon afterward to perform a detailed survey belowdecks, and the gunnery officer led a team to inspect the magazines. At the end of the day the ship's navigator and a seventeen-man security detail came on board to spend the night. By this time most of the ship had been cleared of concern for radioactivity.

The inspection teams found *Nevada* a shambles, at least topside. A two-and-a-half-ton Army truck had been crushed like a children's toy, and a Navy seaplane mangled beyond recognition. Cases of canned goods were tossed around the deck; some of the cans had exploded from the intense heat of the explosion. Surprisingly, the teak deck held up very well with only minor scorching in a few places. The magazines were in acceptable condition. (Temperature was more of a worry in the hot tropical climate than was the effect of the blast on these well-protected areas.)

Indeed, the ship suffered only "moderate damage" according to the Navy's official accounts of the test. Captain Adell wrote in his report, "The overall condition of the ship is good."[13] The sides of the superstructure facing the blast were bent inward slightly, and a part of the aft portion of the deck was split open, exposing the compartments below. Radar and radio antennae were gone—blown overboard. Perhaps most significant, the outer casing of the smokestack was demolished and the inner smoke pipe partially crimped at the top.

Nevada's all-or-nothing armor scheme had proved its worth against the biggest bomb in the world—below the armored second deck there was little damage beyond a thick coating of dust blown through the ventilators. The draft of the ship was the same before and after the explosion; flooding occurred in only a few isolated compartments. The greatest damage was in the engine rooms, where a pressure pulse down the boiler uptakes had ruptured all six boiler casings.

In actual combat, the combined effects of the explosion would have rendered *Nevada* dead in the water with heavy damage topside and all boilers disabled. Everyone in the engine rooms would likely have been killed. Engineers figured it would take on the order of forty-eight hours to get the boilers back on line, after which time the ship might slowly steam to a Navy yard for repair. Communications would have been limited to short-range radio, signal lights, and flags until makeshift antennae could replace those on the downed masts.

The worst damage would have been the profound physical and psychological effects on the crew. Everyone on the upper decks and in the armored gun turrets would have received a fatal dose of radiation. Even those deep in the ship would have absorbed far more than the maximum safe dose. *Nevada* would still be afloat, but she would be of little value as a fighting vessel.

———

The days following Able took on a carnival-like atmosphere. The bar at the officers' club on Bikini Island opened the day after the test, and Vice Admiral Blandy took Secretary of the Navy Forrestal ashore for a drink. *Nevada* became a tourist attraction. The undersecretary of war for air came on board on July 4 along with attendant generals and admirals, a bevy of photographers, and a congressional delegation. The Navy's public relations officer brought ninety-four members of the press, and President Truman's personal evaluation board members saw for themselves how a battleship, albeit an old one, fared in an atomic attack.

Meanwhile, the ship's force worked to get two boilers back on line, one of which could supply auxiliary power to the ship. The starboard engine was spun up on July 9, and 81,606 gallons of fuel were loaded on July 10. While she was damaged, *Nevada* could have moved under her own power and, with operating guns, put up a fight. Minor problems continued to arise. The ship developed a 3-degree list, the result of a flooded compartment. But divers found little damage below the waterline when they went over the side on July 13.

———

July 19 was designated "William Day," the final dry run for Baker. Men began evacuating the ship two days before the test, leaving only the technical people on board to make final adjustments to their instruments. By 1530 on July 19 the dry runs were finished and the captain and part of the crew returned to the ship. There was still a week to go before the actual event.

Since water transmits a pressure pulse better than air, a detonation ninety feet underwater was expected to produce a much stronger shock wave than Able had created. While the crew had anticipated a quick return to the ship after Able, they took all of their personal belongings with them prior to Baker on the expectation that they might never return. By Thursday afternoon, July 24, only a few men were left on board to ensure that *Nevada* was properly sealed and that everyone was evacuated. Captain Adell left at 1432 to join his crew on *George Clymer*.

Baker was detonated at 0835 on July 25. If Able had been rather a disappointment, Baker was nothing less than spectacular. The atomic explosion instantly vaporized thousands of tons of water, creating an enormous bubble of superheated steam. The bubble broke the surface as a brilliant white dome illuminated from within by the still-hot products of the explosion. Seconds later, the water displaced by the huge gas bubble roared back into the area of the detonation. When it reached the center it sent up a two-thousand-foot-diameter column of water rising at a rate

The Baker test covered the ship with radioactive debris. *National Archives Photo Collection, RG 80, no. 396228*

of one mile per second. Events happened so fast that observers could only watch in awestruck silence—there wasn't time to utter a word before the next astonishing phenomenon occurred.

The fast-rising column contained an estimated 2 million tons of water along with rock and coral from the bottom of the lagoon. As the column fell back upon itself it sent a rolling cloud—the base surge—outward along the surface of the lagoon. Observers watched in horror as ship after ship was engulfed, mere toys in the path of the three-hundred-foot-tall juggernaut.

While all of this was happening above the surface, the underwater shock wave from the explosion was speeding toward the unprotected steel bottoms of the target ships. Closest were *Arkansas* and *Saratoga*, each about five hundred feet from the blast. There is an apocryphal story that the explosion upended *Arkansas*, which appeared to be visible in photos as a black smudge against the rising water column. It is more likely that the smudge was soot and dirt blown out of her engine rooms. Another story had *Nevada* tossed up into the air with light showing beneath her bottom. This too was likely an optical illusion resulting from the advancing shock wave and other features of the blast. The amount and type of damage observed on *Nevada* were not consistent with such violent acceleration.

The base surge—the misty remains of the water column collapsing back into the lagoon—turned out to be the kiss of death to the target fleet.[14] The radioactivity produced by the atomic explosion was concentrated in this rolling cloud, including the fission products from the nuclear chain reaction as well as radioactive particles in the seawater and lagoon bottom activated by neutrons from the bomb. More than 1 million cubic yards of coral and rock were blasted from the bottom of the lagoon. Chunks of various sizes fell on the decks of the target vessels, presenting tempting but deadly souvenirs for recovery parties. Ships were literally showered with a radioactive soup that penetrated every crack, crevice, and joint and thoroughly soaked into every rope, piece of wood, and canvas covering.

The landing ship below which the bomb had been suspended was completely obliterated. *Arkansas* went down moments after the blast as she flooded from the massive damage the underwater shock wave did to her hull. *Nagato* followed four hours later, and *Saratoga* three hours after that. "Sara" had been built on the hull of a battle cruiser that was canceled due to the Washington Naval Treaty. She was exceptionally strong, with good watertight compartmentalization, but she could not withstand being only five hundred feet from a twenty-three-kiloton nuclear explosion. Immediately after being hit by the shock wave she began to settle by the stern. When her end came, loudspeakers on the observation ships called men to the rails to salute a gallant lady who had hosted more than 100,000 Sailors during her nineteen-year career.

Radio-controlled boats containing Geiger counters were sent into the lagoon almost as soon as the waves died down. They reported a nightmarish tale—radiation levels were 80,000 times the maximum level permitted for humans. Despite this warning, manned patrol boats followed just forty-one minutes after the detonation, and technicians were soon boarding the target ships to recover instruments and make a quick assessment of damage. By day's end, the support fleet containing some 15,000 men was back in the lagoon, soaking up radiation from the water through shipboard water distillation plants and condensers.

Unpleasant surprise followed unpleasant surprise. No one had anticipated the degree to which the base surge would make the target ships radioactive. Fireboats tried to hose the ships down, but it was like washing a car with muddy water—the radioactivity in the lagoon water merely made the radiation worse. Numerous other methods were employed, including spraying with various chemical solutions and sand blasting. Sailors were eventually sent on board to try the time-honored method of scrubbing with brushes, but the only result was exposure of the men to radioactive debris.

Medical doctors appreciated the danger of nuclear radiation to humans and animals. Early-twentieth-century experiments with radium and x-rays led to a host of cancers and early deaths among researchers. The destruction at Hiroshima and Nagasaki took that danger to a completely new level, clearly demonstrating the lingering effects of radioactivity from a nuclear explosion. Nevertheless, the U.S. government officially downplayed the danger at Bikini, insisting that every safety measure had been taken and no one was in danger. General Groves, who led the Manhattan Project, went so far as to say that death by radiation poisoning was "a very pleasant way to die."[15] He must have known better—deaths caused by radiation accidents at Los Alamos were slow and excruciatingly painful.

Some officers could not fathom this new and silent danger. *New York*'s CO complained that the decks of his ship were clean enough for an admiral to eat off of—where was all this radioactivity that the scientists kept reporting?[16] But over time the full impact of the problem became apparent; the ships were contaminated beyond any hope of cleansing. On August 8 Vice Admiral Blandy requested permission from CNO Chester Nimitz to decommission thirty-nine of the target vessels, including *Nevada*. German shore batteries, Japanese bombs and torpedoes, and two twenty-three-kiloton nuclear blasts had failed to sink her. Her useful life was ended by an invisible poison, the product of a brave new world in which she seemed to have no place. Nimitz approved the request.

On August 9 Captain Adell, along with five officers, led the first of several teams on board that performed quick and cursory inspections. As expected, they found that Baker did more damage to the structure of the ship than had Able. The aft generator room and high-pressure compressor compartments were filled with water, and the steering room was partially flooded. The shock wave had opened seams in the hull plating, and water was trickling slowly into various compartments, much as leaky ventilation shafts had allowed water to seep throughout the ship after she sank in Pearl Harbor.

Evidence of Baker's intense shock wave was everywhere. Boilers repaired after the Able test were wrecked, and Captain Adell concluded that all personnel in the fire rooms would have been killed instantly.[17] Heavy machinery was lifted off its foundations, evidenced by cracks in restraining bolts and along paint lines between the equipment and the deck. While most of the damage was below the waterline, the shock wave was sufficient to lift the heavy main turrets off their tracks—the connecting bolts holding down turret 2 were sheared off, and shell-handling equipment under both aft turrets was thrown out of alignment.

Men returned to *Nevada* over the coming days to recover instruments and continue the damage assessment. More than two hundred boarded on August 17. Working in shorts, T-shirts, and canvas shoes, they had virtually no protection from the radiation. Even multiple showers could not wash away the contamination.

Radiation monitors recognized that working in the contaminated waters of Bikini lagoon was only exacerbating the danger to the support ships and men. Blandy ordered the fleet to retire to Kwajalein, to be followed by those target ships that could be moved. On August 19 the Navy tug *Preserver* towed *Nevada* out of Bikini Lagoon and on to Kwajalein. The remaining crewmembers accompanied their stricken vessel on board the support ship USS *Cortland*.

Blandy's next concern was the ammunition stored on the contaminated ships. He worried that some of the more sensitive high explosives would cook off in the hot tropical climate by reaching a temperature at which rapid chemical reactions led to detonation. He ordered the most worrisome charges removed but was forced to leave the big 14-inch shells where they were. Their presence constituted less of a risk to life than the intense radiation field permeating the ships.[18] *Nevada* still had two-thirds of her normal allowance of ammunition on board when the unloading was terminated.

She was near her end. On August 26 the ship's post office was discontinued, its equipment forwarded to the postmaster in New York. A work party visited the ship on August 27 to recover last-minute items, but the men stayed only a few hours. Finally, on August 29, while *Nevada* was anchored in Berth A-11 at Kwajalein Atoll, with her captain, officers, and men on *Cortland*, the following entry was made in the log: "1030[:] In accordance with Commander Advance Echelons letter, serial 914 of 22 August 1946, the USS NEVADA was decommissioned this date in Kwajalein

Lagoon, Marshall Islands." A later hand underlined "USS NEVADA was decommissioned" in blue pencil, one of only a few annotations made in the official logbooks over the ship's thirty-year history.

With no ship to man, crewmembers were assigned to other duties. Medal of Honor recipient Donald K. Ross was sent to Pearl Harbor for his next job. Captain Adell was ordered to report as chief of staff of the Operational Development Force after a one-month delay. He signed the last page of the logbook before departing. "It was a sad business," Captain Sims had said when he left his ship in 1916. Many men felt the same thirty years later.

═══ 15 ═══

Death of a Warrior

Ships, like those who sail in them, have personalities. Some lead charmed lives, others unhappy ones—a gift or a curse of fate. *Nevada* was a happy ship and a lucky ship. She was born proud—the most powerful battleship in the U.S. Navy, and by some measures the world. Her first captain, William Sims, was a reformer bent on getting the most out of the men and machines entrusted to his care. All of *Nevada*'s commanding officers put their own stamp upon her, but Sims set the tone; he made her the Cheer Up Ship and established a standard of excellence that was passed down from generation to generation of officers and enlisted men.

Nevada saw the emergence of America from a small-town, isolationist country to a global superpower. When her keel was laid the U.S. Army consisted of a few tens of thousands of poorly equipped men and the U.S. Navy was purposely constrained to avoid tempting a president toward adventures abroad. When *Nevada* went down for the last time, the American military was the guarantor of democracy and freedom around the world.

Nevada was never just another ship. All of her nicknames—the Cheer Up Ship, the Old Maru, Old Imperishable—were terms of affection. She was the Sweetheart of the Marine Corps, a sharpshooter who would brave enemy gunfire to protect American troops fighting their way ashore.

Twice she was given a new lease on life—first in her rebuild in 1928–30 and then in a major overhaul after the attack at Pearl Harbor. Some people criticized spending so much money on such an old ship. Subsequent events proved them wrong. She refused to be considered old, even though her turbines, salvaged from *North Dakota*, slowly lost their vim and vigor. Her guns were always ready to fire at the enemy, her armor always ready to absorb whatever was thrown against her. In later years she sported radar and an impressive array of the latest antiaircraft guns. She was always the best ship her design allowed her to be.

Nevada was also a lucky ship. At Pearl Harbor her main magazines were empty of volatile smokeless powder because the raid came in the interval between unloading old charges and loading new ones. More than that, the attack came at the very

260

moment when the crew was preparing her antiaircraft guns for routine inspection. She was ready for a fight.

Her luck persisted. Bad weather, rocky pinnacles, and Japanese submarines failed to deter her from supporting the recapture of Attu. German shore batteries did their best to silence her at Normandy. She was hit by a kamikaze and by Japanese shore batteries at Okinawa, the latter partly due to her skipper's determination to stay close inshore in support of the Marines. She was a *battleship*, after all, designed to engage with the enemy. Most impressive, she survived not one but *two* atomic bombs.

Not all ships were so fortunate. Her sister *Oklahoma* caught fire while under construction, endured collisions at sea, and capsized at Pearl Harbor. After the incredible engineering feat of righting and refloating her, *Oklahoma* was deemed too old and too damaged to be of any use to the Navy. She sank while being towed across the Pacific to the breakers, perhaps out of sheer weariness from the calamities that had befallen her.

Time is the enemy that no warrior can defeat. By the end of World War II *Nevada* was too slow and her guns too small to sail in any future line of battle. The atomic

Nevada arrives back at Pearl Harbor too radioactive even for scrap. *National Archives Photo Collection, RG 80, no. 370949*

Her last departure from Pearl Harbor, July 26, 1948. *National Archives Photo Collection, RG 80, no. 396328*

tests had left her too radioactive for repair or even scrapping. After being decommissioned, she was towed to Pearl Harbor for further decontamination studies. Everything that could be learned about the effect of atomic bombs on armored ships was gleaned from her. And then it was time for her final voyage.

On July 26, 1948, the Old Maru was towed out of Pearl Harbor, past the scene of her first sinking, to a point 65 miles southwest of Oahu where 15,000 feet of ocean were considered a suitable repository for her radioactive steel. Powerless to move on her own, *Nevada* floated freely on the currents, awaiting her fate.

The Navy was characteristically thorough in planning her demise, perhaps recognizing that any ship that could withstand two atomic blasts was no pushover. First, demolition charges using a new type of explosive were set off in the hull. They were expected to sink *Nevada*, but they seemed to have little effect beyond some dented plates and holes in the hull. Aircraft fired radio-controlled "bat-bombs" at her. All of them fell well astern, inflicting no damage. Destroyers launched salvos into her, but to no one's surprise the diminutive guns barely scraped *Nevada*'s heavy armor.

Next up was the modern battleship *Iowa* with her 16-inch guns. It was the pounding that *Nevada* was designed to take—large-caliber shells fired from a battleship. *Nevada* stood her ground. The light cruisers *Pasadena*, *Astoria*, and *Springfield* went at her with their 6-inch main batteries. By this time *Nevada*'s superstructure was a wreck, but her armor held. Some thought they detected a bit of settling, but Old Imperishable remained defiantly afloat.

After she had endured the worst that surface forces could dish out, it was back to aircraft-delivered weapons. Rockets from fighter planes hit her again and again. Observers could hardly see her for the smoke, but when it cleared, she was still there. Men who had served on her watched with a mixture of admiration and regret, taking great pride in their ship yet dismayed that she should have to suffer so. After four and a half days of pounding, it was time to put her out of her misery.

The same weapon that sank her on December 7, 1941, ended her days on July 31, 1948. A flight of Navy torpedo bombers took off from Barbers Point, next to Pearl Harbor, and hit her with a brace of torpedoes amidships at about 1400. She listed slowly to starboard and capsized. She settled by the stern, and the sea claimed her at 1434.

An officer who had served on *Nevada* recalled, "It seemed that we of the *Nevada* had lost a dear friend—more than that, a family member—indeed, a surrogate mother. The ship had never been an impersonal thing to us; she was always an entity, emitting power, pride and security to all those, friends or enemies, who came into contact with her."[1]

Iowa moved slowly over the spot where *Nevada* went down, her crew lined up in dress whites as a brief service was read. Adm. DeWitt Ramsey, commander of the Pacific Fleet, gave her epitaph: "She was a grand old ship."[2]

Bombs land nearby. *Nevada*'s famous good luck seems to hold as she takes everything the Navy can throw at her. *National Archives Photo Collection, RG 80, no. 498258*

Nevada in flames from friendly fire. *National Archives Photo Collection, RG 80, no. 498259*

She rolls over, showing holes in her hull. *National Archives Photo Collection, RG 80, no. 498282*

Nevada slips beneath the waves. *National Archives Photo Collection, RG 80, no. 498260*

It was dark inside the hull as she took the pounding. The galley was empty, and no hammocks swung in the crew's quarters. After so many trials and tribulations in shifting from steam to electric steering and back again, her rudder was still. Never again would engineers turn over her turbines to ensure that she was ready to move at an hour's notice. Her fractured decks were covered in smoke, but no damage control parties raced to the scene of her wounds. Perhaps her greatest indignity: no flag flew from her mast. *Nevada* had done her best for the country that built her and the men who loved her. If a ship has a soul, then *Nevada* surely loved them in return. She rests silently now in the Pacific—her grave undisturbed.

She died a warrior's death.

Notes

Chapter One. Building a Better Battleship

1. Letter from Andrews to Wood, January 23, 1911, National Archives, RG 19.
2. Steward Wood, Memorandum responding to Andrews letter, January 23, 1911, National Archives, RG 19.
3. Department of the Navy, *Characteristics Recommended and Adopted for Nos. 36 to 41*, January 15, 1912, National Archives, RG 19.
4. Norman Friedman, *U.S. Battleships: An Illustrated Design History* (Annapolis: Naval Institute Press, 1985).
5. Memorandum from Adm. George Dewey, President General Board, to the Navy Department, Subject: Criticisms of Battleship Design by Flag Officers and Captains of the Atlantic Fleet, May 24, 1911, National Archives, RG 80.
6. Memorandum from Chief of Bureau of Construction and Repair to the Secretary of the Navy, Subject: Battleship No. 36; Design, May 3, 1911, National Archives, RG 19.
7. An additional $50,000 and 5 months of construction time were added on July 31, 1914, to pay for new gearing for the turbine engines. See Ormond L. Cox, "U.S.S. NEVADA: Description and Trials," *Journal of the American Society of Naval Engineers* 28, no. 1 (1916): 20.
8. Annual Report of the Secretary of the Navy for the Fiscal Year 1917 (Washington, D.C.: Government Printing Office), 425.
9. Annual Report of the Navy Department for the Fiscal Year 1912 (Washington, D.C.: Government Printing Office), 233.
10. Anthony F. Sarcone and Lawrence S. Rines, *A History of Shipbuilding at Fore River*, http://thomascranelibrary.org/shipbuildingheritage/history.htm; letter from David W. Taylor, Bureau of Construction and Repair, to Secretary of the Navy Josephus Daniels, January 10, 1916, Subject: Honorable A. P. Gardner, M.C., Requests Information as to Length Time that NEVADA and OKLAHOMA Have Been Delayed because of Unsatisfactory Turbines, Fires, or Other Exceptional Circumstances, National Archives, RG 19.
11. Roy Willmarth Kelly and Frederick J. Allen, *The Shipbuilding Industry* (Boston: Houghton Mifflin, 1918).
12. R. H. M. Robinson, *Naval Construction* (Annapolis: Naval Institute Press, 1914).
13. "Biggest Battleship Keel-Laying Today," *New York Times*, March 9, 1909.
14. "Keel of the *Nevada* Laid," *Boston Globe*, November 5, 1912.

15. Robinson, *Naval Construction*.

16. "Reminiscences of John C. Niedemair (Naval Architect—Bureau of Ships)," (U.S. Naval Institute Oral History, 1978), 8–9.

17. Cox, "U.S.S. NEVADA: Description and Trials."

18. Annual Report of the Navy Department for the Fiscal Year 1912, 211.

19. "Queen of the Navy Launched," *Boston Globe*, July 12, 1914.

20. Memorandum from T. G. Roberts to Bureau of Construction and Repair, July 23, 1914, Subject: NEVADA—Launching, National Archives, RG 19.

21. "Queen of the Navy Launched."

22. Annual Report of the Navy Department for the Fiscal Year 1912, 212.

23. Ibid.

24. Annual Report of the Navy Department for the Fiscal Year 1915 (Washington, D.C: Government Printing Office), 300.

25. Annual Report of the Navy Department for the Fiscal Year 1913, 242.

26. Letter from Josephus Daniels to Representative A. P. Gardiner, January 12, 1916, National Archives, RG 19.

27. Letter from Josephus Daniels to Bureaus of Construction and Repair and Steam Engineering, April 21, 1916, Subject: Extension of Contract Time, National Archives, RG 19.

28. Letter from J. W. Powell to Superintending Constructor, USN, Fore River Shipbuilding Co., May 29, 1915, National Archives, RG 19.

29. Letter from Superintending Constructor, USN, Quincy, to Bureau of Construction and Repair, September 22, 1915, Subject: NEVADA—Docking, National Archives, RG 19.

30. Letter from Acting Secretary Franklin D. Roosevelt to Fore River Shipbuilding Company (no date), National Archives, RG 19.

31. Letter from H. G. Smith, Manager Fore River Shipbuilding Company, to Superintending Constructor, USN, Fore River Shipbuilding Company, Subject: NEVADA—Docking, October 4, 1915, National Archives, RG 19.

Chapter Two. Trials at Sea

1. Letter from Lt. R. W. Mathewson to Superintending Naval Constructor, Fore River Shipbuilding Corporation, October 25, 1915, Subject: NEVADA—Trials, National Archives, RG 19.

2. "Boston Claims World Champion Skipper, Capt. Joe Kemp, Test Pilot, 66," *Milwaukee Journal*, September 8, 1939.

3. "Sea Fighter *Nevada* Ready for Her Test," *New York Times*, October 26, 1915.

4. Letter from T. G. Roberts to Secretary of the Navy, October 23, 1915, Subject: NEVADA—Docking and Trials, Unfinished Work, National Archives, RG 19.

5. Letter from David W. Taylor to Superintending Naval Constructor, Fore River Shipyard, October 25, 1915, National Archives, RG 19.

6. Letter from Lt. R. W. Mathewson to Superintending Constructor, Fore River Shipbuilding Corporation, November 2, 1915, Subject: USS NEVADA—Preliminary Trial, Consumption of Auxiliaries, National Archives, RG 19.

7. Ibid.

8. Elting E. Morison, *Admiral Sims and the Modern American Navy* (Boston: Houghton Mifflin, 1942), 292.

9. Letter from H. G. Smith, Fore River Shipbuilding Company, to Superintending Constructor, USN, Fore River Shipbuilding Company, February 29, 1916, Subject: USS NEVADA—Delivery of, National Archives, RG 19.

10. Letter from T. G. Roberts to the Bureau of Construction and Repair, March 10, 1916, Subject: NEVADA—Delivery, National Archives, RG 19.

11. Notarized statement by H. G. Smith, Fore River Shipbuilding Corporation, March 11, 1916, National Archives, RG 19.

12. Morison, *Admiral Sims and the Modern American Navy*, 326.

13. This and other unattributed quotations are from *Nevada*'s logbook.

14. "Dreadnought *Nevada* in Commission," *Boston Globe*, March 12, 1916.

15. Quotations from Morison, *Admiral Sims and the Modern American Navy*, 330.

16. Ibid., 331.

17. Ibid., 329.

18. Ibid., 334.

19. Paul Stillwell, *Battleship* Arizona*: An Illustrated History* (Annapolis: Naval Institute Press, 1991), 62.

20. Herbert Corey, "Across the Equator with the American Navy," *National Geographic* 39, no. 6 (1921): 590.

Chapter Three. The Great War

1. Harold Sprout and Margaret Sprout, *The Rise of American Naval Power 1776–1918* (London: Oxford University Press, 1939), 336.

2. Ibid., 344–45.

3. Memorandum from Commander in Chief Atlantic Fleet to Secretary of the Navy, December 17, 1917, Subject: Annual Report; 1 July 1916 to 1 July 1917, National Archives, RG 45.

4. General Board No. 425, Memorandum from Senior Member Present to the Secretary of the Navy, February 3, 1917, Subject: Steps to Be Taken to Meet a Possible Condition of War with the Central European Powers, National Archives, RG 80.

5. Confidential Memorandum from Secretary of the Navy to Commanders in Chief of Fleets, March 23, 1917, Subject: Mobilization Plan, National Archives, RG 80.

6. S. E. Wilkinson, *The* Nevada *Manual: Published on Board the* USS *NEVADA in the Interests of Her Officers and Crew* (USS *Nevada*, 1919), 9, National Archives, RG 45.

7. Paul Stillwell, *Battleship* Arizona*: An Illustrated History* (Annapolis: Naval Institute Press, 1991).

8. *Nevada* war diary, July 5, 1917, National Archives, RG 45.

9. War diary, U.S. Atlantic Fleet, vol. 6, September 25, 1917, Subject: Recognition Signals—Importance of, National Archives, RG 45.

10. Jerry W. Jones, *U.S. Battleships in World War I* (Annapolis: Naval Institute Press, 1998).

11. Testimony of Rear Adm. H. T. Mayo, U.S. Navy, before the U.S. Senate, Subcommittee of the Committee on Naval Affairs, March 30, 1920, 601, *Congressional Record* (Washington DC: Government Printing Office).

12. Author unknown, Data for commander in chief's Annual Report, July 1, 1917, to June 30, 1918, National Archives, RG 45.

13. Syd. E. Wilkinson, *The USS* Nevada *and Her Experiences in the War: A Diary by Chief Yeoman Syd. E. Wilkinson* (privately printed, 1919), 7.

14. Jones, *U.S. Battleships in World War I*, 103.

15. Memorandum from Commander in Chief U.S. Fleet to Secretary of the Navy, June 30, 1919, Subject: Annual Report of Commander-in-Chief United States Fleet—1 July 1918 to 30 June 1919, National Archives, RG 45.

16. Wilkinson, *USS* Nevada *and Her Experiences in the War*, 8.

17. Wilkinson, Nevada *Manual*, 8.

18. Wilkinson, *USS* Nevada *and Her Experiences in the War*, 8.

19. Ibid., 9.

20. Nicholas Best, *The Greatest Day in History: How the Great War Really Ended* (London: Weidenfeld & Nicolson, 2008).

21. Cablegram from Sims to OpNav Washington, November 19, 1918, National Archives, RG 45.

22. "Dared Germans to Come Out," *Boston Globe*, January 5, 1919.

23. Wilkinson, *USS* Nevada *and Her Experiences in the War*, 12.

24. "Ovation to Sea Fighters," *New York Times*, December 28, 1918.

25. Ibid.

Chapter Four. Battleship Diplomacy

1. Memorandum from Commander Battleship Division Seven to Commander Battleship Force Two, March 27, 1919, Subject: Visit of Squadron Three (Exercise Organization) to Bridgetown, Barbados, National Archives, RG 45.

2. Annual Report of the Commander in Chief, U.S. Atlantic Fleet—1 July 1919 to 30 June 1920, National Archives, RG 45.

3. Ibid.

4. Robert Shenk, ed., *Playships of the World: The Naval Diaries of Admiral Dan Gallery, 1920–1924* (Columbia: University of South Carolina Press, 2008), 97.

5. Ibid., 99.

6. Memorandum from Commander in Chief, Atlantic Fleet to Chief of Naval Operations, November 26, 1920, Subject: Organization for Exercises of the Combined Atlantic and Pacific Fleets, National Archives RG 45.

7. Shenk, *Playships of the World*, 67.

8. Herbert Corey, "Across the Equator with the American Navy," *National Geographic* 39, no. 6 (1921): 571–624.

9. Ibid.

10. Ibid., 619.

11. Shenk, *Playships of the World*, 101.

12. Alfred Hurley, *Billy Mitchell: Crusader for Air Power* (Bloomington: Indiana University Press, 2006), 47.

13. Thomas C. Hone and Trent Hone, *Battle Line: The United States Navy 1919–1939* (Annapolis: Naval Institute Press, 2006), 4.

14. Harold Sprout and Margaret Sprout, *The Rise of American Naval Power 1776–1918* (London: Oxford University Press, 1939), 383.

15. Harold Sprout and Margaret Sprout, *Toward a New Order of Sea Power: American Naval Policy and the World Scene 1918–1922* (Princeton: Princeton University Press, 1940), 149.

Chapter Five. The Great Cruise

1. Memorandum from Commanding Officer USS *Nevada* to the Secretary of the Navy, November 17, 1922, Subject: Report on Special Service, USS *Nevada*, October 18 to November 16, 1922, National Archives, RG 45.

2. Annual Report of the Secretary of the Navy for 1923 (Washington, D.C.: Government Printing Office), 453.

3. Albert A. Nofi, *To Train the Fleet for War: The U.S. Navy Fleet Problems* (Newport, R.I.: Naval War College Press, 2010).

4. Trent Hone, "Building a Doctrine: U.S. Navy Tactics and Battle Plans in the Interwar Period," *International Journal of Naval History* 1, no. 2 (2002): 8.

5. Ibid., 11.

6. Nofi, *To Train the Fleet for War*, 53.

7. Ibid., 76.

8. Samuel Wheeler Beach, *The Great Cruise of 1925* (San Francisco: International Printing, 1925), 80–85.

9. "The Reminiscences of Rear Admiral Charles J. Wheeler, U.S. Navy, Retired" (U.S. Naval Institute Oral History, 1970), 136.

10. Ibid., 137.

11. I would like to share an incident involving my son, then a U.S. Navy petty officer second class, that occurred more than seventy years after the Great Cruise. After asking how much he owed for a beer at a local pub, he was told, "Your money's no good here." The proprietor then proceeded to expound on the history of American-Australian naval cooperation and to thank my son for the U.S. Navy's participation in the Battle of the Coral Sea.

12. Beach, *The Great Cruise of 1925*, 178.

13. Telegram from Commandant, Navy Yard Puget Sound to Bureau of Engineering, November 7, 1923, National Archives, RG 45.

14. Memorandum from Commander in Chief Battle Fleet to Chief of the Bureau of Ordnance, June 17, 1924, Subject: Spring Tubes—3 Gun Turrets—Damage to—NEVADA, National Archives, RG 45.

15. Memorandum from Chief of Naval Operations to Commander in Chief Atlantic Fleet, May 8, 1922, Subject: Schedule of Employment 1 July 1922 to 5 January 1923, National Archives, RG 45.

16. Annual Report of the Secretary of the Navy for 1926 (Washington D.C.: Government Printing Office), 242.

17. Annual Report of the Secretary of the Navy for 1924 (Washington D.C.: Government Printing Office), 14.

18. From Commander Battleship Division Three to Chief of Naval Operations, June 2, 1926, Subject: USS *NEVADA*—MATERIAL READINESS, National Archives, RG 45.

Chapter Six. Rebirth

1. "Votes for Elevating Guns of Battleships," *Boston Daily Globe*, March 1, 1927.

2. Annual Report of the Secretary of the Navy for Fiscal Year 1927 (Washington, D.C.: Government Printing Office, 243).

3. From Board of Inspection and Survey, Pacific Coast Section to President, Board of Inspection and Survey, Navy Department, January 22, 1926, Subject: USS NEVADA (BB 36)—Material Inspection—Report of, National Archives, RG 19.

4. Memorandum for the Chief Constructor from E. L. Cochrane, December 30, 1927, Subject: OKLAHOMA and NEVADA—Maximum Beam, National Archives, RG 19.

5. From Chief of the Bureau of Construction and Repair to Commanding Officer, USS *NEVADA*, August 24, 1929, Subject: USS NEVADA (BB 36) and OKLAHOMA (BB 37)—Resistance in Transiting through the Panama Canal, National Archives, RG 19.

6. From Commandant, Norfolk Navy Yard to Chief of the Bureau of Construction and Repair, February 14, 1928, Subject: USS NEVADA (BB 36)—Special Treatment Steel—Second Deck, National Archives, RG 19.

7. Ibid.; signal from Bureau of Construction and Repair to Commandant, Norfolk, February 21, 1928, National Archives, RG 19.

8. From Chiefs of the Bureau of Construction and Repair and Engineering to Navy Department, April 21, 1927, Subject: USS NORTH DAKOTA—Transfer of Main Propelling Machinery to USS NEVADA, National Archives, RG 19.

9. From Board of Inspection and Survey, Pacific Coast Section to President, Board of Inspection and Survey, Navy Department, January 22, 1926, Subject: USS NEVADA (BB 36)—Report of, National Archives, RG 19.

10. From Commandant to Chief of Bureau of Construction and Repair, August 15, 1927, Subject: NEVADA—Structure Material Required for Work on Reboiling, National Archives, RG 19.

11. From Bureau of Engineering to Bureau of Construction and Repair, December 16, 1927, Subject: USS NEVADA, Propeller, New, Forwarding Plan of, National Archives, RG 19.

12. From Bureau of Construction and Repair to Secretary of the Navy, May 12, 1928, Subject: OKLAHOMA (BB 37) and NEVADA (BB 36)—Installation of Anti-aircraft Machine Guns; from Chief of the Bureau of Construction and Repair to Commandant, Norfolk, July 23, 1928, Subject: USS NEVADA (BB 36) and OKLAHOMA (BB 37)—Installation of Anti-aircraft Machine Guns, National Archives, RG 19.

13. Memorandum from C. B. C. Carey to Chief of Bureau of Ordnance, January 28, 1928, Subject: Above Water Torpedo Tubes on OKLAHOMA and NEVADA, National Archives, RG 19.

14. From General Board to Secretary of the Navy, February 8, 1928, Subject: Installation of Torpedoes on USS OKLAHOMA and NEVADA, National Archives, RG 19.

15. From Bureau of Ordnance to Bureau of Construction and Repair, March 3, 1928, Subject: Class A Armor—Information regarding Cutting, National Archives, RG 19.

16. From Commandant, Norfolk Navy Yard to Chief of the Bureau of Construction and Repair, March 28, 1928, Subject: USS NEVADA (BB 36) and OKLAHOMA (BB 37)—Method to Be Used for Cutting Turret Armor, National Archives, RG 19.

17. From Commandant to Chief of Bureau of Construction and Repair, May 14, 1928, Subject: USS NEVADA and OKLAHOMA—Method to Be Used for Cutting Turret Armor, National Archives, RG 19.

18. From Chief of the Bureau of Construction and Repair to Commandant, Norfolk, February 10, 1928, Subject: USS NEVADA and OLKAHOMA—Major Alterations—Elevation of Turret Guns, National Archives, RG 19.

19. Weekly Report of Progress on Ships, Norfolk Navy Yard, for week ending March 31, 1928, USS NEVADA, National Archives, RG 19.

20. From Commandant, Norfolk Navy Yard to Bureau of Construction and Repair, July 23, 1928, Subject: USS NEVADA (BB 36)—Berthing and Messing—Installation of Bunk System, National Archives, RG 19.

21. From Commandant, Norfolk Navy Yard to Bureau of Construction and Repair, July 23, 1928, Subject: USS NEVADA (BB 36)—Bunks and Lockers for, National Archives, RG 19.

22. From Geo. H. Rock to Commandant, Norfolk, December 4, 1928. Subject: USS NEVADA (BB 36)—Bunks and Lockers for, National Archives, RG 19.

23. From Commanding Officer to Chief of the Bureau of Construction and Repair, 22 October 1928, Subject: Bunks and Mattresses, USS NEVADA, National Archives, RG 19.

24. From Chief of the Bureau of Construction and Repair to Commanding Officer, October 25, 1928, Subject: USS NEVADA (BB 36)—Bunks and Mattresses, National Archives, RG 19.

25. From Chief of the Bureau of Construction and Repair to Commanding Officer, USS NEVADA, October 17, 1928, Subject: USS NEVADA (BB 36)—Installation of Enameled Iron Lavatories in Crew's and Firemen's Washrooms, National Archives, RG 19.

26. From Chief of the Bureau of Construction and Repair to Commandant, Norfolk, March 5, 1929, Subject: USS NEVADA (BB 36)—Lavatories, National Archives, RG 19.

27. From Chief of the Bureau of Construction and Repair to Commandant, Norfolk, May 6, 1928, Subject: USS NEVADA (BB 36) and USS OKLAHOMA (BB 37)—Dish Washing and Dish Sterilizer Machines, National Archives, RG 19.

28. From Chief of Bureau of Construction and Repair to Bureau of Supplies and Accounts, February 4, 1928, Subject: USS NEVADA (BB 36)—Silverware, Refinishing, National Archives, RG 19.

29. From Commanding officer to Chief of the Bureau of Construction and Repair, October 26, 1928, Subject: USS NEVADA (BB 36) and OKLAHOMA (BB 37)— Captain's Quarters—Arrangement of, National Archives, RG 19.

30. From Chief of the Bureau of Construction and Repair to Commanding Officer, USS NEVADA, November 10, 1928, Subject: USS NEVADA (BB 36) and OKLAHOMA (BB 37)—Captain's Quarters—Arrangement of, National Archives, RG 19.

31. From Commander of Battleship Division Three to Chief of the Bureau of Construction and Repair, December 3, 1929, Subject: Flag Accommodations— USS NEVADA—Request for Temporary Installation of, National Archives, RG 19.

32. Weekly Report of Progress on Ships, Norfolk Navy Yard, for week ending November 17, 1928, USS NEVADA, National Archives, RG 19.

33. Weekly Report of Progress on Ships, Norfolk Navy Yard, for week ending February 2, 1929, USS NEVADA, National Archives, RG 19. Weekly Report of Progress on Ships, Norfolk Navy Yard, for week ending May 18, 1929, USS NEVADA, National Archives, RG 19.

34. Weekly Report of Progress on Ships, Norfolk Navy Yard, for week ending August 17, 1929, USS NEVADA, National Archives, RG 19.

35. From Commandant[, Norfolk] to Chief of the Bureau of Construction and Repair, February 13, 1930, Subject: USS NEVADA—Special Report on Expenditures, National Archives, RG 19.

36. Letter from Curtis D. Wilbur to Honorable Fred A. Britten, M.C., Acting Chairman, House Naval Affairs Committee, April 21, 1928, National Archives, RG 19.

37. Annual Report of the Secretary of the Navy for Fiscal Year 1929 (Washington D.C.: Government Printing Office), 270.

38. From Senior Member of Board to Commanding Officer, USS NEVADA, September 6, 1928, Subject: OKLAHOMA & NEVADA, Main Battery Tests of, National Archives, RG 19.

39. From Chief of Naval Operations to various recipients, August 23, 1929, Subject: NEVADA and OKLAHOMA, Main Battery Tests of, National Archives, RG 19.

40. From the Chiefs of the Bureaus of Ordnance and Construction and Repair to the Chief of Naval Operations, March 1, 1929, Subject: NEVADA and OKLAHOMA, Batteries, Tests of, National Archives, RG 19.

41. From Bureau of Construction and Repair to Board of Inspection and Survey, October 9, 1929, Subject: USS NEVADA (BB 36)—Trial Displacement of, National Archives, RG 19.

42. Signal from USS NEVADA to Board of Inspection and Survey, October 11, 1929, National Archives, RG 19.

43. Memorandum for Chief of Naval Operations, October 23, 1929, Subject: USS NEVADA (BB 36)—Advance Report of Standardization, Fuel Consumption Trials, and Material Inspection, National Archives, RG 19.

44. From Board of Inspection and Survey to Chief of Naval Operations, October 18, 1929, Subject: USS NEVADA (BB 36)—Report of Trials and Material Inspection— Report of Trials—Part II, National Archives, RG 19.

Chapter Seven. Fleet Problems

1. Report of Material Inspection of USS NEVADA (BB36) Held 26 September 1932 by the Board of Inspection and Survey, National Archives, RG 38.

2. From Commanding Officer, USS OKLAHOMA to Commander Battleship Division Three, February 15, 1930, Subject: Rudder Angle during Tactical Exercises, National Archives, RG 19.

3. Albert A. Nofi, *To Train the Fleet for War: The U.S. Navy Fleet Problems* (Newport, R.I.: Naval War College Press, 2010), 135.

4. From Commander Battleship Divisions, Battle Fleet, to Chief of Naval Operations, July 19 1930, Subject: Quarterly Inspection of USS NEVADA, National Archives, RG 38.

5. From Commander Battle Force to Chief of Naval Operations, Commander in Chief, U.S. Fleet, December 27, 1934, Subject: USS NEVADA—Short Range Battle Practice, 1934–35, National Archives, RG 313.

6. From Commanding Officer [*Nevada*] to Chief of the Bureau of Ordnance, December 29, 1932, Subject: 14" Projectile Service, National Archives, RG 313.

7. Thomas C. Hone and Trent Hone, *Battle Line: The United States Navy 1919–1939* (Annapolis: Naval Institute Press, 2006).

8. William F. Jurens, "The Evolution of Battleship Gunnery in the U.S. Navy, 1920–1940," NavWeaps.com: Naval Weapons of the World, accessed March 11, 2014.

9. Lt. F. S. Withington, "United States Fleet, Battle Force, Battleships Division Three, USS NEVADA, Shooting the Main Battery" (unpublished, 1934) National Archives, RG 313.

10. From Board of Inspection and Survey to Chief of Naval Operations, October 13 1929, Subject: USS NEVADA (BB 36)—Report of Trials and Material Inspection—Material Inspection Part I, National Archives, RG 19.

11. Sadao Asada, "The London Conference and the Tragedy of the Imperial Japanese Navy," in John H. Mauer and Christopher M. Bell, eds., *At the Crossroads between Peace and War: The London Naval Conference of 1930* (Annapolis: Naval Institute Press, 2014), 91.

12. Saburo Ienaga, *The Pacific War 1931–1945* (New York: Random House, 1978), 39–40.

13. Asada, "The London Conference and the Tragedy of the Imperial Japanese Navy," 120.

14. "Drinks Poison to Offset Disgrace," *Boston Daily Globe*, December 21, 1931.

15. Nofi, *To Train the Fleet for War*, 144.

16. From Commandant, Puget Sound Navy Yard to Chief of the Bureau of Construction and Repair, April 16, 1931, Subject: USS NEVADA—Arrival Conference Report and Recommended Overhaul Costs (C&R), National Archives, RG 19.

17. From Commandant, Puget Sound Navy Yard to Bureau of Construction and Repair, November 18, 1932, National Archives, RG 19.

18. Report of Material Inspection of USS NEVADA (BB 36) Held 26 September 1932 by Board of Inspection and Survey, National Archives, RG 38.

19. From Bureau of Ordnance to the Chief of Naval Operations, May 9, 1933, Subject: USS NEVADA—Defects Found in Armament Installation during Recent Overhaul, National Archives, RG 74.

20. From Commandant, Norfolk Navy Yard to Chief of the Bureau of Ordnance and Chief of the Bureau of Construction and Repair, April 17, 1933, Subject: USS NEVADA—Defects Found in Armament Installation during Recent Overhaul, National Archives, RG 74.

21. "The Reminiscences of Rear Admiral Frederick Stanton Withington, U.S. Navy (Retired)" (U.S. Naval Institute Oral History, 1972), 34.

22. Nofi, *To Train the Fleet for War*, 187.

23. Rear Adm. T. T. Craven, Commander Battleship Division One, April 25, 1934, Memorandum of Operations from 12 April, 1934 to 21 April, 1934, Battle Exercise "K"—12 April, 1934, National Archives, RG 313.

24. From Assistant Umpire, USS NEVADA to Chief Umpire, April 14, 1934, Subject: Battle Exercise "K," April 13, 1934, National Archives, RG 313.

25. From Commanding Officer, USS *Nevada*, to Commander Battleships, Battle Force, April 21, 1934, Subject: Report of Tactical Exercises Enroute San Pedro–San Diego to Panama Canal, National Archives, RG 313.

26. From Commander-in-Chief, United States Fleet to FLEET, April 23, 1934, Subject: Report of Tactical Exercises Enroute San Pedro–San Diego Area to Panama Canal, National Archives, RG 313.

27. From Commander Battleships to Chief of Naval Operations (Division of Fleet Training), April 2, 1934, Subject: Long Range Battle Practice "TURRETS," Special Firing Units (USS NEVADA, USS TENNESSEE, USS CALIFORNIA), National Archives, RG 313.

28. From Commandant, Puget Sound Navy Yard to Bureau of Construction and Repair, March 8, 1934, Subject: USS NEVADA (BB 36)—Unsatisfactory Steering Qualities, National Archives, RG 19.

29. From Bureau of Construction and Repair to Commandant, Puget Sound Navy Yard, April 6, 1934, Subject: USS NEVADA—Unsatisfactory Steering Qualities, National Archives, RG 19.

30. From Commander in Chief, U.S. Fleet to Commanding Officer, USS NEVADA, November 13, 1934, Subject: Short Range Battle Practice—USS NEVADA, National Archives, RG 313.

31. From Commanding Officer, USS NEVADA to Chief of Naval Operations (Division of Fleet Training), October 17, 1934, Subject: USS NEVADA—Short Range Battle Practice, 1934–35, Main and Secondary Batteries, National Archives, RG 313.

32. From Chief Observer to Chief of Naval Operations, September 28, 1934, Subject: Report of Scores, Short Range Battle Practice, National Archives, RG 313.

33. Report of Material Inspection of USS NEVADA (BB 36) Held November 19, 1935, by Board of Inspection and Survey, National Archives, RG 38.

Chapter Eight. Oranges and Chrysanthemums

1. Edward S. Miller, *War Plan Orange: The U.S. Strategy to Defeat Japan, 1897–1945* (Annapolis: Naval Institute Press, 1991).

2. Ibid., 202.

3. Lynne Olson, *Those Angry Days: Roosevelt, Lindbergh, and America's Fight over World War II, 1939–1941* (New York: Random House, 2013).

4. Albert A. Nofi, *To Train the Fleet for War: The U.S. Navy Fleet Problems* (Newport, R.I.: Naval War College Press, 2010), 282.

5. Ibid.

6. From Commander Battleship Division One to Commander Battleships, Battle Force, April 10, 1937, Subject: Narratives of Division Practices Conducted by Commander Battleship Division One, 1936–37, National Archives, RG 313.

7. Piers Brendon, *The Dark Valley: A Panorama of the 1930s* (New York: Vintage, 2000), 342.

8. Ibid., 438.

9. Samuel Eliot Morison, *Oxford History of the American People* (New York: Oxford University Press, 1965), 990.

10. Brendon, *The Dark Valley*, 514.

11. Nofi, *To Train the Fleet for War*.

12. Report of Gunnery Exercise Gunnery Year 1938–39, Short Range Practice, Santa Barbara Island, September 1, 1938, National Archives, RG 313.

13. From Board of Inspection and Survey, Pacific Section, to President, Board of Inspection and Survey, Navy Department, October 13, 1938, Subject: USS NEVADA (BB 36)—Material Inspection of, National Archives, RG 38.

14. From Chief of the Bureau of Ordnance to Commander Battleships, Battle Force, December 30, 1938, Subject: 14"/45 Caliber Battery—Care of Gun Bores, National Archives, RG 74.

15. Pearl Harbor Survivors Association, http://www.pearlharborsurvivorsonline.org, accessed April 6, 2014.

16. Walter Lord, *Day of Infamy* (New York: Henry Holt, 1957), 51–52.

17. W. S. Wyatt, *Cruise Book USS* Nevada, *1916–1946* (San Francisco: James H. Barry, 1946), 140.

18. John T. Kuehn, *Agents of Innovation: The General Board and the Design of the Fleet That Defeated the Japanese Navy* (Annapolis: Naval Institute Press, 2008), 162.

19. Walter R. Borneman, *The Admirals: Nimitz, Halsey, Leahy, and King—the Five-Star Admirals Who Won the War at Sea* (New York: Back Bay Books, 2012), 190.

20. Sadao Asada, *From Mahan to Pearl Harbor: The Imperial Japanese Navy and the United States* (Annapolis: Naval Institute Press, 2006), 235.

21. H. P. Willmont, *Pearl Harbor* (London: Cassell, 2001), 53.

22. From Commander Battleships, Battle Force, to Flag Officers in Command of Units, U.S. Fleet, Battleships U.S. Fleet, Aircraft Carriers, U.S. Fleet, October 5, 1940, Subject: Report of Exercise No. 124, Inter-type Exercises, Battleline and Battleline Carrier, National Archives, RG 313.

23. Report of Gunnery Exercise Gunnery Year 1937–38, T.P.D. (Dive Bombing) Practice VO, San Pedro, May 11, 1938, National Archives, RG 313.

24. Wyatt, *Cruise Book USS* Nevada, 137.

25. Naval History and Heritage Command, http://www.history.navy.mil.

26. Jeff Phister, Thomas Hone, and Paul Goodyear, *Battleship* Oklahoma, *BB-37* (Norman: University of Oklahoma Press, 2008), 54.

27. Lord, *Day of Infamy*, 6.

28. Phister, Hone, and Goodyear, *Battleship* Oklahoma, 56.

29. "Reminiscences of Captain Charles J. Merdinger" (U.S. Naval Institute Oral History, 1974), 31–32.

30. Lord, *Day of Infamy*, 4.

Chapter Nine. Pearl Harbor

1. From Commanding Officer to Commander Battleships, Battle Force, December 19, 1941, Subject: Information regarding USS NEVADA, National Archives, RG 313.

2. Gordon W. Prange, *At Dawn We Slept: The Untold Story of Pearl Harbor* (New York: Penguin, 1991), 491–92.

3. From Commander in Chief, U.S. Pacific Fleet, to Secretary of the Navy, February 15, 1942, Subject: Report of Japanese Attack on Pearl Harbor, December 7, 1941, National Archives, RG 313.

4. Edwin S. Swaney, *Operation Crossroads* (Montezuma, Iowa: Sutherland Publishing, 1986), 9.

5. Taussig had family ties to *Nevada*. His father, who had risen to flag rank, had commanded the first destroyer flotilla sent to Britain during the Great War and was a friend of William Sims, *Nevada*'s first captain.

6. Walter Lord, *Day of Infamy* (New York: Henry Holt, 1957), 67.

7. Swaney, *Operation Crossroads*, 18.

8. Joseph K. Taussig Jr., "A Tactical View of Pearl Harbor," in Paul Stillwell, ed., *Air Raid Pearl Harbor! Recollections of a Day of Infamy* (Annapolis: Naval Institute Press, 1981), 134.

9. From Commanding Officer to Commander Battleships, Battle Force, December 19, 1941, Subject: Information regarding USS NEVADA, National Archives, RG 313.

10. Taussig, "A Tactical View of Pearl Harbor," 135.

11. Mitsuo Fuchida, *For that One Day: The Memoirs of Mitsuo Fuchida Commander of the Attack on Pearl Harbor* (Kamuela, HI: eXperience, 2011), 96.

12. Walter Stratton Anderson, "Worse than Dante's Inferno," in Paul Stillwell, ed., *Air Raid Pearl Harbor! Recollections of a Day of Infamy* (Annapolis: Naval Institute Press, 1981), 128.

13. Bureau of Ships, Navy Department, War Damage Report No. 17, September 18, 1942, USS NEVADA Torpedo and Bomb Damage, December 7, 1941, Pearl Harbor, 7, National Archives, RG 19.

14. Paul H. Backus, "Why Them and Not Me," in Paul Stillwell, ed., *Air Raid Pearl Harbor! Recollections of a Day of Infamy* (Annapolis: Naval Institute Press, 1981), 164.

15. Lord, *Day of Infamy*, 73.

16. H. P. Willmott, *Pearl Harbor* (London: Cassell, 2001), 140.

17. Theodore C. Mason, *Battleship Sailor* (Annapolis: Naval Institute Press, 1982), 228.

18. Fuchida, *For that One Day*, 66.

19. Bureau of Ships, Navy Department, War Damage Report No. 17.

20. Homer N. Wallin, "The Raising and Salvaging of the *Nevada*," in Paul Stillwell, ed., *Air Raid Pearl Harbor! Recollections of a Day of Infamy* (Annapolis: Naval Institute Press, 1981), 148.

21. Lorenzo Sabin, "The Cheer-Up Ship," in Paul Stillwell, ed., *Air Raid Pearl Harbor! Recollections of a Day of Infamy* (Annapolis: Naval Institute Press, 1981), 145–46.

22. Lord, *Day of Infamy*, 180–81.

23. Edward C. Raymer, *Descent into Darkness: Pearl Harbor, 1941, a Navy Diver's Memoir* (Annapolis: Naval Institute Press, 1996), 23–24.

24. From Commanding Officer to Commander in Chief, U.S. Pacific Fleet, December 15, 1941, Subject: Report of December 7, 1941 Raid, National Archives, RG 19.

25. Bureau of Ships, Navy Department, War Damage Report No. 17.

26. Samuel Eliot Morison, *The Rising Sun in the Pacific*, vol. 3 of *History of United States Naval Operations in World War II* (Boston: Little, Brown, 1948), 125.

27. Willmott, *Pearl Harbor*, 203.

28. Fuchida, *For that One Day*.

29. Willmott, *Pearl Harbor*, 145.

30. Ibid., 76.

31. Morison, *The Rising Sun in the Pacific*, 125.

Chapter Ten. Back in the Fight

1. Edward S. Miller, *War Plan Orange: The U.S. Strategy to Defeat Japan, 1897–1945* (Annapolis: Naval Institute Press, 1991), 320.

2. Daniel Madsen, *Resurrection: Salvaging the Battle Fleet at Pearl Harbor* (Annapolis: Naval Institute Press, 2003).

3. Edward C. Raymer, *Descent into Darkness: Pearl Harbor, 1941, a Navy Diver's Memoir* (Annapolis: Naval Institute Press, 1996), 23–24.

4. Bureau of Ships, Navy Department, War Damage Report No. 17, September 18, 1942, USS NEVADA Torpedo and Bomb Damage, December 7, 1941, Pearl Harbor, National Archives, RG 19.

5. Homer N. Wallin, "The Raising and Salvaging of the *Nevada*," in Paul Stillwell, ed., *Air Raid Pearl Harbor! Recollections of a Day of Infamy* (Annapolis: Naval Institute Press, 1981), 151.

6. *Nevada* war diary, April 3, 1941, National Archives, RG 38.

7. *Nevada* war diary, April 7, 1941, National Archives, RG 38.

8. Peggy Hughes Ryan, "A Navy Bride Learns to Cope," in Paul Stillwell, ed., *Air Raid Pearl Harbor! Recollections of a Day of Infamy* (Annapolis: Naval Institute Press, 1981), 237.

9. Norman Friedman, *U.S. Battleships: An Illustrated Design History* (Annapolis: Naval Institute Press, 1985), 368.

10. See Anthony Tully, *Shattered Sword: The Untold Story of the Battle of Midway* (Washington, D.C.: Potomac Books, 2005), 44–45.

11. Brian Garfield, *The Thousand-Mile War: World War II in Alaska and the Aleutians* (Anchorage: University of Alaska Press, 1995), 286.

12. Ibid., 291.
13. Samuel Eliot Morison, *The Atlantic Battle Won: May 1943–May 1945*, vol. 10 of *History of Unitd States Naval Operations in World War II* (Boston: Little, Brown, 1956), 134–35.

Chapter Eleven. The Atlantic

1. Craig L. Symonds, *Neptune: The Allied Invasion of Europe and the D-Day Landings* (New York: Oxford University Press, 2014), 249.
2. Ibid., 193.
3. Walter J. Buckley, "The Silver Mine," in Paul Stillwell, ed., *Air Raid: Pearl Harbor! Recollections of a Day of Infamy* (Annapolis: Naval Institute Press 1981), 156.
4. Samuel Eliot Morison, *The Invasion of France and Germany, 1944–1945*, vol. 11 of *History of United States Naval Operations in World War II* (Boston: Little, Brown, 1957), 83.
5. Symonds, *Neptune*, 248.
6. Charles T. Sehe, "Operation Neptune" (unpublished manuscript in Nevada State Museum, 2013).
7. Ibid., 259.
8. Stephen E. Ambrose, *D-Day June 6, 1944: The Climactic Battle of World War II* (New York: Simon and Schuster, 1994), 268.
9. Symonds, *Neptune*, 263.
10. Ambrose, *D-Day June 6, 1944*, 290.
11. W. S. Wyatt, *Cruise Book USS* Nevada, *1916–1946* (San Francisco: James H. Barry, 1946), 30.
12. Unreferenced quotes in this chapter and chapters 12 and 13 are taken from *Nevada's* logbook and war diary.
13. Wyatt, *Cruise Book USS* Nevada, 94.
14. Charles Moldenhauer, handwritten diary (Nevada State Museum).
15. Edwin S. Swaney, *Operation Crossroads* (Montezuma, Iowa: Sutherland Publishing, 1986), 35.
16. Moldenhauer diary.
17. Symonds, *Neptune*, 340.
18. *Nevada* war diary, June 25, 1944, 41 National Archives, RG 38.
19. Swaney, *Operation Crossroads*, 36.
20. *Nevada* war diary, August 15, 1944, National Archives, RG 38.
21. Wyatt, *Cruise Book USS* Nevada, 105.
22. H. A. Yeager, "Memorandum to All Hands" (Nevada State Museum, no date).
23. Tony DiGuilian, "United States of America, 14"/45 (35.6 cm) Marks 8, 9, 10, and 12," http://www.navweaps.com/Weapons/WNUS_14–45_mk10.htm.
24. Swaney, *Operation Crossroads*, 38.
25. Wyatt, *Cruise Book USS* Nevada, 43.
26. Swaney, *Operation Crossroads*, 40.
27. Wyatt, *Cruise Book USS* Nevada, 105.

Chapter Twelve. The Pacific: Iwo Jima

1. Edwin S. Swaney, *Operation Crossroads* (Montezuma, Iowa: Sutherland, 1986), 41.
2. Samuel Eliot Morison, *Victory in the Pacific 1945*, vol. 14 of *History of United States Naval Operations in World War II* (Boston: Little, Brown, 1960), 110.
3. W. S. Wyatt, *Cruise Book USS* Nevada, *1916–1946* (San Francisco: James H. Barry, 1946), 93.
4. Swaney's *Operation Crossroads* (51) gives an exciting account of *Nevada* charging full speed to within eight hundred yards of the beach and then executing a sharp turn to starboard, firing her aft turrets at Mount Suribachi and her forward turrets at a cliff north of the invasion beaches. Unfortunately, this account is not supported by the ship's logbook or the war diary, both of which record more methodical firing and do not indicate such a close approach to the beach.
5. Morison, *Victory in the Pacific 1945*, 31.
6. Ibid., 40.
7. Unreferenced quotes in chapters 12 and 13 are taken from *Nevada*'s logbook and war diary.
8. Swaney's *Operation Crossroads* (59) reports that *Nevada* did not retire for the night and relates a conversation between Rear Admiral Rodgers and General Schmidt that resulted in *Nevada* firing illumination rounds over Iwo Jima. The ship's logbook and war diary both give details of night retirement and do not indicate any firing of star shells. Indeed, the war diary reports, "remainder of night quiet."
9. Swaney, *Operation Crossroads*, 63.
10. Morison, *Victory in the Pacific 1945*, 44, 48, 69.

Chapter Thirteen. The Pacific: Okinawa

1. Samuel Eliot Morison, *Victory in the Pacific 1945*, vol. 14 of *History of United States Naval Operations in World War II* (Boston: Little, Brown, 1960), 130.
2. W. S. Wyatt, *Cruise Book USS* Nevada, *1916–1946* (San Francisco: James H. Barry, 1946), 58.
3. Ibid., 54.
4. Edwin S. Swaney, *Operation Crossroads* (Montezuma, Iowa: Sutherland Publishing, 1986), 78.
5. "Piece of Japanese Kamikaze Plane That Hit U.S.S. *Nevada* on March 27th, 1945 at Okinawa" (Nevada State Museum).
6. Wyatt, *Cruise Book USS* Nevada, 59.
7. Swaney, *Operation Crossroads*, 80–81.
8. Wyatt, *Cruise Book USS* Nevada, 146.
9. Morison, *Victory in the Pacific 1945*, 89–90.
10. Swaney, *Operation Crossroads*, 83.
11. Ibid., 91.
12. Ibid., 93.
13. Mitsuru Yoshida, *Requiem for Battleship* Yamato (Annapolis: Bluejacket Books, 1999), 37.

14. Swaney, *Operation Crossroads*, 99.

15. Ibid., 98.

16. Morison, *Victory in the Pacific 1945*, 231.

17. Wyatt, *Cruise Book USS* Nevada, 67.

18. Swaney, *Operation Crossroads*, 107.

19. Ibid.

20. Morison, *Victory in the Pacific 1945*, 272, 276, 282.

21. Swaney, *Operation Crossroads*, 108.

22. Edward S. Miller, *War Plan Orange: The U.S. Strategy to Defeat Japan, 1897–1945* (Annapolis: Naval Institute Press, 1991), 366.

23. D. M. Giangreco, *Hell to Pay: Operation Downfall and the Invasion of Japan, 1945–1947* (Annapolis: Naval Institute Press, 2009), 50, 62.

24. Ibid., 124.

25. Swaney, *Operation Crossroads*, 114.

Chapter Fourteen. Operation Crossroads

1. Lewis Strauss, *Men and Decisions* (Garden City, N.Y.: Doubleday, 1962), 208–9.

2. *New York Times*, January 25, 1946.

3. W. A. Shurcliff, *Bombs at Bikini: The Official Report of Operation Crossroads* (New York: William H. Wise, 1947).

4. "A-Bomb May Finish Job Japs Couldn't Complete," *Honolulu Advertiser*, 1946.

5. Edwin S. Swaney, *Operation Crossroads* (Montezuma, Iowa: Sutherland Publishing, 1986), 120.

6. Shurcliff, *Bombs at Bikini*, 42.

7. Jonathan M. Weisgall, *Operation Crossroads: The Atomic Tests at Bikini Atoll* (Annapolis: Naval Institute Press, 1994), 157.

8. Swaney, *Operation Crossroads*, 122.

9. Ibid., 125.

10. "Operation Crossroads," Defense Nuclear Agency Report DNA 6032F, 1947.

11. Weisgall, *Operation Crossroads: The Atomic Tests at Bikini Atoll*, 184.

12. Ibid., 199.

13. Capt. C. C. Adell, "Commanding Officer's Report," Bureau of Ships Group Technical Inspection Report, Operation Crossroads, USS *NEVADA* (BB 36), Test Able, vol. 1, XRD-19, 1947.

14. Shurcliff, *Bombs at Bikini*, 159.

15. Weisgall, *Operation Crossroads: The Atomic Tests at Bikini Atoll*, 229.

16. Ibid., 234.

17. Capt. C. C. Adell, "Commanding Officer's Report," Bureau of Ships Group Technical Inspection Report, Operation Crossroads, USS *NEVADA* (BB 36), Test Baker, XRD-88, 1947.

18. "Operation Crossroads," Defense Nuclear Agency Report DNA 6032F, 1947, 124.

Chapter Fifteen. Death of a Warrior

1. Edwin S. Swaney, *Operation Crossroads* (Montezuma, Iowa: Sutherland Publishing, 1986), 130.

2. "Navy Finally Sinks Tough BattleWagon after Four Days," Associated Press, July 31, 1948.

Bibliography

Original Sources

Annual Reports of the Navy Department. Various years. Washington, D.C.: Government Printing Office.

Bureau of Construction and Repair General Correspondence. Record Group 19, National Archives, Washington D.C.

Bureau of Ordnance Correspondence. Record Group 74, entry 25, National Archives, Washington, D.C.

Division of Fleet Training, Reports of Efficiency of Inspection of Naval Vessels. Record Group 38, National Archives, Washington, D.C.

General Records of the Department of the Navy, General Board. Record Group 80, National Archives, Washington, D.C.

Naval Operating Forces, U.S. Fleet Battle Force, Commander Battleships. Record Group 313, National Archives, Washington, D.C.

Office of the Chief of Naval Operations. Fleet Training Division General Correspondence. Record Group 38, National Archives, Washington, D.C.

Records Collection of the Office of Naval Records and Library. Record Group 45, National Archives, Washington, D.C.

Records of the Bureau of Naval Personnel. Record Group 24, Logbooks of USS *Nevada*, National Archives, Washington, D.C.

U.S. Navy War Diaries. USS *Nevada*, Record Group 38, National Archives, Washington, D.C.

Battleships

Friedman, Norman. *U.S. Battleships: An Illustrated Design History*. Annapolis: Naval Institute Press, 1985.

Phister, Jeff, Thomas Hone, and Paul Goodyear. *Battleship* Oklahoma, *BB-37*. Norman: University of Oklahoma Press, 2008.

Stillwell, Paul. *Battleship* Arizona: *An Illustrated History*. Annapolis: Naval Institute Press, 1991.

Histories of USS *Nevada*

Beigel, Harvey M. *Two Ocean Battleship*. Missoula, Mt.: Pictorial Histories, 2002.

Cox, Ormond L. "U.S.S. *NEVADA*: Description and Trials." *Journal of the American Society of Naval Engineers* 28, no. 1 (1916): 20.

Henley, David C. *Battleship* Nevada: *The Epic Story of the Ship That Wouldn't Sink*. Murray, Utah: Western Military History Association, 1991.

Niedemair, John C. "Reminiscences of John C. Niedemair (Naval Architect—Bureau of Ships)." U.S. Naval Institute Oral History, 1978.

Scarpaci, Wayne. *Battleship* Nevada: *The Extraordinary Ship of Firsts*. CreateSpace Independent Publishing Platform, 2013.

Wren, Charles L. *Battle Born: The Unsinkable USS* Nevada *BB-36*. Bloomington, Ind.: Xlibris, 2008.

Ship Construction in the Early Twentieth Century

Kelly, Roy Willmarth, and Frederick J. Allen. *The Shipbuilding Industry*. Boston: Houghton Mifflin, 1918.

Robinson, R. H. M. *Naval Construction*. Annapolis: Naval Institute Press, 1914.

Sarcone, Anthony F., and Lawrence S. Rines. *A History of Shipbuilding at Fore River*. http://thomascranelibrary.org/shipbuildingheritage/history.htm. Accessed December 7, 2012.

World War I

Best, Nicholas. *The Greatest Day in History: How the Great War Really Ended*. London: Weidenfeld & Nicolson, 2008.

Jones, Jerry W. *U.S. Battleships in World War I*. Annapolis: Naval Institute Press, 1998.

Morison, Elting E. *Admiral Sims and the Modern American Navy*. Boston: Houghton Mifflin, 1942.

Sprout, Harold, and Margaret Sprout. *The Rise of American Naval Power 1776–1918*. London: Oxford University Press, 1939.

Wilkinson, S. E. *The* Nevada *Manual: Published on Board the* USS *NEVADA in the Interests of Her Officers and Crew*. USS *Nevada*, 1919. National Archives, RG 45.

Wilkinson, Syd. E. *The USS* Nevada *and Her Experiences in the War: A Diary by Chief Yeoman Syd. E. Wilkinson*. Privately printed, 1919.

Wyatt, W. S. *Cruise Book USS* Nevada, *1916–1946*. San Francisco: James H. Barry, 1946.

The Interwar Period

Asada, Sadao. *From Mahan to Pearl Harbor: The Imperial Japanese Navy and the United States*. Annapolis: Naval Institute Press, 2006.

———. "The London Conference and the Tragedy of the Imperial Japanese Navy." In John H. Mauer and Christopher M. Bell, eds., *At the Crossroads between Peace and War: The London Naval Conference of 1930*. Annapolis: Naval Institute Press, 2014.

Beach, Samuel Wheeler. *The Great Cruise of 1925*. San Francisco: International Printing, 1925.

Brendon, Piers. *The Dark Valley: A Panorama of the 1930s*. New York: Vintage, 2000.

Corey, Herbert. "Across the Equator with the American Navy." *National Geographic* 39, no. 6 (1921): 571–624.

Hone, Thomas C., and Trent Hone. *Battle Line: The United States Navy 1919–1939*. Annapolis: Naval Institute Press, 2006.

Hone, Trent. "Building a Doctrine: U.S. Navy Tactics and Battle Plans in the Interwar Period." *International Journal of Naval History* 1, no. 2 (2002).

Hurley, Alfred. *Billy Mitchell: Crusader for Air Power*. Bloomington: Indiana University Press, 2006.

Kuehn, John T. *Agents of Innovation: The General Board and the Design of the Fleet That Defeated the Japanese Navy*. Annapolis: Naval Institute Press, 2008.

Mauer, John H., and Christopher M. Bell, eds. *At the Crossroads between Peace and War: The London Naval Conference of 1930*. Annapolis: Naval Institute Press, 2014.

Miller, Edward S. *War Plan Orange: The U.S. Strategy to Defeat Japan, 1897–1945*. Annapolis: Naval Institute Press, 1991.

Morison, Samuel Eliot. *Oxford History of the American People*. New York: Oxford University Press, 1965.

Nofi, Albert A. *To Train the Fleet for War: The U.S. Navy Fleet Problems*. Newport, R.I.: Naval War College Press, 2010.

Olson, Lynne. *Those Angry Days: Roosevelt, Lindbergh, and America's Fight over World War II, 1939–1941*. New York: Random House, 2013.

Shenk, Robert, ed. *Playships of the World: The Naval Diaries of Admiral Dan Gallery, 1920–1924*. Columbia: University of South Carolina Press, 2008.

Sprout, Harold, and Margaret Sprout. *Toward a New Order of Sea Power: American Naval Policy and the World Scene 1918–1922*. Princeton: Princeton University Press, 1940.

Wheeler, Charles J. "The Reminiscences of Rear Admiral Charles J. Wheeler, U.S. Navy, Retired." U.S. Naval Institute Oral History, 1970.

Wyatt, W. S. *Cruise Book USS* Nevada, *1916–1946*. San Francisco: James H. Barry, 1946.

World War II

Ambrose, Stephen E. *D-Day June 6, 1944: The Climactic Battle of World War II*. New York: Simon and Schuster, 1994.

Anderson, Walter Stratton. "Worse than Dante's Inferno." In Paul Stillwell, ed., *Air Raid Pearl Harbor! Recollections of a Day of Infamy*. Annapolis: Naval Institute Press, 1981.

Backus, Paul H. "Why Them and Not Me." In Paul Stillwell, ed., *Air Raid Pearl Harbor! Recollections of a Day of Infamy*. Annapolis: Naval Institute Press, 1981.

Borneman, Walter R. *The Admirals: Nimitz, Halsey, Leahy, and King—the Five-Star Admirals Who Won the War at Sea*. New York: Back Bay Books, 2012.

Buckley, Walter J. "The Silver Mine." In Paul Stillwell, ed., *Air Raid: Pearl Harbor! Recollections of a Day of Infamy*. Annapolis: Naval Institute Press 1981.

Fuchida, Mitsuo. *For that One Day: The Memoirs of Mitsuo Fuchida Commander of the Attack on Pearl Harbor*. Kamuela, Hawaii: eXperience, 2011.

Garfield, Brian. *The Thousand-Mile War: World War II in Alaska and the Aleutians*. Anchorage: University of Alaska Press, 1995.

Giangreco, D. M. *Hell to Pay: Operation Downfall and the Invasion of Japan, 1945–1947*. Annapolis: Naval Institute Press, 2009.

Ienaga, Saburo. *The Pacific War 1931–1945*. New York: Random House, 1978.

Lord, Walter. *Day of Infamy*. New York: Henry Holt, 1957.

Madsen, Daniel. *Resurrection: Salvaging the Battle Fleet at Pearl Harbor*. Annapolis: Naval Institute Press, 2003.

Mason, Theodore C. *Battleship Sailor*. Annapolis: Naval Institute Press, 1982.

Merdinger, Charles J. "Reminiscences of Captain Charles J. Merdinger." U.S. Naval Institute Oral History, 1974.

Morison, Samuel Eliot. *The Atlantic Battle Won: May 1943–May 1945*. Volume 10 of *History of United States Naval Operations in World War II*. Boston: Little, Brown, 1956.

———. *The Invasion of France and Germany 1944–1945*. Volume 11 of *History of United States Naval Operations in World War II*. Boston: Little, Brown, 1957.

———. *The Rising Sun in the Pacific*. Volume 3 of *History of United States Naval Operations in World War II*. Boston: Little, Brown, 1948.

———. *Victory in the Pacific, 1945*. Volume 14 of *History of United States Naval Operations in World War II*. Boston: Little, Brown, 1960.

Prange, Gordon W. *At Dawn We Slept: The Untold Story of Pearl Harbor*. New York: Penguin, 1991.

Raymer, Edward C. *Descent into Darkness: Pearl Harbor, 1941, a Navy Diver's Memoir*. Annapolis: Naval Institute Press, 1996.

Ryan, Peggy Hughes. "A Navy Bride Learns to Cope." In Paul Stillwell, ed., *Air Raid Pearl Harbor! Recollections of a Day of Infamy*. Annapolis: Naval Institute Press, 1981.

Sabin, Lorenzo. "The Cheer-Up Ship." In Paul Stillwell, ed., *Air Raid Pearl Harbor! Recollections of a Day of Infamy*. Annapolis: Naval Institute Press, 1981.

Sehe, Charles T. "Operation Neptune." Unpublished manuscript in Nevada State Museum, 2013.

Stillwell, Paul, ed. *Air Raid Pearl Harbor! Recollections of a Day of Infamy*. Annapolis: Naval Institute Press, 1981.

Swaney, Edwin S. *Operation Crossroads*. Montezuma, Iowa: Sutherland Publishing, 1986.

Symonds, Craig L. *Neptune: The Allied Invasion of Europe and the D-Day Landings*. New York: Oxford University Press, 2014.

Taussig, Joseph K., Jr. "A Tactical View of Pearl Harbor." In Paul Stillwell, ed., *Air Raid Pearl Harbor! Recollections of a Day of Infamy*. Annapolis: Naval Institute Press, 1981.

Tully, Anthony. *Shattered Sword: The Untold Story of the Battle of Midway*. Washington, D.C.: Potomac Books, 2005.

Wallin, Homer N. "The Raising and Salvaging of the *Nevada*." In Paul Stillwell, ed., *Air Raid Pearl Harbor! Recollections of a Day of Infamy*. Annapolis: Naval Institute Press, 1981.

Willmott, H. P. *Pearl Harbor*. London: Cassell, 2001.

Withington, Frederick Stanton. "The Reminiscences of Rear Admiral Frederick Stanton Withington, U.S. Navy (Retired)." U.S. Naval Institute Oral History, 1972.

Wyatt, W. S. *Cruise Book USS* Nevada, *1916–1946*. San Francisco: James H. Barry, 1946.

Yoshida Mitsuru. *Requiem for Battleship* Yamato. Annapolis: Bluejacket Books, 1999.

Atomic Tests

Shurcliff, W. A. *Bombs at Bikini: The Official Report of Operation Crossroads*. New York: William H. Wise, 1947.

Strauss, Lewis. *Men and Decisions*. Garden City, N.Y.: Doubleday, 1962.

Swaney, Edwin S. *Operation Crossroads*. Montezuma, Iowa: Sutherland Publishing, 1986.

Weisgall, Jonathan M. *Operation Crossroads: The Atomic Tests at Bikini Atoll*. Annapolis: Naval Institute Press, 1994.

Index

About the Author

Stephen M. Younger is the president of Sandia National Laboratories in Albuquerque, New Mexico. He previously served as president of National Security Technologies, LLC, and director of the Defense Threat Reduction Agency. He has written extensively on national security, anthropology, and physics.